Multi-Choice Policing
in Africa

Bruce Baker

NORDISKA AFRIKAINSTITUTET, UPPSALA 2008

Indexing terms:

Police

Conflicts

Crime prevention

Violence

Safety

Human security

Social implications

Africa south of Sahara

Uganda

Sierra Leone

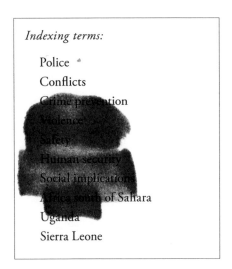

Cover photo: Bruce Baker
*A crowded street in Malakal, southern Sudan,
with the police station in the background.*

Language checking: Elaine Almén

Index: Margaret Binns

ISBN 978-91-7106-603-9

Printed in Sweden by Elanders Gotab AB, Stockholm 2008

Contents

— CHAPTER 1 —

Introduction

Local actors can choose – to a certain extent – the insitution they
approach to resolve problems… it is tempting … to refer to this as
'institutional shopping'.
(Bierschenk and de Sardan, 2003)

Policing, in this book, is any organised activity, whether by the state or
non-state groups, that seeks to ensure the maintenance of communal order,
security and peace through elements of prevention, deterrence, investigation of breaches, and punishment. Its condition in Africa is largely unknown. Surprisingly, state policing has scarcely been researched in Africa
outside of South Africa and there is an even greater dearth of studies on
non-state policing. The neglect is all the more unexpected, given the large
output of studies on democracy and good governance in Africa and the fact
that non-state policing agencies are valuable assets for advancing safety and
security among the poor. Policing is surely crucial to how citizens enjoy the
freedoms of democracy and the protection of government, and how they
view their government.

This book sets out to redress the neglect. Based on extensive fieldwork
in Africa, it offers an exploration of the nature and implications of state and
non-state policing across sub-Saharan Africa and, in particular, closely examines the two states of Uganda and Sierra Leone.[1] The account describes
and explains the kaleidoscope of overlapping policing agencies that are formal and informal, legal and illegal, effective and inept, fair and partisan,
restrained and brutal. The governance of policing is a contested terrain in
which various nodes of governance bargain and negotiate with each other
over the nature of the order to be established and the mechanisms for ac-
complishing protection. Policing may be authorised by a variety of sponsors: economic interests (both legal and illegal); residential communities;
cultural communities; individuals; and governments. In terms of policing

---

1. The research was funded by the Economic and Social Research Council (Award
   Reference: R000271293) and Coventry University.

provision, commercial companies, non-state authorisers of policing, individuals, and governments are all involved.

Together these multiple authorisers and providers form a complex set of choices for Africans as they seek to negotiate a measure of protection from crime and abuse in their daily lives. A focus on government agencies can, and often does, direct attention away from the full range of governmental authorisers and providers that exists, particularly at the local level. There are advantages, instead, in focussing on the consumers of governance through a 'multi-choice' approach, which examines the choices citizens face from a variety of policing providers to meet differing security requirements. Despite individuals' economic and social constraints, there is a striking variety of policing alternatives available. Many academics have noted a diversification away from the state, but this is not the only change taking place. At times it is a diversification away from the state police but not from state policing for it is still within the influence and control of the state.

The degree to which these patterns and relationships are dynamic, intricate and subtle can only be established by empirical research. I have sought, therefore, to ask Africans across the continent, 'To whom do you look for protection from crime?' and 'To whom do you turn for investigation of crime?' The answers have sometimes been surprising, but by this method I have begun to piece together the extent of policing agencies; the degree of state control over such policing bodies; and why individuals, groups (and even governments) turn to alternatives to state policing. The research has then led to my reflection on what the implications are of this fragmentation of policing and range of choice to citizens.

I begin in Chapter 2 by tracing the genealogy of policing. The roots of African state policing are found in the history of policing in Europe, where policing concepts and practices were forged over centuries of state development, urbanisation and industrialisation, before being imposed on African nations. The historical survey reveals a picture of changing policing patterns to meet changing communal needs and a rich diversity of authorisers and providers of policing. The many paradigms that have been proposed to capture this diversity and complexity are then examined. These include neo-feudalism with its distinct separation between private and public orders of policing; 'multilateral policing' with its emphasis on the two distinct layers of diversity, namely auspices and providers of policing; and plural networked policing emphasising the relationship and co-operation between the diverse policing groups. I offer my own multi-choice policing that stresses the competitive and parallel alternatives that are available to citizens, offering different levels of service.

To understand the policing solutions that have been chosen by Africans, the current social context and the historical background need to be examined. Chapter 3 explores the context in which policing is required. Two shadows are cast over Africans today: the shadow of conflict and the shadow of crime. Nearly a fifth of Africa's people live in countries disrupted by wars and civil unrest. Further, Africa is currently viewed as the most violent continent on the basis of crime victimization rates. Wars and victimization are manifestations of marginalisation, impoverishment and relative deprivation. Hence, though the violence of war may cease, violence itself may simply transmute itself from the political to the criminal. Both are products of the same fractured societies. Understanding in more detail what those underlying factors of violence and crime are explains the nature of the policing that has developed to counter them. The factors examined in the chapter are material poverty and social inequality; youth marginalisation; political transition; liberalisation and globalisation; urbanisation; availability of weapons; inadequate state criminal justice systems; and the crisis of informal social control.

Chapter 4 turns to the historical background. The enduring traditions, colonial impositions, autocratic oppressions and commercial exploitations that have swept across Africa have played a major role in shaping the contemporary policing responses. The chapter explains the paths followed with respect to the authorisers and providers of policing from pre-colonial days to the 1980s. The details of how policing was organised by pre-colonial governments are not altogether clear, but it can be shown that in the early phases of European domination commercial interests acted with little supervision and were quick to resort to force to achieve their ends. It was under colonial rule that centrally controlled regime policing established itself. Yet though colonial states were authoritarian regimes, with police being given a repressive role, they were often weak structures and the colonial state by no means had a monopoly of policing. It is evident that, for the average African, colonialism did little to relieve them from the prevailing violence, and fear of violence from criminal elements, ethnic disputes and religious conflicts. With independence there were expectations that the police would be reorganised and re-orientated from regime policing to a force committed to serving the people. Instead, as the chapter demonstrates, little changed. Policing remained militarised and, due to the insecurity of the regimes, was kept weak, fragmented, dependent and with an uncertain future, through under-funding. In areas outside the main towns, meanwhile, traditional procedures of policing and social control continued largely untouched.

With the background and context provided, Chapter 5 turns to contemporary African policing patterns. The perceptions of failing state police and rising crime have created a situation today where a plethora of non-state policing groups have emerged across sub-Saharan Africa. Some adhere to the law and have police support, some are lawless and violent in their assault on crime; some are spontaneous, short lived or evolving, some are more permanent commercial enterprises. They are authorised and provided by an array of civil and commercial groups besides governments, including economic interests (legal and illegal), residential communities, cultural communities, and individuals. It is this changing variety and complexity that the chapter explores.

The next two chapters, 6 and 7, record the results of fieldwork undertaken in Uganda and Sierra Leone. They provide a detailed understanding of the degree of multi-choice policing in the two countries and the contrasts between the two. The key issues addressed are: Who are delivering policing? Who are responsible for authorising policing? How many non-state providers of policing are there, what do they do, and whom do they serve? Are the nature and scope of public policing changing? Are the state police defining their responsibilities differently from in the past? How do the various policing agents interact on the ground?

Having looked at the patterning of policing in Africa, Chapter 8 turns to the social consequences of multi-choice policing. It asks: How variable is the quality of the different authorisers and providers of policing available; to what degree is policing choice and quality determined by class and geography; are the rights of individuals more at risk when policing is provided by some groups rather than others; and who gains and loses in terms of public safety as a result of multi-choice policing?

Finally, Chapter 9 considers the political implications of multi-choice policing. What does multi-choice policing mean for African governments? What opportunities and what challenges does it present them? If community and private providers are willing to respond to public demand for policing, should this be a matter for concern? What controls and mechanisms of accountability and public-private relationships are going to be necessary to maximise the benefits and minimise the dangers? How much influence will states have in this process? What do policy makers say is required for the policing of the new democracies of the twenty-first century?

Multi-choice policing is not a new phenomenon arising from economic liberalisation and the privatisation of state functions in the post-cold war period. The presumption of policing as a public good never made much ground in Africa outside the political elite in the capital. For most Africans policing has almost always been a private commodity and they have long been investigating alternatives to state policing. Some thirty years of authoritarianism provoked alienation from the state police and the development of informal legal orders that by-passed it. Going back before independence, alternative security arrangements predate state (and colonial) policing and were never totally displaced by it. Although it is no novelty, it has not been systematically studied before across the sub-continent. It is hoped that this book will introduce the reader to what crime prevention and crime response is on offer for Africans in the first decade of the new millennium.[2]

---

2. Further information on African policing can be found on the author's website: www.africanpolicing.org.

CHAPTER 2

The Genealogy and Analysis of Policing

In any given society there will be as many legal systems as there are functioning social units.
(Pospisil, 197:24)

Policing has always existed. Communities everywhere have sought to maintain communal order and to correct and discipline those who depart from communally acceptable behaviour. In the largely rural population of pre-industrial Europe, for instance, crime control and order maintenance was a local community affair. Policing was fulfilled by collective tasks (scrutiny; hue and cry; posse) and sometimes also through voluntary community service on a rotating basis (as a constable; a watchman; patrols) (McMullan, 1987; Draper, 1978; Salgado, 1977). It relied on close and regular contacts within restricted spaces.

> The basic weapon that the citizens of the early modern era learned to use to defend their security and combat danger was their own intense sociability – a complex of human relations and institutions predicated on collective, local, informal and voluntaristic reactions to disorder and law breaking ... As a concept, police was a community duty (McMullan, 1998:95).

The formal provision of policing through political authorities came later. The shift from collective responsibility to a public policing system parallels the rise of state power in Europe and the desire to centralise and monopolise the forces of coercion under state control.

Yet even as the European concept of state policing was being forged over centuries of state development, urbanisation and industrialisation, private policing, both communal and commercial, never fully died out. Though histories of policing have largely overlooked them, there has always been a rich diversity of authorisers and providers of policing in Europe. States were never strong enough to live up to their claims of a policing monopoly and into the security vacuum other provision was inevitably drawn.

The colonisation process in Africa exported the state controlled concept of policing. The even more limited penetration of the colonial state into African societies, compared with the European state, meant, however, that security provision was even weaker. Not only did the colonisers fail to eradicate non-state policing, but their own inadequacies promoted a fresh spate of alternative policing.

When policing is analysed, therefore, whether in the present or the past, or whether in Europe or Africa, it has to take into account this fragmentation. The account of the construction of state policing in Europe and its failure to secure a monopoly is recorded in this chapter, whilst the story of policing in Africa is given in chapter four. Together they share a complex pattern of policing. A number of paradigms have been proposed to capture this heterogeneity and these are reviewed and assessed at the end of the chapter.

The construction of state policing
in the colonising countries

Policing was a collective responsibility in pre-industrial Europe. Yet by the 18th century this policing system was under stress due to the profound social and economic changes taking place. These included urbanisation, industrialisation and populations growing faster than the economies. The social and economic transformation meant that many were left destitute, unemployed and homeless. There emerged increasing numbers of 'masterless' people beyond the reach of local supervision and large numbers of mobile 'vagabonds' begging and stealing. It was no longer sufficient for a local community to undertake the responsibility for watching the conduct of each other. Hence personal interests began replacing public spirit (informal and voluntary) as the motivation of communal control. Yet for the state the issue was not just that without central supervision the quality of contract security, whether private security guards or bounty hunters, was variable and its activities unaccountable. Nor was it simply that the current security arrangements could not handle the upsurge of crime and rioting in the growing cities. The crucial factor was that without centralisation the state was unable to assert its authority (Spitzer and Scull, 1977).

The political classes of France were one of the first in Europe to appreciate the need for strong central control to contain social unrest and migrant populations looking for work and the threat this posed to the state. During the late 1700s and throughout the 1800s the country saw revolutionary upheaval, coups, uprisings, wars, industrial unrest, food shortages and rapid rural change. Inevitably the state was focussed on how to maintain its order and to suppress rising political threats. If the army was not acceptable as a means of internal control, nor were the local civilian security provisions. Though provincial towns and cities had local forces ('sergent de ville') and rural areas employed 'gardes-champetres' to enforce rural codes, these local security organisations were thought to be too localised and inefficient and not sufficiently independent of local rivalries. They were unable to cope with social groups like vagrants, gypsies, escaped felons and deserters or with more violent crimes like highway robbery, murder, riots and brigandary. The state concluded, therefore, that it needed a centrally organised military force, which had sworn its allegiance to the state and which, unlike local security forces, was armed, mobile, efficient, disciplined and above local influence. It sought a coercive force that penetrated the whole nation and brought the state's demands, authority and norms to the people. It would be one that could deal with brigands and rioters, tax evaders and conscript dodgers; one that could patrol roads and protect tax and ammunition convoys.

The French state turned, therefore, to what had begun as a system of mounted military police. Initially this was extended in the sixteenth and seventeenth centuries to jurisdiction over civilians. By the late eighteenth century it was decided to institutionalise the mounted military police as a national military-style organisation that had a civilian character. The 'marechausses' were mainly assigned to the rural areas, with a separate company assigned to Paris. Their role, according to their training handbook, was 'to maintain public peace, facilitate commerce and enforce the execution of laws'. The Revolution of 1789–99 did nothing to lessen the attraction of a national professional military force that made regular patrols of main roads, fairs and markets to watch over public safety and follow up information on crime that the state required. So the 'marechaussée' was reformed in 1791 as the 'Gendarmerie Nationale', to ensure, according to the authorities, 'the maintenance of order and the execution of laws. A constant, ever-watchful surveillance constitutes the essence of its service' (Emsley, 1999:54).

They were not always so popular with the population, however. Gendarmerie brigades found difficulty enforcing legislation that had little or no legitimacy in rural areas. This included preventing people from taking wood from state forests, poaching, and pursuing refractory conscripts and deserters. There was also strong resistance to their attempts to enforce taxes, such as those for the upkeep of roads. In the towns their unpopularity was particularly associated with the exercise of force during political protests and industrial confrontations. Nevertheless, though regimes changed repeatedly in the late 1700s and 1800s from monarchies, to republics, to Empires, all found the civilian-military hybrid of the gendarmerie essential for surveillance of vagrants, vagabonds, political agitators and potential conscripts.

As revolution and social unrest led to a review of French policing, city riots and rising crime in England led to similar calls for a state sponsored policing system, but one that was civilian, full time, public based and that could both keep the peace using minimal force, as well as prevent and detect crime. While the state hesitated to take this step, private initiatives were undertaken. The Marine Police Establishment was a private police force set up in London in 1798. Its 60 armed men, financed mainly by the West India Company, kept surveillance of the docks and warehouses along the River Thames. Two magistrates at Bow Street, London, set up in 1750 a body of paid full time constables to detect and arrest criminals, known as the 'Bow Street Runners'. Though paid a salary, they were also hired out as private security guards and bounty hunters. With the British parliament's reluctance to provide a state authorised force for London, the Bow Street Runners expanded in number, though never to more than 450 men in a London of about 1.5 million people. They also began undertaking both foot patrols and in an effort to curb highwaymen, mounted patrols in the rural margins.

Alongside these changes in formal policing in Europe there continued, of course, informal communal control under the threat of sanctions, such as public chastisement, dismissal from work, ostracism or expulsion from the community. Sometimes it was no more than citizens spying on one another or those detained under suspicion being 'encouraged' to inform on their accomplices. At other times victims used intermediaries or the offer of rewards to recover property (see Beattie, 1986 for 17th and 18th century England;). In France:

> Rural communities had their own means of dealing with offenders and minor trouble before the arrival of the gendarmes. This could involve using the law. But the law was costly and time consuming, and at times was seen more as an instrument for perpetuating a feud than for the quick resolution of an offence. A quick resolution was much preferred, especially if the offender was known. Sometimes problems were resolved through individual or community violence; sometimes there was recourse to magic, or more often, to agreements

negotiated by influential figures within the community, possibly the seigneur, but more likely his agent, the curé, or the mayor (Emsley, 1999:253).

Even as late as the early 19th century, policing in Europe was still primarily 'a socio-political function (rather than merely a formal legal one) and was still exercised in civil society (rather than merely within the confines of the state)' (Johnston, 1992:4). Inevitably, therefore, policing was authorised and provided by an array of persons. Authorisers included political, religious and economic authorities or family heads; providers included individuals acting either on the behalf of others or themselves, or authorised units that were usually part-time volunteers, but sometimes were paid watchmen and militias. Diversity and plurality of authorisation and provision was still the norm.

Whilst states in Europe, as part of their nation-building project, sought to concentrate authority for all aspects of policing within a single state body, there was a reluctance in England. In a country where there was widespread suspicion of state control and interference, and jealousy of civil liberty, such centralised and militarised policing was suspect. Thus when, in 1785, William Pitt asked Parliament to create a police force in London, it was rejected, being seen as too much like the French system. For many, a degree of disorder was the price for freedom. John Ward wrote in 1811:

> They have an admirable police in Paris, but they pay for it dearly enough. I had rather half a dozen people's throats should be cut in Radcliffe Highway every three or four years than be subject to domiciliary visits, spies and all the rest of Fouche's [Minister of Police] contrivances (Halevy, 1974:146).

Despite Ward's reservations, the concept took hold across Europe that policing was 'the role of a uniformed body of men concerned with the maintenance of public order, riot control and crime prevention' (Sheptycki, 1999:218). The success of London's Bow Street Runners and other private policing initiatives enabled Robert Peel (British Home Secretary, that is, Minister of the Interior) to successfully introduce the 'new police' in 1829. They began as a uniformed full time force of 1,000 officers responsible for a seven-mile radius from the centre of London. They were unarmed, exemplifying their civilian character and policing by consent. Anxious that local authorities should accept greater responsibility for law and order, the British state introduced legislation that allowed (1833), urged (1839, 1842) and then compelled (1856) boroughs to establish town police forces (Davey, 1983).

In Europe, German and Italian states and Austria, followed the mixed policing route of the French with both civilian and paramilitary structures. Nationalised gendarmeries were seen as a means of guaranteeing a semblance of order during tumultuous times. They alone could handle the undesirables in the countryside and the industrial agitation in the cities, whilst at the same time helping to construct some kind of political identity for the new states.

Yet for all these European attempts to impose state defined order, there remained, 'the rural provinces, often primitive, the last frontier for the nation states', resisting the state justice systems (Emsley, 1997:157). The local lord or his representative was still there to resolve complaints and injuries through negotiating agreed restitution or recompense, as was the local priest. For discovering the culprit there was still the 'cunning' person's skills. Commonly the victim was expected to exact their own punishment on the offender, provided that the physical punishment kept within certain tolerated levels. Not that the limits were always adhered to. Family revenge punishments for family honour slighted could provoke long-standing feuds. Shaming punishments included parading through the village or shaving the beard. It was outsiders who received the most severe penalties and brutal killings of horse thieves and the like were not unknown. These practices did not mean that the state law was totally ignored. It was indeed used, but as and when it suited and not because rural communities accepted the claims for it being the only or final authority. But it might be used as a means of last resort to press a claim over land, to uphold customary rights, or to break the power of a local lord to prevent justice. Yet even this recourse presupposed that gendarmes or magistrates were available and the fact was that though they began to appear in increasing numbers during the nineteenth century in Europe, in many areas they remained very thin on the ground (Emsley, 1997:166–74).

Many historians argue that 'it was the threat posed by the disenfranchised and economically marginalized 'dangerous classes' at the beginning of the Industrial Age that galvanized Europe's political classes into creating the police institution and giving it a mandate to secure public space through various legal instruments aimed at public disorder, theft and violence' (Sheptycki, 1999:218; cf. Steedman, 1984; Chesney, 1972; Gurr et al., 1977; Linebaugh, 1991; Jones, 1984; Vogler, 1991). Civil police certainly filled the vacuum left by increasing restrictions on the use of capital punishment and of the military in internal affairs. The role of police forces in the mid-1800s in England was, on behalf of local populations (or rather property owning ratepayers), to maintain the peace; put down riot and insurrection; and watch (if not protect) private property. This role, however, meant that those outside the property owning classes were not so enthusiastic about them. Indeed, the unpopularity of the British police with the working classes led to frequent violent attacks against them (Chesney, 1972:44; Read, 1979:53) and protests to preserve:

> popular recreations or customs, prevent interference in strikes, protect wanted individuals, protest against police interference in political activities, protest against instances of police brutality, rescue arrested persons (Storch, 1981:95).

It was not long before English ratepayers came to expect their local police forces to regulate their local communities more extensively, as Poor Law relieving officers, inspectors of 'nuisances', market commissioners, impounders of stray animals, inspectors of weights and measures, recorders of animal diseases, controllers of vagrants, and inspectors of common lodging houses, shops and licensees (Steedman, 1984:8). Their activity was, in other words, done as much in accordance with local bye laws as with national statutory legislation, using if necessary the legitimate use of force that had been granted to them.

By the mid-19th century inconsistent provision and a need for universal inspectorates led central government in London to oblige provincial communities to organise police forces and undertake crime prevention and local administrative roles. The process had begun whereby local police forces came to be regarded as agencies of central government as well as of rural local magistrates and town watch committees.

Yet whether from the local or central perspective, policing in the late 19th century was still concerned as much with population surveillance, control, local administrative services and civil law, as with the use of repression and force to curtail crime and uphold criminal law. Such a diverse workload, however, was not sustainable and by the 1880s the mood had changed and the call was for police who were professionals in investigating criminal offences. Yet the new objective was never fully realised on the ground. In reality 'the "monopoly" enjoyed by the police was only a symbolic one' (Newburn, 2001:830). Effective informal communal control continued as it had for centuries through the sanctions of chastisement or dismissal of employers and landowners, the rebukes of heads of homez and priests and the threat of ostracism or expulsion by the community (Roberts, 1973; Davis, 1989; Cohen, 1979; Shapland and Vagg, 1987).

Likewise, though the concept of policing as a state service was more and more entrenched during the course of the nineteenth century, private policing never completely died out. 'Associations for the Prosecution of Felons' that had first emerged in England in 1760, flourished there until 1840. These local citizen policing groups shared the costs of rewarding informers and taking suspects to court or even at times of posse and patrol activity (Philips, 1989; Shubert, 1981; Halevy 1974:146). Until at least the 1920s there were a variety of such voluntary and subscription forces in operation throughout England using local people or initially, professional police officers sent from London (Johnston, 1992:17; Emsley, 1987; Storch, 1981; Davey, 1983). Some of those who were paying rates or subscriptions to provide policing for themselves welcomed the state's intervention in providing policing, but others were reluctant to pay taxes to support the protection of other people's property.

The story of the transfer of these European forms of policing to Africa is told in Chapter 4. Ironically governments in developed states, having taken over communal control functions that once belonged to the institutions of the community, and having transferred this system to their colonies, came to question the system by the end of the twentieth century. They found that even the richest state could not meet popular expectations of crime control. The welfare state could not curb or cure crime simply through social improvement. Both citizens and state in the West have had to review their options. Victimisation surveys reveal citizens are reporting less than half of all crimes and very few file civil law suits even when significant sums of money are at issue. Instead 'people prefer to handle their disputes by other means', using sanctions of avoidance or of violence or the threat of it (Cooney, 1994:33). The response of the developed state to its own failure has been to look to public-private partnerships and to devolving responsibility for crime prevention to non-state agencies, organisations, and individuals. This is not simply the privatisation of crime control, but an attempt to exercise governance at a distance and indirectly. States now appear to be seeking to restrict themselves to the role of security in coordinating and activating.

What does this review of the construction of state policing in the European colonising powers reveal? Over the centuries three institutions of policing have been constantly active. There is the local collective voluntary policing alongside informal communal control: it sees local solutions as the answer to local problems and may function on the basis of rules and values at variance with the state. Then there is client based contract policing as individuals specialising in policing offer their services on a fee basis.

Finally there is a public policing that offers to serve all on the basis of state law. The community, business and the state have constantly been the authorisers and providers of policing. Only the relative dominance and the inter-relationships between the three institutions have changed. As regards underlying mentalities, all three institutions have responded to crime and disorder through the application of force for punishment and as a means of constraint. Likewise all have engaged in surveillance and preventative approaches. In terms of technologies these have altered over the years and with increased sophistication has come an increasing use of specialist security personnel. Many have characterised the last 50 years as a period of increasing fragmentation in policing. It might be more accurate to see fragmentation, not so much as a new process, but the speeding up of an old one.

The ideology and definition of policing

With all the new developments in policing, plus the continuation of older traditions of self-provision, theorising has struggled to keep pace with reality. The mid-19th century ideology of policing, that it was a public good and therefore deserved a state monopoly, was largely unchallenged intellectually until the early 1990s. It was regarded as self-evident that functions such as regulating society and maintaining order, preserving security, preventing crime, responding to crime and restoring order, and the use where necessary of instruments of coercion to assist in any of these, were matters for the state to undertake and the state alone. Only in the state's hands, it was argued, could policing activities be required to be accountable, consistent and humane. The ideological hegemony was such that invariably the practice in debate was, as Johnston puts it, 'to conflate policing (a social function) with police (a specific body of personnel)' (Johnston, 1999a:177). Thus, what had only been the experience for 150 years in the West, was regarded as 'natural' and 'right', whilst the longer historical pattern of diversity and plurality by non-state authorisers and providers was unimaginable. Those proposing its revival were vilified as promoting morally suspect vigilantes, mercenaries and commercial interests.

Today the 'state monopoly' discourse does not fit people's experience in the West, which is one of multiple authorisers and providers. The public are more likely to look to and meet private security guards and CCTV operators at their workplace and in retail parks, than the civil police; to find local council wardens supervising vehicle parking and recreation areas, and to anticipate protection in their street from electronic security and the neighbourhood watch more than civil police on the beat. Nor are they averse to organising their own patrols to keep prostitutes off their streets, taking part in protests to evict paedophiles from their neighbourhoods and to informing telephone hotlines of security, fraud and other suspected criminals. The days of the state monopoly in policing have gone. Nor, for that matter, does the discourse fit outside Europe.

In Africa, where the post-colonial state has always been much weaker than in the West, this is even more the case. Faced with an absent, inefficient, corrupt and at times brutal state police service, citizens never ceased to provide their own local solutions and have initiated new forms with or without the approval of the state. A whole array of formal and informal groups in Africa exercise policing functions as part of, or as their primary, role (Baker, 2002a–c; 2003; 2004a–d; 2005; 2007a). State policing bodies include not only the State police and gendarmerie, but internal security units, presidential guards, local militias, anti-corruption police, anti-organised crime paramilitaries, forest guards and tax fraud officers. State-approved community-based policing can include customary structures, Neighbourhood Watch groups, Community Policing Forums, local government crime prevention bodies and street patrols. Informal or autonomous citizen groups (that do not have official approval), such as anti-crime groups, religious police, ethnic militias, car guards and vigilantes are also common. Finally there are the commercial security operations, offering armed or unarmed protection, debt collectors and security equipment installers.

In Africa, as in the West, it is common to see non-state agencies engaged in street patrolling, guarding private and public property, order maintenance, arrest, search, detection, surveillance, inspection and personal escort/protection. In fulfilling many of these duties they commonly bear firearms and other means of coercion, such as handcuffs, truncheons and pepper spray to, if necessary, enforce their activities. In other words, such policing groups do everything that the public police force does and do it as the police do it. Or, put another way, law enforcement is a broader activity than simply what 'The Police' do. As Bayley and Shearing note:

> Without close scrutiny it has become difficult to tell whether policing is being done by a government using sworn personnel, by an agent using a private security company, by a private security company using civilian employees, by a private company using public police or by a government employing civilians (Bayley and Shearing, 2001).

Law enforcement in the last 20 years in developed and developing countries has been undergoing reconstruction, with not only a separation between those who authorise it from those who provide the service, but a dispersal of both functions away from the state police or even away from the government (Bayley and Shearing, 2001). Policing for business interests, residential communities, cultural communities, individuals as well as the state, is now provided by commercial security companies, formal voluntary non-governmental groups, individuals and even governments themselves as private suppliers of protection. Research into policing, therefore, has to look beyond the state and beyond the formal. As Hills rightly observes, 'the focus should be on policing (as in the provision of order and enforcement) rather than on what organizations call themselves. How police style themselves is less important than what they do or do not do' (Hills, 2000:6). Across the developed and the developing world there is a broad and diverse network of policing that not only works through government but, above, below and beyond government (Loader, 2000:328; Baker, 2005).

This view of policing as a heterogeneous function undertaken by a plurality of providers using an array of techniques confirms that it is not simply a form of government (though the state police have that function), but a form of governance or governmentality, by which is meant 'ways in which agency is structured through public and private attempts to realize a way of doing things' (Valverde, quoted in Johnston 2001:959). In Johnston's words, policing is 'an act of governance (or 'rule') directed towards the promotion of security' (Johnston 1999a:179). The failure to recognise the difference between policing and police, or to put it another way, the mistaken conflation of governance and government, leads to the popular assumption 'that any solution to the governance of crime/fear will, inevitably, be a state-led one' (Johnston, 2001:959).

Is there any way of defining this particular form of governmentality that has a mandate to maintain communal order? Stimulated by the argument that policing is not synonymous with the police, some have stretched the concept of policing to mean communal control in all its forms. However, when this is done, the term is left explaining everything and nothing. In response to this danger Cohen (1985:2) has proposed restricting the term policing to 'organised', that is purposive, actions undertaken by communities to deal with problematic behaviour. Similarly, Reiner argues that policing involves 'the creation of systems of surveillance coupled with the threat of sanctions … *directed* at preserving the security of a particular social order' (Reiner, 1997:1005; emphasis in the original).

The purposive element is a necessary part of the definition, but not everyone thinks it is sufficient. For instance, it still leaves the issue of whether policing must involve 'a conscious exercise of power', as Jones and Newburn claim (1998:18). Yet to add this extra element excludes, in Johnston's estimation, the significant area of 'civil' modes of policing and actions by corporate bodies that are engaged in techniques of behavioural surveillance (Johnston, 1999a:178). In addition it can be argued, as does Shearing, that policing fundamentally is not so much about the exercise of power/coercion as about the establishment of security and peace; security being the preservation of some established order against threat (Shearing, 1992). This thinking underlies the Community Safety partnerships being developed by the British Government and the Community Safety Forums implemented by the South African Government (Schärf, 2000). Policing in this formulation is not only about a network of agencies and community groups rather than about a single state police force, but is clearly focussed on governance rather than coercion. Bayley and Shearing, in a similar vein, argue that policing is 'the self-conscious process whereby societies designate and authorise people to create public safety' (1996:586). Johnston also supports this security emphasis, on the grounds that it is wider than crime and reflects people's concern for more than just protection from crime. He defines policing as 'a purposive strategy involving the initiation of techniques which are intended to offer guarantees of security to subjects' (Johnston, 1999a:178–79). The advantage of putting security, peace and order at the centre of what constitutes policing is that it removes policing from being an exclusively criminological activity, confined to the domain of criminal justice. Crime is only one source of people's insecurity (Johnston, 1999a:178–79). The security framework is also a reminder of why the state police service is only one provider of policing and can never be the sole one. Indeed 'people spend more time in their daily lives in places where visible crime prevention and control are provided by non-governmental groups rather than by governmental police agencies (Bayley and Shearing, 2001). The public peace of the villages, townships and city centres across Africa cannot possibly be kept solely by the state police. As Jacobs observed: 'it is kept primarily by an intricate, almost unconscious, network of voluntary controls and standards among the people themselves … No amount of police can enforce civilization where the normal, casual enforcement of it has broken down (Jacobs, 1961, quoted in Newburn, 2001:845).

Accepting the arguments that policing contains the elements of purposive action and the provision of security, I propose to use the following definition of policing throughout this book: any organised activity, whether by the state or civil groups, that seeks to ensure the maintenance of communal order, security and peace through elements of prevention, deterrence, investigation of breaches, resolution and punishment.

Policing paradigms

How is this dispersed mechanism of governance that is called policing to be captured conceptually? Several related paradigms have been suggested in recent years and although some were primarily proposed with the Western world in view, they still have value in the African context. The first may be called *neo-feudalism*. When private policing was 'rediscovered' in the mid-1970s in North America (Shearing et al., 1974; Shearing and Farnell, 1977; Shearing and Stenning, 1981; Spitzer and Scull, 1977) and a little later in the UK (South, 1988; Johnston, 1992), private and public policing were sharply divided, with the former being primarily thought of as commercial security. After an initial interest in security guards, research on private policing began to note gated residential communities, mass retail outlets, and sporting/leisure complexes that suggested 'fortified fragments' where a privately defined order was administered by private security. It was an order where 'undesirables' were excluded through methods other than state law and largely through the consensus of participants and the design of the environment (Shearing and Kempa, 2000:207). In other words, semi-exclusive communities/spaces were arising where a different order of law and its administration was applied to that of the state in public places. The parallel was drawn with feudal society and that of mediaeval city-states, since the fortified enclaves of privilege deployed a system of exclusionary justice. However, the neo-feudal paradigm suggested a clear-cut separation between private and public orders of policing that did not fully fit the world of overlapping and co-operative patterns of security.

To capture the complexity more effectively, Bayley and Shearing (2001) use the term *multilateral policing*. They draw attention to the fact not only that private policing consists of the informal as well as the formal, but that there are two distinct layers of diversity, namely auspices and providers of policing. This division of labour, they argue, is more significant than the traditional distinction between 'public' and 'private' policing, since the roles of state and non-state policing often overlap. According to their definition:

Auspices are groups that explicitly and self-consciously take upon themselves the responsibility for organizing their protection. Providers are the groups that actually do the policing asked for. Sometimes auspices and providers coincide. A defining characteristic of the new paradigm of policing, however, is that auspices and providers may not be the same (Bayley and Shearing, 2001).

Their review suggested that policing is authorised by a variety of sponsors: economic interests (both formal and informal, legal and illegal), residential communities, cultural communities, individuals and governments. Policing provision is equally diverse in their view. It includes commercial companies, non-state authorisers of policing, individuals and governments. On the one hand, a variety of non-governmental groups have assumed responsibility for their own protection, whilst on the other hand a variety of non-governmental agencies have undertaken to provide security services. As the boundaries have blurred,

> Both public and private entities have assumed responsibility for authorizing policing; both public and private entities provide policing to these auspices. Even government's role is no longer exclusively public. It authorizes policing, encourages non-governmental groups to authorize policing, and provides policing to specialized consumers on a fee-for-service basis. Similarly, private providers are not exclusively private, since they sometimes work under public auspices and are sometimes staffed by public police personnel (Bayley and Shearing, 2001).

The (re)entry of citizens into policing functions, whether with or without the state police's blessing, has also been noted by Johnston. Commenting on the active role of citizens in both authorising and/or providing policing, he writes:

> Citizens, rather than being the passive consumers of police services, engage in a variety of productive security activities. Such 'co-production' ranges from individual/household activities undertaken with police co-operation (property marking, becoming a special constable) to those lacking such co-operation (buying a fierce guard dog, surrounding one's property in razor wire); and from group activities supported by the police (liaison groups, neighbourhood watch groups) to those denied such support (hiring a private security patrol to protect a group of residences, engaging in citizen patrol) (Johnston, 2001:965).

Though it may be true that the boundary between public and private has lost its distinctiveness, some insist that collapsing the whole field of law enforcement is to merge phenomena that are inherently separate. There are indeed significant differences in the authority, organisational structure, legality, and working definitions of communal deviance and 'order'. Nevertheless both public and private policing have important features in common. They are both forces of coercion engaged to preserve internal communal order and they draw on similar control and investigative techniques. It is, then, increasingly hard to separate them analytically.

A third paradigm, proposed by Loader, speaks of *plural networked policing*. It, too, recognises that the state is not (and cannot be) the sole source of both provision and accountability in policing, but emphasises the relationship and co-operation between the diverse policing groups. In other words it is not just that the boundaries between state and non-state institutions have 'blurred' but that they have been transformed by new partnerships. Though diverse, Loader argues that policing groups are not to be seen as isolated autonomous groups, but as together providing a security network across society. He talks of the 'network of power' in which the state is but one node:

> This network continues to encompass the direct provision and supervision of policing by institutions of national and local government. But it now also extends to private policing forms secured *through* government; to transitional police arrangements taking place *above* government; to markets in policing and security services unfolding *beyond* government; and to policing activities engaged in by citizens *below* government. We inhabit a world of plural, networked policing (Loader, 2000:323–24).

This is a framework that recognises a multiplicity of state, market and community groups loosely networked to provide shared control, order and authority. In this tradition some prefer to talk about security networks rather than policing (Newburn, 2001:830). In a similar vein, Kempa et al. speak of 'a concept of "policing" as a process of "networked nodal governance", understood as a complex of interlaced systems of agencies which work together to produce order' (Kempa, Carrier, Wood and Shearing et al., 1999:199). The many 'permutations of private policing involve the forging of connections between numerous agencies to form extended networks of regulatory power' (Kempa, Carrier, Wood and Shearing et al., 1999:207).

Though many nodes are acknowledged, this paradigm assumes the primacy of state law and still regards the government as the primary node. This security network tends to be defined in terms of the variable relationships with the state. By way of illustration, attention is drawn to government initiatives to 'voluntarise' and 'civilianise' security provision. So called 'responsibilization strategies' encourage individuals and organisations out-side of the state apparatus to take responsibility for crime prevention and security (Newburn, 2001:837; Jones and Newburn, 2002:138; the termi-nology belongs to Garland, 1996). It is now common to see governments, who until recently labelled citizen participation in policing as vigilantism, encouraging citizen participation in self-policing schemes like Neighbour-hood Watch and urging a 'private prudentialism' (O'Malley, 1997). Thus individuals are, in effect, being incorporated as private agents in a net-worked policing process, though with their central relationship still being to the state police. The prominence of the state may well fit current Western patterns, but in Africa and other parts of the developing world, where the state police are largely absent in the rural areas and poorer neighbourhoods of the towns, this paradigm is unsatisfactory. Further, the 'junior partner' theory of the relationship of private policing to public policing is very often a convenient myth. Private policing does not simply tackle lesser offences. It may often prefer to tackle the most serious offences itself and leave the state police to lesser offences. Nor does the state police always determine what private policing does, but is often found following private policing in terms of its techniques (Shearing and Stenning, 1983).

The *security governance* paradigm of Johnston and Shearing (2003) in-corporates all the insights of the earlier paradigms, but is prepared to deny conceptual priority to the state in any security network. They argue that it is important to carefully separate what policing is in essence from the historical forms which policing has taken, in terms of its underlying men-talities and their related institutions, technologies and practices. That the traditional historical pattern has been one where policing is conceived as being about the application of punishment by state officers is beyond dis-pute. However, as they point out, this is not the only way of approaching policing. Other mentalities to policing also exist, such as problem solving, risk management and remedial/restorative approaches operated through alternative institutions of the state, business or voluntary bodies. It is this historical baggage associated with 'policing' that makes them prefer to speak of security and its governance. They define security governance as 'the application of any means that will promote safe and secure places in which people live and work' (Johnston and Shearing, 2003:71). The lack of specificity about the agents and the means they use is quite deliberate.

This approach makes no 'essentialist' assumptions about *inter alia* the func-tions of the police, the ends which they serve, the objectives which they pursue, the means by which they pursue them or the historical trajectory through which police institutions develop (Johnston and Shearing, 2003:60).

The attraction of this paradigm is that it eschews preconceptions of policing and insists that only empirical research can establish the exact nature of the security governance network in any given area and the relationships of the various nodes, the state sector, the business sector, the non-government organisation (NGO) sector and the informal sector (2003:147).

The only paradigm that specifically has Africa in mind is that proposed by Christopher Clapham (1999). It is one that, on empirical grounds, abandons the private/public division and makes the case for *the universality of private policing*. He contends that most African states (though not exclusively so) have never developed 'public' security systems in the first place, in the sense of security systems that protect all citizens without discrimination and which are accountable to them. Essentially the state security systems, in his view, have been developed to support the ruling elite in their hold on power and wealth. Clapham believes it is naive to imagine that, generally speaking, African states actually represent the populations of the territories ascribed to them. Their 'public' security is little different from the 'privatised' security systems controlled by groups and individuals. In the context of Africa, therefore, he sees no basis for retaining the dichotomy between 'public' and 'private' security. All security systems are private to the extent that they all serve less than the whole population. What does divide these essentially private security systems is the degree to which they are efficient and accountable.

> The management of security by at least a substantial number of African states is in practice essentially 'private', in that such security as exists is primarily concerned to protect the lives, power and access to wealth of specific groups and individuals who control the state, and is not substantially different from the security provided, say, by a warlord who is not formally recognised as representing a state. Many of the claims that are made for the provision of public security through states are actually little more than special pleading, designed to appropriate a veneer of legitimacy for attempts by people who control states to use them for their own interests (Clapham 1999:33).

Failing to find true public policing in Africa, Clapham abandons the distinction between public (or state-managed) security systems and private (commercial or even criminal) ones. His collapsing of all law enforcement into one category challenges those who claim public authority for state policing to prove that such forces serve the interests of all the citizens and are accountable to the public. To him it is not just that African policing groups, whether called private or public, may engage in similar activities (a point that could be contested), but that they have a similar purpose to promote private interest. We are left, therefore, with a spectrum of private security systems. Each system displays a combination of the two basic criteria of any security system: 'its efficiency in maintaining some kind of order on the one hand, and its accountability to those people whose security is at stake on the other' (Clapham, 1999:24).

My own preference is to consider security from the point of view of the experience of the citizen rather than from the governance perspective of the political authorities. There is considerable value in undertaking participatory mapping as the tool to explore policing on the ground. Individuals and groups are in a unique position to depict and analyse their own experience of policing. It is a view now beginning to be recognised by development agencies:

> One of the problems with many justice sector reform programmes in the past is that they have often looked at the operation of the institutions from the perspective of officials rather than from the perspective of the poor. It is critical to the success of a Safety, Security and Access to Justice programme that the operation of the institutions is understood from the bottom up (Department for International Development, DFID, 2002:37).

Starting from this perspective, the fluidity of policing becomes very apparent, for people are rarely users of either private or public policing, as if these were mutually exclusive categories. As people move about their daily business, or as the time of day changes, so they may move from the sphere of one security agency to which they would naturally look for protection, to another; or they may be faced at times with a choice of agency which has to be made in terms of personal experience, preference for mentality (surveillance or punishment), cost or traditional acceptability. The reality is that *multi-choice policing* exists. The extended family may protect the compound, but it is the street committee that resolves the assault at the bar, the sorcerer that detects the culprit, the headman or local priest that mediates a settlement over damages caused by a neighbour, a spontaneous mob that handles the bus station pickpocket, the commercial security guard that secures the entrance to the city centre office, and the state police that are called if a colleague is murdered at the bank at lunchtime. Policing, as it is experienced, is not just diverse or private, it is a complex pattern of overlapping policing agencies. What applies to protection and detection also applies to resolution and punishment. A whole array of organisations provides 'courts' to handle disputes through conciliation and/or sanctions. Research in Uganda found that:

> Most personal problems are usually taken to family, in-laws or relatives, friends and church leaders. More serious offences like serious injuries or maiming during the fight, fraud or theft are referred to either the police or local administration. Matters of succession and land are normally first referred to clan leaders, opinion leaders and neighbours while simple squabbles especially among the youth are settled by friends and/or peers (DANIDA, 1998).

In Benin, Bierschenk and de Sardan describe an accumulation of local political institutions in rural areas that has resulted, as far as dispute resolution is concerned, in local people engaging in what they call 'institutional shopping', choosing the institution that appears most suited to resolving the particular problem:

> A case of theft can be taken to the traditional chief, the village 'chief' or district mayor, the national gendarmerie, the courts, the office of the village association, the other ethnic associations, the association of village producers or, yet again, the local church or mosque authorities... (2003:158).

The authors found no single legitimacy, no institution that had a monopoly of regulation, and no institution that was capable of imposing its law and norms on other institutions. The reality of a choice of policing (or at least the availability of alternatives) is also described by Tshehla's research in the Western Cape townships of South Africa. In contrast to rural areas where a single (chieftainship) dispute resolution institution existed, in the townships, 'there is a freedom as to what structure to approach' (2001:34). He found a wide range of organisations from those comprising traditional leaders, to those run by local groups or NGOs from outside. There was of course a corresponding variation in the cases handled and the modus operandi. Individuals chose any of these or the formal courts according to which was deemed to be able to serve their interests best in a given time and dispute. Yet it was not a totally rational choice. He found evidence of confusion in that many did not know the full range of non-state ordering structures that existed in their communities or what they offered, since many of them were new and had a competitive relationship (2001:55)

Much academic literature on policing constructs the choice as one between accountable public policing and minimally accountable private policing (cf. Stenning, 2000). However, for Africans their experiences, or choices in as much as they have them, are based on 'what is available', 'what works best' and 'what is affordable', more than issues of who controls the policing body and to whom are they accountable (the same point is made about peasants in nineteenth century Europe; see Emsley, 1997). Also within this paradigm, familiar security terminology becomes problematic as popular understanding gives different shades of meaning or different applications. Thus 'public' and 'private' do not exist as straightforward terms in popular experience. Public policing not only fails to serve all equally, as Clapham pointed out, but neither is it free. To secure the interest, investigation and prosecution of a criminal case may well necessitate people offering bribes. Further, daily encounters with public policing at roadblocks and at roadside vending pitches is costly (on the violent street battles between hawkers and police officers in Nairobi in July 2002, see *Daily Nation*, 28 July, 2002). Research in 2002 showed that on average each Kenyan had been forced to bribe the police 4.5 times a month, paying them on average US$16 per month. Over 95 per cent of dealings with the police had resulted in a bribe (*Transparency International*, 24 January, 2002). Not only do practices overlap, but the relationship itself can be blurred. In Lund's words, policing organisations resemble 'twilight institutions' (Lund, 2001). Whilst opposing the state, they also draw symbols, paraphernalia (e.g. uniforms) and legitimacy from mimicking the state and its procedures. Further, as Jensen observed in northeastern Mpumalanga, South Africa, the state and especially its local representatives, negotiate, appropriate and sometimes even shed their 'stateness'. For example police officers 'saw' violence as state employees, but not as civilians participating in communal discipline of 'criminals'. He found state representatives needed to negotiate danger (they live in the area they patrol) and notions of morality where they often agree personally with the contraventions of the law (Jensen, 2003). And yet, 'public' and 'private' may well mean something in terms of the law and communal mores being enforced and the methods of enforcement, despite the evident contradictions and confusions in their formal relationships.

Though this paradigm recognises overlapping provisions, it downplays both the co-operation and state police dominance of policing networks, since in Africa at least, there is often an element of competition between policing groups within the same geographic space. For example, in Sagamu, the capital of Ogun State, Nigeria, a vigilante group with the support of the traditional rulers in effect displaced the Nigeria Police after the latter had failed to prevent armed robberies. However after their killing of a student, a youth group challenged the vigilantes and in a pitched battle burnt down the residence of their patron traditional leader. The conflict drew in a federal government delegation. This took policing out of the hands of the vigilante group and returned it to the Nigeria Police (*This Day*, Lagos, 18 and 24 March, 2003).

If there is not competition, there may be parallel provision that offers choice based on performance and cost. There is a sense in which residents shop around for the type of policing they want (Schärf, 2001:49; Bierschenk and de Sardan, 2003). For instance, in an attempted rape case in a township in South Africa, a street committee (vigilante group), without consulting the victim, punished her assailant by ordering that he buy alcohol for the street committee members. The victim complained, not to the state police, but to an alternative informal justice body, a restorative justice committee, about the vigilantes' conduct. After all sides had been brought together the members of the street committee apologised for their conduct (Roche, 2002:521). In another situation, a Hausa young man who stole money from a market woman in the Yoruba city of Ibadan, Nigeria, was chased by a crowd bent on violence, but was arrested by a policeman after a struggle. Both the policeman and the market woman believed that both justice and their own interests would best be served if they took the accused to the lo-cal Hausa community's court, presided over by Hausa elders and the local Emir's deputy. After both had given testimony, the informal court found the young man guilty, fined him a large sum of money, lent him this money to pay the fine to the woman and policeman, and warned him that any further trouble and he would be exiled to his home town in the North and confined there (Salamone, 1998). In any situation there are often a surpris-ing number of policing agencies – non-state and state, offering localised protection of different levels of legality, effectiveness, availability, meth-ods and services. Each, of course, enforces their own code of conduct and standards. 'In any given society', as Pospisil puts it, 'there will be as many legal systems as there are functioning social units (Pospisil, 1971:24). These agencies create on the ground spheres of influence that overlap and change like a kaleidoscope. To what extent security provisions overlap in competi-tive or co-operative modes is a matter for further participatory research.

The complexity of African policing is no accident. It is the product of intense social and political upheaval brought about by colonial conquest, self-serving and predatory rulers, weak states, violent rebels and economic transformation and hardship. Chapter three explores the social context of contemporary African policing and chapter four the historical context.

CHAPTER 3

Conflict, Crime and the Context of Policing in Africa

Most Togolese now literally go to sleep with at least one eye virtually open.
(*Ghanaian Chronicle*, 28 July, 2003)

Freedom lies in not having to calculate the risk to oneself on every journey outdoors. (Patricia Morgan, quoted in Goldsmith, 2003)

To understand the policing solutions that have been chosen by Africans it is essential to understand the policing needs that confront them. The state's failure to deliver a universal police force that is fair, respectful, efficient and effective has been repeatedly documented. The BBC's 'Africa Live' programme ran a series in September 2003 called 'Africa's police: Friend or enemy?' inviting listeners to evaluate their state police. The overwhelming number of respondents on their web site were negative.[1] According to a 2004 poll by Steadman Research Services, owing to lack of confidence in the police, only 45 per cent of the incidents in Kenya were reported to them.[2] The nicknames alone used of the police are informative. In Nigeria, police officers from the mobile unit are referred to as 'Kill and go'; the traffic police in Kenya are called TKK – Toa Kitu Kidogo – Swahili for 'give something small'; in Ghana, police are often chided as 'Koti' because of their tendency to harass the public; in Sierra Leone during the APC era the Internal Security Unit (ISU) was known as 'I Shoot You' and when they changed their name to Special Security Division (SSD) they became known as 'Siaka Stevens' [the President's] Dogs'; in Cameroon police are referred to as 'mange-milles' – thousand eaters – in reference to the customary bribe of 1000 CFA. Even police chiefs and presidents bemoan the police corruption.[3]

---

1. http://news.bbc.co.uk/go/pr/fr/-/1/hi/world/africa/3081515516.stm.

2. *The East African Standard,* Nairobi, 5 April, 2004.

3. In Zambia, Assistant Commissioner of Police and Copperbelt Deputy Police Chief, Grace Chipalila, said there were many criminal elements within the ranks (*The Times of Zambia*, Ndola, 24 July, 2003); President Mwanawasa of Zambia expressed disappointment at the police service that had failed and needed serious cleansing.

Their inadequacies could be the result of many factors, including under-funding that itself has a political motive (Hills, 2000); the product of endemic corruption amongst those who are associated with the state and possess the means of coercion (Bayart et al., 1999); the result of lingering cultures of authoritarianism and disciplinarianism (Baker, 2002b); and the colonial origins of the police and decades of military rule that together produced militarised police forces that acted as instruments of oppression on behalf of the government (Chukwuma, 2001:127). Whatever the exact causes, 'The proven inability of the police to single-handedly produce security within the nation has created a vacuum in security' (Shearing and Kempa, 2000:206). It is a vacuum that is commonly filled by non-state policing. Africans wary or dismissive of the state police look elsewhere for security.

The shortcomings of the state police forces have to be set against a context where security is fragile and threatened on all sides. Africans today are faced with two evils: conflict and crime. Many would say that they have both become more serious threats in the last generation. All would say that Africans are in a weak position to counter them. The two are related, for both are manifestations of marginalisation, impoverishment and relative deprivation. Hence though the violence of war may cease, violence may simply transmute itself from the political to the criminal. Both are products of the same fractured societies.

Widespread conflict

The rule of law is possible only in an orderly state. Before enforcing law, government must establish order, yet unfortunately this has been seriously challenged in Africa over the last decades. 281 million, 45 per cent of the population of sub-Saharan Africa, live in countries that have been disrupted (at least in part of their territory) by wars, insurgencies and civil unrest in the last ten years. Since 1970 Africa has endured more than 30 wars, whilst during the past decade more than 17 countries of sub-Saharan Africa have experienced significant periods of violent conflict. These have been both inter-state (Ethiopia/Eritrea, Democratic Republic of Congo/Uganda/Rwanda) and intra-state (Ethiopia, Somali 1997ff., Sudan 1983ff., Chad 1994ff., Uganda 1995–2006, Rwanda 1990–94, Burundi 1993–2006, Democratic Republic of Congo (DRC) 1998ff., Angola 1975–2002, Sierra Leone 1991–2001, Liberia, 1989–96, 2000–04, Senegal 1990ff., Côte d'Ivoire 2002ff., Congo-Brazzaville 1992ff., Guinea Bissau 1998–99, Comoros 1997).

The crises have been of a multi-layered nature, with *inter alia*, humanitarian, livelihood, ethnic, political and international relations dimensions. In addition, they typically have multiple causes, whether an underlying economic, political and institutional breakdown or the absence of sufficiently effective alternative institutions for the resolution of intense competition or disagreement. Hence the term 'complex emergency' has been coined to capture their nature more effectively than the simplistic 'internal conflict' (Cliffe and Luckham, 1999). Many of these complex emergencies are now in the process of moving through the transition to peace, but the knot of cause and effect rarely unties with a military peace agreement. In fact, even after a peacemaking phase, some degree of violent conflict often continues, as certain interested parties seek to secure leverage in the settlement process. Conflict may return despite a peace agreement, as has happened in Sudan, Angola, DRC, Sierra Leone and Liberia; or a coup takes place, as in the case of Central African Republic (CAR) and Guinea Bissau. And 'no war/no peace' situations are not infrequent (e.g. DRC, Côte d'Ivoire, Burundi). Hence it is preferable to conceptualise the presumed final phase of conflict as one 'emerging from conflict', rather than as 'post-conflict', or simply 'post-settlement'.

Complex emergencies, by definition, require complex solutions, that is, radical and comprehensive ones. They have to address the political, military, security, humanitarian, developmental and international aspects of the problem in an integrated fashion. Yet it is no easy matter to seek to rapidly reform the economic and political system in the absence of those institutions and agencies that are designed to achieve this. Unfortunately, an inadequate response may only provoke a renewed outbreak of conflict. Inevitably, therefore, political issues come to the fore as a fundamental ingredient for constructing lasting settlements to internal conflict.

Even before the process of conflict resolution following the cessation of hostilities, there is a need for security and the restoration of the rule of law. Without that there can be no building of political institutions, no economic growth and no social reconciliation. Policing, therefore, has a key role to play in post-conflict reconstruction (Call, 2002; CSIS/AUSA, 2002; Plunkett, 2005; WOLA 2002; Woodrow Wilson 2003; Baker, 2006). Or put another way, policing in many parts of Africa has to begin from scratch in circumstances where there is a recent history of disregard for the rule of law and little respect for human rights. It must do so when the resources of policing authorisers are at a minimum and when their structures have been severely disrupted by the loss or displacement of personnel in the conflict.

Further, many of those who have been police providers in the past will have taken part in armed activity during the conflict and will be disqualified by vetting programmes or may have problems in re-integrating with their former communities. It is also a fact that there is always an abundance of arms left over from any conflict that quickly finds itself used for criminal activity.

Sadly, one of the regular features of violent internal conflict is the withering of the formal legal infrastructure and the murder of prominent judges and lawyers, either because the professions were seen to be dominated by a particular ethnic group or because they threatened punishment for wartime atrocities. It is often necessary, therefore, to train significant numbers of court officers, magistrates and judges, ensuring not just their grasp of the principles of justice, but also of human rights issues; the historical problems of justice for women, children and minorities; and the complexities of disputes arising from resettlement and reintegration of communities.

As regards the state police, their return to civilian policing is rarely straightforward. The state police face working in a very difficult social context. It is one where there is a surfeit of weapons left over from the conflict and where relaxed international border controls allow a sudden growth in organised crime (Schärf, 2001; Mondelane, 2000). Yet the police are likely to have been seriously under-resourced compared with the military during the conflict years. Indeed, during a civil war state civilian policing ceases to exist over large areas and, where it does continue, it commonly assumes a paramilitary nature. This may mean the police imagine that they have a licence to act with brutality against enemies of the state and to use torture to secure information that would preserve state security. Such practices mean that they are not well equipped for civilian duties or familiar with the procedures of evidence-based investigations, as opposed to confession-based methods (Schärf, 2001). In addition, if the previous regime has been authoritarian (e.g. Liberia) there is the issue of the political neutrality of the police force. Authoritarian regime police are unfamiliar with the concept of being accountable to the public rather than to the state. As agents of the regime they grow accustomed to immunity from prosecution themselves and to granting immunity to the powerful. They have to learn to use appropriate civilian methods of riot control and crowd management.

It is not surprising that conflict undermines the expectations of the African public towards the state police. Years of state police neglect or abuse produce a wariness and lack of confidence. Since it was often human rights abuses by the state security forces that constituted one of the causes of armed conflict, capacity-building programmes for them raise the fear of strengthening their repressive capabilities. Even though the public are told of human rights training for existing state police, as in Mozambique, Rwanda, Uganda, Liberia and Sierra Leone, they are acutely aware of the unsolved question as to how governments assuming office after the destruction wrought by conflict are to find and finance enough qualified police to offer nation-wide coverage. Nor do they see much progress in reducing the prohibitive costs and undue delays of the formal justice system. Complex emergencies invariably require the creation of a new state police force that is accountable through the disciplinary procedures of internal management, the oversight of the courts, performance monitoring by the internal affairs ministries, and critical appraisal by civil rights organisations and the media. Unless the state police forces are fair, accessible, efficient and incorruptible, there is little hope that citizens will have confidence in them or in the state that authorises them. Yet though no one doubts that improved state civil policing is a national priority following conflict, few states emerging from conflict have made much progress.

Growing crime rates

Crime against the person and property is an ever-present reality for Africans and one where they themselves must take responsibility for security against it. Africa is currently viewed as the most violent continent on the basis of crime victimization rates (Zvekic et al., 1995; see also UN-HABITAT Safer Cities Programme, 1996). According to one survey of Uganda, South Africa and Tanzania, three Africans out of every four in the cities had been victims of violence during 1991–95. This is nearly twice as many as in the cities of Asia and South America (Van Dijk, 1996). Though crime data based on reported and recorded crime is not totally reliable, the evidence suggests that many countries' crime rates have increased rapidly in the last two decades. However there may be many fluctuations within the overall trend. In Rwanda there is clear evidence that armed robberies in the provinces have declined but that in Kigali rape, organised crime and violent assaults have risen 2003–05 (Baker, 2007a). A rural Ethiopian study reported a crime increase first during 1990–91, when there was a government transition, and during 1994–95, when a rise in unemployment was accompanied by 'loose police control'. But in 1996–97 there had been a dramatic decline as the result of an increase in the numbers of police at the local level (World Bank, 1998).

Malawi's official crime statistics show that reported crime increased steadily between 1995 and 1999. Between 1997 and 1999, the number of reported armed robberies rose by nearly 40 per cent, while the number of murders per year increased slightly, even though many other reported crimes such as general theft and break-ins, assaults, and mob justice declined in the same period.

> All these indicators, and the testimony of local police officers interviewed, suggest a steady growth of more organised crime and a decrease in petty crime. The general rise in the crime rate after 1994 and the recent decline in many types of crime left a disproportionate fear of some types of non-violent crime (Wood, 2000).

South African Police figures for 2002–03 show high levels of crime. 60 South Africans are murdered each day, giving murder rates of 47.4 per 100,000 of the population. More than half of all murders were committed with firearms. Rape is at 115.3 per 100,000, although it is probably much higher since only one in three rape cases is reported to the police.[4] Since 1983 at least 3,049 policemen have been murdered. Despite some drops in crime rates over recent years, the fear of crime in South Africa is widespread. Data from the November 1999 Human Sciences Research Council National Opinion Survey showed 44 per cent 'personally felt safe or very safe most days', whilst 47 per cent 'felt unsafe or very unsafe' (Humphries, 2000:1).

Figures for Accra, Ghana, show similar large increases in the last decade. Total crimes recorded by the police jumped from 26,946 in 1990 to 44,567 in 1996. Taking selected offences, murder rose from 20 per year to 51; assault from 9,551 to 17,905; and theft from 7,659 to 12,911 (Appiahene-Gyamfi, 2003:17).

In a nation-wide survey in Nigeria, conducted in October 2000, the public was asked, 'Has crime abated in your area within the past one year?' 66 per cent said crime in their areas had worsened. Of the 34 per cent who said the rate of crime had dropped in their areas, most attributed this decline to the emergence of vigilante and anti-crime groups.[5]

A 2001 Victimization Survey in Kenya reported 37 per cent of Nairobi's residents had been victims of robbery; 40 per cent of victims had been injured as a result of violence used in the robbery. About 50 per cent of the

---

4. *Business Day,* Johannesburg, 23 September, 2003.

5. *Post Express,* Lagos, 16 October, 2000.

victims did not report their injury to the police because they felt it was a waste of time (UN-HABITAT, 2001).

This sample of surveys does suggest that crime rates may be growing, though of course they are closely related also to a greater willingness to report crime to the police. This willingness may be part of the 1990s transformation of state police into civilian policing serving the public rather than the regime or it may be a response to sensitisation programmes among the public and the police that have made them more willing to treat seriously certain crimes such as those that involve gender violence. On the other hand, the decline in the use of intrusive and violent methods by state police may have allowed crime to grow. Beyond the activities of the police however, there are major social upheavals going on in Africa that are likely to affect crime. Earlier it was suggested that violence and crime were related, both being manifestations of marginalisation, impoverishment and relative deprivation. Understanding in more detail what those underlying factors are explains the nature of the policing that has developed to counter violence and insecurity. Eight factors are examined below as significant contributors: material poverty and social inequality; youth marginalisation; political transition; liberalisation and globalisation; urbanisation; availability of weapons; inadequate state criminal justice systems; and crisis of informal social control.

Material poverty and social inequality

Poverty not only provides a motive for crime and rebellion, but also undermines some attempts to police it. The world economic slowdown at the beginning of the 21st century pushed the number of unemployed in Africa (based on the jobless who have some form of social protection) to a new high. Over 50 per cent of the populations in most African cities live in absolute poverty (Kisia, 2004:8). In sub-Saharan Africa the open unemployment rate had risen to 14.4 per cent by 2002, and was expected to rise higher due to the food crisis (International Labour Office, 2003). A Tanzanian government survey 2000/1 found that one million Tanzanians were unemployed and another two million under-employed (i.e. working less than the normal 40 hours per week). In Kenya unemployment levels are close to 60 per cent (Kisia, 2004:8). Even in South Africa, which has a stronger economy than most African countries, unemployment soared from 16 per cent in 1995 to almost 30 per cent in 2003, with 60 per cent of the unemployed under 30 years of age. Further, the rapid spread of HIV/

AIDS, faltering aid and investment flows, and weak commodity prices undermined African economic growth and left many countries in severe poverty with little hope of escape. It is true that the picture is not uniform across the continent. In some 12 or more countries, average income per head has risen at 1 per cent or more a year over the decade. However at least another 20 countries experienced falling income per head during the same period. 16 of these 20 were involved in conflict, such as Sierra Leone, Liberia, Angola, Democratic Republic of Congo, and Côte d'Ivoire; others saw political turmoil, such as Zimbabwe, and Central African Republic (World Bank, 2003).

Even those with formal jobs are often poorly paid and high inflation undermines the value of salaries and savings. In South Africa incomes from work have declined, so that whereas in 1995 39 per cent of workers earned less than R1000 a month in nominal terms, by 2003 (when R1000 could only buy about half as much) the figure had risen to 42 per cent. In addition to falling wages, there is the issue of the inequality of income distribution across the continent. Three factors have aggravated inequalities. First, the HIV epidemic has placed higher economic and human burdens on the poor. It has forced more and more children and juveniles aged 10–19 into the labour force as adults fell ill or died. The burden of caring for family members who are ill, and the likelihood of losing a home when a wage earner dies, all entrench poverty. Second, sharp increases in user fees have jeopardised the extension of government services to the poor, which had been important in cushioning income inequalities. School fees, in particular, have had an adverse effect in maintaining inequalities and limiting the access of poor children to essential education. In South Africa, though many more households have received basic services since 1994, one survey suggested 13 per cent of households have had their water cut for at least some period of time, with a similar proportion for electricity (International Labour Office, 2003). Thirdly, in the aftermath of conflict there are, of course, the additional economic challenges of large numbers of returning internally displaced persons (IDPs) and demobilised soldiers seeking employment.

Millions, therefore, struggle to survive by legal means. With more and more people unemployed, underemployed, and employed in the insecure informal economy, there has been an increasing attraction to acquiring goods by theft or on the black-market, though this only feeds corruption and theft. As poverty and inequality grow, so does the likelihood of crime and rebellion. Of course the state police are not immune to this economic struggle. A Nigerian newspaper that bemoaned the 'brazen arrogance and shamelessness' of police that collected 20 Naira off motorists at illegal checkpoints, admitted that,

> It is no secret that an average policeman lives in poverty and penury with very poor monthly salary and living in a dilapidated ramshackle building for accommodation. Again, he operates in a filthy and health-threatening environment with obsolete equipment most of which was inherited from the fleeing colonial masters.[6]

Youth marginalisation

Some criminologists argue that crime is a young person's behaviour. If this is so, then the larger the proportion of young people in society, the more criminogenic it becomes (Schonteich, 1999b; Agnew, 1990; Brantingham and Brantingham, 1984, 1993; Kennedy and Forde, 1990; Igbinovia 2000: 543; cf. Samara, 2005). In Accra it was found that over 96 per cent of police suspects were young males and 74 per cent were between 18 and 32 years of age. Most were single with little formal education (Appiahene-Gyamfi, 2003:20). In Africa young people typically constitute 50 per cent of the total population; they are tomorrow's parents, business owners and agricultural workers; or tomorrow's fighters and criminals. Young people constitute a particularly difficult challenge for African states. They can feel disenfranchised and, as a result, resentful and hopeless without the provision of constructive social incentives such as cohesive communities, accessible education and recognition of their right to participate in the political process. They face a range of substantial problems: unemployment, child labour, inadequate education and loss of parents through AIDS. A national survey in Tanzania showed that 1.6 million of the 4.7 million children in the country were labourers. A majority of the children between 5 and 17 years worked for more than four hours a day and were not attending school due to poverty. This lack of skills later penalised them in the formal labour market. The same survey found that unemployment was most severe among the youth aged 10 to 34 years (Integrated Labour Force Survey, 2000/01).

Those young people who have lived in the midst of armed conflict face still greater problems: the loss of parents through war, and the trauma of having been directly involved with the fighting forces in the war as combatants or sex slaves. In 2003 the United Nations Children's Fund estimated

---

6. *Vanguard,* Lagos, 6 October, 2003.

that the rebel LRA in Northern Uganda had abducted 8,500 children. Children have been exposed to more trauma, responsibility and experience of power than ever before. As a result, they are more politically aware and carry greater expectations for involvement in decision making and desire for economic opportunity than ever before. Unless African states foster in youth a real stake in society by building social fabric, they will turn to the thrill and reward of deviance. They will be outside of the reach of the law and their identities will not be shaped by the law (Altbeker, 2001). The most recurring factors amongst the social causes of youth crime are all too familiar in Africa. They are social exclusion due to long periods of unemployment or marginalisation; dropping out of school or illiteracy; and the lack of socialisation within the family. The nihilism of the young unemployed draws them to gangs because they offer quick material reward and, perhaps most importantly, they turn these youngsters into objects of attraction and respect, rather than disdain in their own communities. The gang offers a cohesive alternative sub-culture to the dominant culture that has marginalized them, and through criminal activity offers alternative forms of wealth creation. These criminal youth gangs may have particular appeal in the aftermath of the war as armed youth seek an alternative place of belonging and social cohesion. As Amadou Touré puts it: 'Young people who are out of school, unemployed and sometimes living at the fringes of their families and of society, form a reserve force of destabilisation' (Touré, 1998:51–52).

Political transition

Evidence from South Africa, as well as several Latin American nations and former Soviet states, suggests a close correlation between the process of political transition and the rise of crime. The explanation commonly offered is that internal security practices employed by totalitarian and authoritarian states to maintain control over political dissidence may also have served to curtail ordinary crime. Liberalising governments are keen to prevent these security practices but do not always show the same degree of enthusiasm when it comes to developing and implementing effective and legitimate alternatives. On the one hand the police are under pressure to reduce crime, to abandon old coercive methods and to offer greater transparency. On the other hand they lack the new skills and institutions to implement democratic means of crime control. The result is a visible failure to limit crime (International Council on Human Rights Policy, 2003). And in the case of post-conflict states they may be confronted with armed groups who have transformed themselves into criminal gangs.

In addition, political transitions can be so sudden as to catch governments unprepared. Major General David Jemibewon, former Nigerian Minister of Police Affairs observed:

> The sudden change that the transition from the long years of military rule to a democratic dispensation brought on the country (Nigeria) was so monumental and managing it was daunting … The Nigeria Police Force that we inherited could be said to have suffered gravely from lack of such regulatory institutions and lack of focus … Our newfound democracy became to some extent a source of insecurity and lawlessness, as rights were misconstrued and exercised without restraint. Views which were considered anti-government and hitherto suppressed out of fear under the military, were now freely expressed and often times violently too. Militant groups that were agitating for one thing or the other, often times armed, sprang up in some parts of the country. The police, who were not adequately prepared for the violent and criminal eruptions that heralded our democratic rebirth, were therefore stretched to the maximum of their capability (Jemibewon, 200:30).

The danger of a failing police service and rising crime in a transition period is that it leads to widespread demands for sterner anti-crime measures and often to calls for retribution from the public and from the police themselves. In such a situation it is a strong temptation for a government seeking to consolidate its legitimacy to instigate a harsh 'war on crime'. Though this can be done quickly and may meet with strong public support, it obviously sends a signal to the police that a blind eye will be turned towards any reversion to the old abusive practices in order to capture criminals.

Liberalisation and globalisation

Crime is commonly linked to social dislocation. As such the social effects in Africa of the opening up of markets and the reduction of the minimal state welfare and job protection have been profound. Currie (1992, 1997) describes the trend towards the market society, a society in which everything is for sale, as eroding all principles of social or institutional organisation and subordinating them to private gain. Individuals and communities become increasingly dependent on the market for all their needs. Yet it is precisely in these societies that the level of dislocation to society, such as the level of crime, has been most marked (Taylor, 1999).

The situation in Africa is not identical to the West, in that the state has never reached the same scale of penetration of society and welfare provision, nor have the levels of industrialisation been such that a shift to services would make as large an impact. Nevertheless, there is evidence that some of these processes and their consequences have been felt in Africa. One negative feature of market society is the manner in which it imposes additional strains on the family unit through its requirements for parents to generate the maximum possible income to sustain the family. In urban Africa it is not uncommon for both parents to take on two or three jobs.

Economic liberalisation is also associated with the withdrawal of public provision of welfare or the offer of welfare through the private market. Thus user fees have been introduced for education and health across Africa. The World Bank argues that the current government provision model of service delivery must be rejected in favour of reforms that largely bypass the state, including private concessions and sub-contracting (World Bank, 2004). The momentum for this service privatisation mainly comes from budget crises and pressure from the International Monetary Fund (IMF) to balance budgets. Another reason is that in many cases public services perform very badly or exclude the poor. African governments at independence spoke of promoting equity and universality through redistributive mechanisms to ensure a minimum level of access to primary education, basic health care, and safe drinking water. In these areas they have fallen far short of their promises. Current policy sees private contracts between governments and providers. However, the most pervasive impact of service privatisation is increased prices, which inevitably lead to social exclusion. In Kenya privatisation, implemented since 1992, has made water more expensive than oil and turned patients away from hospitals untreated (Kenya: Integrity Assessment Comments, 23 June, 2004, www.public-i.org/). And in South Africa almost 10 million people had their water service disconnected between 1994 and 2002, primarily as the result of non-payment.

Such economic policies also have criminological consequences. On the one hand, commercial security companies have rapidly appeared all over Africa since the 1990s offering armed and unarmed guards. On the other hand, the cost means that those who can take advantage of their services tend to be commercial interests and the wealthy. There is a cheaper end of the security market, but users are faced with poor quality and stories of collaboration between guards and criminals. For most, however, the liberalisation of policing has offered little more than a guard outside their place of formal employment. In such a market society there will, by definition, be 'winners' and 'losers'. This will exacerbate inequality and in the process generate destructive concentrations of very pronounced economic deprivation. The experience of losing out or failing in a market society can become a defining moment for an individual and an alternative and criminal path may be seriously considered

Urbanisation

Across the world, cities stand out as having the highest crime rates. Part of the explanation must lie in the very nature of cities as bodies of shared public space amongst unequal citizens. Poverty and wealth are brought together in close proximity, both in trade and in housing, and yet in a space where, as far as developing countries are concerned, a governing authority is minimal and poorly managed. The availability of portable goods of value also creates enormous attractions, vulnerabilities and opportunities.

Africa is far less urbanised than other continents, although there are considerable variations across countries. Urbanisation levels are 81 per cent in Gabon and 50 per cent in South Africa and Botswana, yet only 18 per cent in Burkina Faso and 24 per cent in Malawi and Chad. Urbanisation is occurring rapidly, however, especially where base levels are low. Everywhere figures of 4–5 per cent growth per annum are typical. Big 'million plus' cities include Addis Ababa, Kampala, Mogadishu, Nairobi, Douala, Yaoundé, Ouagadougou, Abidjan, Accra, Conakry, Bamako, Ibadan and Dakar. Three giant cities are Johannesburg with 4 million, Kinshasa with 5 million and Lagos with more than 13 million. The rapid urban growth since the 1960s has been the result of the growth of existing urban populations and migration to urban centres of people, either pushed by civil conflict and poverty or pulled by prospects of employment, improved security, and available welfare amenities.

The demand for housing brought about by these rapidly increasing populations is far beyond the capacity of available land for controlled development. Inevitably the cities are experiencing widespread development of illegal occupation on sites unplanned, overcrowded, inadequately serviced, and often unsafe. In Nairobi, for instance, over 55 per cent of the population are living in unplanned settlements. Most African municipalities do not have the resources to keep pace with the demand for basic services such as housing, roads, piped water, sanitation and waste disposal. Nor have health services, education services and electricity supply been expanded sufficiently to cope with the growing populations. Hence in sub-Saharan

Africa the proportion of urban residents in slums is the highest in the world at 71.9 per cent, whereas in developing regions as a whole, slum dwellers account for 43 per cent of the population (UN-HABITAT, 2003).

The picture of communities of crime in the informal settlements threatening the wealthier residential areas is far from the reality. In fact the poor of the informal settlements are more the victimised than the perpetrators of crimes. A victim survey in Johannesburg in 1997 revealed that people who live in informal settlements and townships are the most likely to be victimised by both property and violent crime. But while the poor are more exposed to crime in areas in which they live, they are far less able to afford protection from physical security measures such as walls, burglar proofing and electronic alarms (Louw et al., 1998). The high crime rates in informal settlements are as much a reflection of their inability to defend themselves as of any predisposition to crime.

Immigrant groups in the cities can have an especially difficult time and their survival strategies may well include crime. Discrete urban territories can readily arise where ethnic minorities reside who are permanently excluded from legitimate employment and where the writ of the authorities, like the police, does not run. Further, social exclusion can erode moral values and break down social support structures, such as family and community. These effects may be concentrated by the racism of the surrounding society, as has been reported against Somalis in Nairobi, Mozambicans in Johannesburg and Burkinas in Abidjan. Yet the chance of escape from racialised enclaves may be minimal. Rather than being zones of transition, they are becoming permanent zones of minorities. The fact that lawlessness in these districts is often left unchallenged by the African state leads to their stigmatisation.

Availability of weapons

Weapons are extensively used in Africa to cause violence in local populations, affecting livelihoods and creating poverty. The availability of small arms in Africa, often from past conflicts within or outside the country, has had a profound effect on crime. The Small Arms Survey research estimates that there are 30 million small arms in sub-Saharan Africa (previous estimates commonly put the total figure at 100 million) (The Small Arms Survey, 2003). The vast majority of these guns are in civilian hands (79 per cent), followed by the military (16 per cent), police (3 per cent) and insurgents (2 per cent). Kenya, Tanzania and Uganda each have an estimated national stockpile of between 500,000 and one million small arms. There are about 77,000 small arms in the hands of major West African insurgent groups. The total number of illicit military-style guns is probably one million or less for all of sub-Saharan Africa.

Illicit production of small arms occurs in a number of countries in sub-Saharan Africa, including Ghana and South Africa (The Small Arms Survey, 2003). The rise in armed robbery appears to be directly linked to the ease with which criminals can access these illicit guns. Police in South Africa revealed that nearly 9,000 people had been held for using guns in crimes during January–August 2003 in Gauteng Province alone – 1,042 were held for murder, 1,324 for attempted murder, 3,548 for armed robbery and 261 for hijacking.[7] Elsewhere elephant poachers use military weapons to slaughter herds and intimidate preserve guards. And in the savannah lands of Kenya, Uganda and Ethiopia historic conflicts between competing cattle herders have escalated to deadly warfare with the introduction of automatic rifles.

Yet though people seek protection from gun-violence, there is often widespread distrust of the police, since it is widely believed in countries such as Mozambique, Kenya and Zambia that they are a principal source of supply of weapons to criminals or are actively involved in the arms trade themselves.[8]

Inadequate state criminal justice systems

When the state cannot offer a system that protects people from crime, and when it cannot guarantee to detect it and punish it if crime does occur, people will resort to their own policing and courts. It is not just that the formal court system is only found in the main towns of Africa, but that the very operation of the formal court system needs to be addressed. It has to become more user friendly and requires a high level of resources to make it fair. Most countries have a very limited number of practising lawyers and few can afford their services (e.g. Namibia 140; Mozambique 180; Tanzania 120; Malawi 300. Baker and Scheye, 2007). People also find courts alienating since they are rarely conducted in local languages and the adver-

---

7. *Sunday Times*, Johannesburg, 24 August, 2003.

8. Reported at Christian Council of Mozambique Conference on, 'The illicit spread of small arms in Mozambique', September, 2001. See also; Bayart et al. 1999: 63; *The Times of Zambia*, 2 July, 2003; *Mail&Guardian*, 21 August, 1998.

sarial procedures are unfamiliar. Such a situation clearly encourages people to use their own justice models and disregard the state system.

The police are also very limited in the service they can offer to the average African. The harsh reality is that in many African states the police are ill equipped in training, resources and numbers to deal with crime. The estimated ratios of police officer to population is DRC, 1:4,377; Guinea Bissau, 1:2,403; Kenya, 1:1,157; Nigeria: 1:1,166; Sierra Leone, 1:612. Baker and Scheye, 2007). It is true that donors have introduced new equipment, from vehicles to radios and computers, but if it is not resisted as a threat to the traditional way of 'doing business' it may well be quickly redundant for lack of servicing or replacement parts (Igbinovia, 2000). The common reputation of the state police for inaccessibility, indifference, inefficiency, extortion and brutality inevitably means that few turn to them for crime prevention or detection. As the Kenyan victimization survey points out, over half of the victims do not bother to report to the police because of the perception that the police are ineffective, and more crucially, because respondents attributed one in three crimes, directly or indirectly, to the police themselves (Ruteere and Pommerolle, 2003:594).

The formal justice system has not only discouraged people from using it, but its very weakness has been exploited by criminals. Transnational and organised crime in particular has been able to exploit the expanded illegitimate opportunity of democratic transitions. Border controls have been relaxed, international trade and tourism have grown, and the police have been slow to reorganise and to acquire criminal investigation skills (Shaw and Louw, 1997; Gastrow, 1998, 1999; Kinnes, 2000). Thus according to the Togo Commissioner of Police, the pattern of crime in Lomé changed during the transition. It moved from petty forms of stealing, to violent armed robberies, as organised crime gangs from neighbouring Benin, Nigeria, and Ghana took over, or established new, local crime networks in the stealing of vehicles.[9]

Conviction rates are one way of measuring how well the criminal justice system is doing. Yet while the number of crimes reported to the police has increased since political transitions, the number prosecuted remains low, as do conviction rates (e.g. in South Africa in 1999, the police recorded 2.4 million crimes, only 200,000 of which resulted in convictions). For some of the more serious crimes, conviction rates were even worse. In South Africa they are only 2 per cent for car hijacking, 3 per cent for aggravated

---

9. *Ghanaian Chronicle,* Accra, 28 July, 2003.

robbery, and 8 per cent for rape. Such low conviction rates are largely due to under-trained and overworked detectives and prosecutors, with inadequate support staff and services. Conviction rate, however, is not the only performance measure of the criminal justice system. The fact is that most crimes reported do not end up in court: they remain 'undetected' due to the absence of leads, or incomplete or poor police investigation.

A study for the South African Law Commission tracked developments in 15,000 cases of violent crime (murder, rape and robbery with aggravating circumstances) and fraud from 1998 for two years. Its findings were that: in 75 per cent of cases, the crime had not been solved; in 4 per cent of cases the criminal trial was still going on after 33 months; about 10 per cent of cases had been withdrawn in court; about 6 per cent of cases reported had ended in a guilty verdict; and about 5 per cent of cases reported had ended in an acquittal. In a more in-depth study (involving about 1,000 cases) in the Western Cape they found that: 74 per cent of cases had never been solved; in 17 per cent of cases the complainant had withdrawn the charge; in another 7 per cent of cases the investigation was ongoing; in 2 per cent of cases a warrant of arrest had been issued, but nobody had been arrested. The Commission's stark conclusion was:

> Violent criminals get away with their crimes. For every 100 violent crimes reported to the police, perpetrators in only six cases had been convicted after more than two years … We cannot expect to see a significantly lower incidence of crime until investigation and prosecution improves dramatically.[10]

Such low detection and conviction rates are an incentive to criminal activity. In addition, a failing police force does not get the required co-operation from members of the public, which in turn reduces their chances of success in crime control initiatives.

Crisis of informal social control

Criminologists have long argued that the real question is not why people commit crimes, but why they do not. In general their answer is not that some rational fear of detection and punishment deters them, but that it is due to the socialising processes at work in society. Informal social controls and natural surveillance are exerted within local communities by, for instance, elders, leaders of faith communities, and extended families. It is

---

10. *Cape Argus,* Cape Town, 5 August, 2003.

suggested that these communal controls may be weakening due to the increasing mobility of people, capital and information, with a corresponding increase in crime. The willingness of people to exert informal communal control, or 'guardianship' (Cohen and Felson, 1979, quoted in Bayley and Shearing, 2001) is being 'disembedded' (Giddens, 1990).

The decline of more indirect and arguably more effective sources of social control is often associated with urbanisation when social relations are removed from local contexts. As Appiahene-Gyamfi notes, following the routine activities theory, the growth of Accra has led to people being dispersed 'away from their families, property, guardians/handlers, and altered … the probability that motivated offenders and suitable targets would converge without the presence of capable guardians, in most parts of the city' (2003:21).

The loosening of informal social control has also been linked to the many disruptive and violent democratic transitions that Africa has experienced in the last 15 years. Shaw, summarising a conference on crime and policing in transitional societies, suggests that internal communal organisation may be dramatically altered in a period of democratic transition (Shaw, 2000). He notes, for example, the impact of prolonged resistance to apartheid, where alternative forms of community cohesion and communal control were built that kept criminality in check until they were disbanded with the opposition's success. Or again, he observes the effect on crime of the loss of a strict state imposed organisational network, as when the socialist states fell.

Reflecting on Western societies, others have linked the loss of informal control to the transition to post-modern or late modern societies. This, it is argued, has produced 'a pluralistic, fragmented and diversified socio-cultural system' (Johnston 1999a:180). These trends are said to have promoted individualism, consumerism and a weakening of traditional forms of communal control that previously supplemented the efforts of the state police. Though elements of these processes can be detected in Africa, for the most part communal identities and values are still prevalent.

Conclusion

Conflict and crime hang as dark clouds over the lives of Africans. Both are fuelled by poverty. Both have blighted the lives of millions and the fear of poverty grips many more. For those trapped in poverty, endemic solutions like migration and home security measures are not available. They need policing provision. In terms of protection from armed rebels the state is an unreliable provider; in terms of protection from criminals the state is often a non-provider. Poverty, therefore, not only determines their exposure to danger, but also the quality of the protection they will be able to put together by themselves or with the help of others. But social conditions are not the only determinant of policing. No explanation of contemporary policing patterns can ignore the role of history, particularly political history, in Africa's story, so the next chapter will address this.

CHAPTER 4

The Historical Path of Policing in Africa

The colonial police were a 'domestic missionary' of the modern 'civilized' order.
(Storch, 1975)

Chapter three sought to portray the social context in which authorisers and providers of policing make their decisions. Conflict and crime as experienced or feared is a major determinant of policing. The other factor shaping it is the historical trajectory, particularly the political history of Africa. Without understanding the enduring traditions, colonial impositions, autocratic oppressions and commercial exploitations that have swept across Africa leaving behind debris of varying harm, it is impossible to understand the contemporary policing responses. This chapter, therefore, will explain the paths followed with respect to the authorisers and providers of policing from pre-colonial days to the 1980s.

Pre-Colonial policing in Africa

It is instinctive for people to take steps to ensure that they and their families are protected from danger. On the basis of offering such protection governments are said to have arisen. The details of how policing was organised by pre-colonial governments in Africa is not altogether clear. According to Alice Hills, no accurate account of policing in pre-colonial Africa before the arrival of the Europeans can be given. She suggests that, in addition to the social control of communities and headmen and age sets, it is likely, 'that many of the most powerful traditional rulers maintained bodies of men whose roles could be likened to those of the police' (2000:29). This seems to have been the case in Botswana by the early nineteenth century. Finding that both male age sets and headmen were not always sufficient for arrests and enforcing order, some chiefs turned to their own appointees to act as policemen (Bouman, 1987:280). Chukwuma argues that in Nigeria it appears that several ethnic nationalities had some form of community-based police services:

> This ranged from the highly developed age-grade system among the Igbos of south-eastern Nigeria, the 'secret societies' – such as the Ogboni and Oro cults found in several Yoruba Communities of the south-west – to the Ekpe cult among the Efiks of the south. All these societies, rooted in the communities, helped to maintain law and order as well as general community development (Chukwuma, 2001:127).

In the north of Nigeria it was customary for every emir to possess bodyguards (the dogarai) who performed policing functions, such as collecting taxes and arresting offenders, as well as delivering messages for the emirs (Ahire, 1991:43). Likewise traditional militia hunters and warriors (for example, the Kamajors of Sierra Leone) are commonly thought to be descendants of the pre-colonial provision of communal policing and defence. The explorer David Livingstone makes reference to chiefs' militias and judicial systems. Writing of Bango, a chief who ruled near Golungo Alto (east of Luanda in modern Angola) he says:

> When any of his people are guilty of theft he pays down the amount of the stolen goods at once, and then reimburses himself out of the property of the thief so effectively as to benefit by the transaction. The people under him are divided into a number of classes ... the carriers are the lowest of free men .... The soldiers and militia pay for the privilege of serving, the advantage being that they are not liable to be made carriers (quoted in MacNair, 1956:131).

It was, of course, a very different legal context from the contemporary one. Livingstone reports the cropping of ears and the selling of people into slavery for the slightest offences. Yet other pre-colonial African societies, especially when the disputants were known to one another, 'aimed less at punishing criminal offenders than at resolving the consequences to their victims. Sanctions were often compensatory rather than punitive, intended to restore victims to their previous position' (Llewellyn and Howse, 2002; Gluckman, 1973; Van Ness and Heetderks, 1997:6).

Though there was considerable variation in laws and customs both within and across ethnic groups, a common concern was 'the restoration of the disturbed social equilibrium within the community' (Mqeke 1995:364). The concept of *ubuntu* denotes a sense of humanity and of the inter-connectedness of people. The notion is enshrined in the Xhosa proverb: *umuntu ngumuntu ngabantu* (a person is a person through persons) (Villa-Vicencio 1996:527). *Ubuntu* is captured in the sayings, 'I am because you are' and 'my humanity is tied up with your humanity'. Hence what makes others worse off also brings harm to oneself. Thus, on this understanding of justice, restoration concerns repairing the damage done to the wrongdoer as well as the wronged (Llewellyn and Howse, 2002). Policing, authorised and provided by chiefs in pre-colonial societies, was seeking to uphold this community wholeness.

The view that policing and law enforcement was a community undertaking was to continue in the rural areas in a modified form throughout the colonial period. It was only with the arrival of the African independent state that steps were taken to remove local community self-policing. What was later to be excoriated as the people 'taking the law into their own hands', was then (and now) seen as the people keeping in their own hands what had always been there.

European commercial policing in Africa

In the early phases of European domination, commercial interests acted with little supervision. They were not slow to resort to force to achieve their ends. For instance, to secure labourers in his new private domain of the Congo (acquired 1885), King Leopold of Belgium used mercenary troops. Later, in 1888, he organised them into the Force Publique, which grew to 19,000 men. It combined the roles of counterinsurgency, occupying army and company labour police force. To secure the necessary rubber tappers and porters for Leopold's enterprise, people were beaten, chained together and forced to carry loads. The Force Publique also supplied much of the firepower to the rubber gathering companies. Villages that refused to submit to producing their quotas of rubber had their entire population shot by the Force Publique or company troops and their hands cut off as 'evidence' to the officers that the job had been done (Hochschild, 1998).

The British South Africa Company was another commercial enterprise that was not averse to using coercion to increase profit. At the time of the Shona Rising of 1896, in what is now Zimbabwe, the company's British South Africa Police (BSAP, formed 1889) were entering villages to collect the hut taxes, lashing people and demanding goats and cattle be slaughtered for them. One headman was recorded as saying that it was the company police who:

Ravished their daughters, and insulted their young men, who tweaked the beards of their chieftains and made lewd jokes with the elder women of the Great House, who abused the law they were expected to uphold, who respected none but the native Commissioners and officers of police, who collected taxes at the point of their assegais, and ground the people in tyranny and oppression (quoted in Schmidt, 1992:37).

Patrolling on horse, the BSAP enforced the company's law and if need be were prepared to fight as a military body. Their two small cavalry regiments were employed in punishing all those implicated in the Shona rebellion. Shona kraals were burnt, their animals seized, their men killed and their women and children were held by the Company's Native Messengers (police).

Further north, the Imperial British East African Company (IBEACO) also had an armed private policing body of mainly Sudanese and Indians. These were deployed along the trade routes to guard them, until the IBEACO transferred its rights to the British Government in 1893. To the west in northern Nigeria, the Royal Niger Company set up the Royal Niger Constabulary in 1888 to protect its property. Being a paramilitary force it was also able to play an important role in British campaigns until it was dissolved in 1900.

A similar pattern prevailed in Portuguese East Africa. Three big trading companies managed it by 1915. They owned all rights to agriculture and mining in their area and could also claim taxes from the local population, who were forced to work on the plantations. They too organised their own policing until 1932 when the Portuguese state took over the companies.

Not all the commercial policing ceased with the establishment of colonial police forces. Some commercial interests, particularly the mines and railways, maintained or asserted their role as authorisers and providers of policing (Killingray, 1997:182; van Onselen 1973:401–18; 1976:139–41). For instance the Sierra Leone Selection Trust formed a Diamond Protection Force in 1935, whilst the Uganda Railways established the Uganda Railway Police in 1902.

Colonial state policing in Africa up to 1945

Whatever the exact nature of the pre-colonial policing systems, many aspects of them continued into colonial times as authority was devolved to indigenous rulers. Indeed the very people that had served pre-colonial authorities in a policing role often became the uniformed Chiefs' Messengers and the Native Authority police under the European colonial system (Bouman, 1987:281).

The rural interiors of the colonies were not normally policed directly by the authorities, because of the size and difficulty of the terrain and, more importantly, because the area was not considered economically vital.[1] Indirect rule ensured that the colonial state was the authoriser, but that in these specified areas it looked to customary authorities to be the providers of security and order.

The main areas of European investment, however, such as the cities, mines and transportation links were to be protected by newly recruited armed forces and armed police. The assumption of policing responsibilities by the public authorities took place in the latter half of the nineteenth century. For example, in Southern Africa a police force was established in Cape Town in the 1850s, the Natal Mounted Police in 1874, the Transvaalsche Rijdende Politie in 1881 and the Bechuanaland Border police in 1885. In East Africa, Uganda had an armed constabulary formed in 1899 and Nyasaland in the mid-1890s. In West Africa in 1854 a detachment of the French National Gendarmerie was formed with jurisdiction over French territories from Senegal to Côte d'Ivoire. As for British territories, the Gold Coast established a small force in the coastal towns in 1865, whilst the Colony of Lagos was given in 1861 an armed Consular Guard, commonly known as the 'Hausa Constabulary'. To the east, the Oil Rivers Protectorate was established in 1891 and given an armed constabulary later known as the Niger Coast Constabulary (Ahire, 1991:35–39; Alemika, 1993).

A degree of shift from military to civilian duties did not alter the European focus of their work, however. In 1952 it could still be said of the Kenyan police that their main work: 'lies in the settled and urban areas of the territory, though detachments have been stationed in the Northern Frontier Province, at the gold mine and in other places where there is special need for their services' (Jeffries 1952:104).

Not unexpectedly, most officers in these early police forces in Africa were Europeans, but neither were the lower ranks necessarily representatives of the communities where they operated. Some came from other colonies (in the British case, particularly India) and those recruited from within the colony were chosen from those sections of the population which were generally least educated, most distant from the centres of power, and

---

1. The French divided Chad into what they described as 'le Tchad utile' and 'le Tchad inutile', useful and useless Chad.

hence least threatening to the colonial government. And they worked out-side their home territory lest they be disinclined to enforce the law harshly. Often, too, they originated from what the colonial authority regarded as a martial race, such as the 'Nubians' of the Kenya Police, the 'Hausa' of the northern territories in the Gold Coast Armed Police or the Yao of the Nyasaland Police (Kirk-Greene, 1980; McCracken 1986). They were alien police enforcing alien rule. Governor Denton of Lagos said in 1893:

> In our Hausa Force we have a body of men dissociated from the counties im-mediately around Lagos both by birth and religion and who are as a matter of fact, the hereditary enemies of the Yoruba. This is such an enormous advan-tage in any interior complication that I should be sorry to see it abandoned (quoted in Ahire, 1991:56).

Since the European overlords, both commercial and state, were alien and invading forces of oppression, control and regulation of the population had to have a strong emphasis on physical coercion through locally recruited military and paramilitary units. Military organisations held quasi-police functions (i.e. they were responsible for internal security as well as defend-ing frontiers and being available for assisting neighbouring colonies) such as the British West African Frontier Force (1898), the East African Rifles and the Uganda Rifles (1899) (the latter two being merged later into the King's African Rifles). Certain regions, such as Northern Uganda and Northern Territories of Gold Coast, remained under military administration beyond the First World War. On the other hand, police forces were paramilitary in nature and often recruited from the military. The intermingling of func-tions is illustrated by the Hausa Constabulary of Lagos. It had its mission expanded to include imperial defence when dispatched to the Gold Coast during the Asante expedition of 1873–74. It performed both police and military duties until 1895, when an independent Hausa Force was carved out of the constabulary and given exclusively military functions.

The model used for the British colonial authorities, therefore, owed more to the Indian, Irish and later, Palestinian paramilitary style of po-licing, than the civilian unarmed law enforcement model of the London Metropolitan Police. First and foremost these forces, both military and police, had to secure and extend colonial rule and to maintain order, in other words they were political in character; the prevention and detection of crime came a poor second.

As the territorial boundaries of the colonial regime were secured and peace largely prevailed, the emphasis of colonial rule inevitably began to shift from military-political security to civilian control using the state police force, though the latter kept their paramilitary organisation. With their urban focus, they handled violations of the newly introduced European criminal codes in areas of European settlement. Not surprisingly, many of the new laws were meant to secure political stability and served the economic interests of the colonial power. Much of the police work was involved in the surveillance of European property (including at times maintaining order among workers at private factories) and persons, the 'persuasion of recalcitrant inhabitants' to pay taxes, the dispersal of anti-tax protesters, the recruitment of wage labour, the return of deserters from the plantations, and in the 1940s and 50s forceful break up of strike demonstrations (Ahire, 1991:68–79, 99). The Bechuanaland Police were accused of only being 'interested in offences under the Masters and Servants Act and the Liquor Act [and] in later years offences under the native pass law and the Native Tax Act… otherwise the force was hardly interested in criminal behaviour unless whites were involved' (Bouman, 1987:283). Of Nyasaland, a Commissioner reported in 1939:

> They are perhaps chiefly engaged in collection of Hut Tax, escorts of cash, accompanying the District Commissioner on ulendo, and other duties that might well be performed by a messenger staff. The actual position is that it is only the areas in the Southern Province where there is European settlement that are policed (McCracken 1986:131).

The role of the police then was regime policing, policing the colonial economy and upholding the authority of colonial rule.

This meant, of course, that while coercion was not used continuously, it was used when deemed necessary. Not only did the Europeans use armed policing, but just as importantly, they equipped themselves with 'a legal arsenal of arbitrary regulations to carry out [their] responsibilities: diverse master-and-servant ordinances, specified periods of obligatory labor service at state defined tasks, plenary powers to local administrators to impose penalties for disobedience' (Young, 1988:47). Charges of 'vagrancy', 'prostitution', 'beer brewing', 'smuggling', 'poaching', membership of an 'unlawful society', 'native witchcraft' and the catch-all 'public nuisance' were used to criminalize Africans, to control their labour and to repatriate them to 'native' areas. This legal framework 'enabled the police to tackle legalistically what it had previously accomplished militaristically. State law provided the technical procedures and the bureaucratic framework that enabled the police to rationalise their activities as law enforcement (Ahire,

1991:137). The supervision of labour, the regulation of indigenous manufacturing, the enforcement of tax payment, all became matters regulated by colonial laws that were enforced by the police. In this way, economic control was gradually rationalised as the enforcement of law directed towards crime fighting.

The social and economic control did not make the police popular with the local population. One group of complainants to the Nyasaland authorities wrote that the average policeman, 'not only carries out the instructions he is given but enters every neighbouring house and puts everything in disorder' (McCracken 1986:146). Indigenous methods of punishment were often retained:

> Communities could be given collective punishments, for example the removal of cattle, enforced labour, or a fine. The punishments for individuals varied considerably. Serious crimes, such as murder, invariably were punished with a death sentence ... For lesser offences flogging was widespread. It was easily administered and cheap and, it was argued, Africans did not feel pain to the same degree as Europeans. Fines were rarely thought to be appropriate (Killingray, 2003).

Inevitably both the direct and indirect policing met social resistance. As early as 1886, African policemen were stoned in Accra, Gold Coast, because they were considered traitors of the native African community. Protests against taxes, low producer prices and low wages also led to conflict with the police. Typically, violent protests led to police brutality, which provoked further violence. Even more frequently, resistance took the form of social crime, such as cattle theft from settler farms, hunting on land enclosed as Game Reserves for the exclusive use of Europeans, and theft and sabotage at colonial companies. Interestingly the Kalenjin in Kenya distinguished between cattle 'raids' on 'outsiders' (Europeans or other Africans) and 'thefts' from fellow section members. For the former there were no sanctions since it benefited the whole community, enabling younger members to acquire stock without the need for redistribution by the community. For the latter there was the strongest public curse and social ostracism (Anderson, 2002).

The colonial police forces were small and urban and so for most of the territories it was local rulers through their agents (messengers and native authority police) that enforced order and who were expected, as a condition of their tenure, to uphold colonial rule. Whether the chiefs were those who had been reconstituted as state appointees or fabricated as the authorities, they combined judicial, legislative, executive, administrative and coercive roles. It was they who defined (or invented) and enforced customary law to regulate non-market relations in land, familial and community affairs (Tignor, 1971; Ranger, 1983). Mamdani aptly calls the delegation of rule and legal authority to local power holders, 'decentralised despotism' (Mamdani, 1996).

The size and ability of the Native Administration police varied considerably. Though many of these forces were too small to be effective in crime control, others like that of Buganda's were large entities. Of the effectiveness of a chief's messengers, a District Officer in Northern Rhodesia, wrote in 1943:

> They are the eyes, the ears and the strong right arm of the District Officer. In Northern Province, some 100,000 square miles in area, there is not a single policeman. The unbroken peace of the country is, I am sure, very largely due to the fact that the routine of administration of the tribal areas has always been carried on through unarmed Messengers who are local men and the friend of the people, but who are at the same time known to be incorruptible and undivided in their loyalty (Jeffries, 1952:109).

The discovery of their existence came as a welcome surprise to administrators struggling to offer colonial policing to large areas. When the British took over the Northern Provinces in Nigeria, Girourard, Lugard's successor, in 1908, admitted:

> We had no knowledge of their native government. Their police and prisons appeared both inadequate and cruelly oppressive, hence we attempted to set up a colonial police force. But faced with shortages of manpower it was a relief to discover that 'a native police organisation not only existed but was undoubtedly the best way of dealing with criminals of the ordinary class' (quoted in Ahire, 1991:42).

Thereafter the Northern Nigerian Police was stationed only in the 'purely pagan communities' that had no clearly defined authority structures. Over time, recognition, supervision, training and additional responsibilities (for maintaining law and order as defined by the colonists) were given to the Native Authority police. Throughout the first decade of the 20th century chiefs in Nigeria were encouraged either to establish native police forces or to expand existing ones (Ahire, 1991: 45–46). Of course many chiefs were not hereditary leaders but appointed by the authorities. In the case of Portuguese territories it is claimed that the 'regulos' were usually former soldiers, policemen or interpreters who had served the authorities well and received the chieftainship as a reward (Ade Ajayi and Crowder, 1974:528). This might also explain why they and their armed police (also recruited from ex-service men) were so infamous for their cruelty.

The native police forces acted on behalf of the colonial powers in recruiting labour, gathering taxes and handing over to them criminal cases that troubled the colonial rule. All else was a matter of indifference to the authorities, a fact that many chiefs and their Native Administration forces took advantage of, seizing livestock and property, demanding forced labour, and enforcing a personal arbitrary rule with fines and beatings (Killingray, 1986:417).

By the 1920s and 30s the emphasis on coercive control had declined and colonial police forces within colonies were amalgamated, whilst forces were co-ordinated and uniformly regulated as part of the newly formed Colonial Police Force (a truly global force). Military troops were reduced (total British Colonial troops in Africa in 1930 were only 12,000) and the relatively small police forces sought to engage more in the enforcement of colonial laws, although Criminal Investigation Departments (CIDs) were (until the formation of the Security Branch) more about investigating political than criminal activities, whilst the finger print bureaux, at least in East Africa, were primarily concerned with migrant labourers. Even so, most police work still focussed on the economic foundations of colonial power, and specifically involved the collection of hut taxes and order maintenance at the European mines and on the European estates. This period up until the end of the Second World War was the time when colonial state policing was most focussed on crime prevention and when the forces' value as upholders of peace and law began to be appreciated by many. The diary of an officer in the Ghana police illustrates the activities that preoccupied him April–June 1944. We read of duties associated with the flooding of a lagoon, the deportation of a number of Nigerian prostitutes, a visit to a village in which stolen property was believed to be hidden and the prevention of a riot over returning exiles (Clayton and Killingray, 1989:18). Civilian duties had come to form a large part of their activities, and the intention was that a paramilitary role would be reduced to a provision for emergency situations only. The increasing civilianisation, however, was to be overtaken by the events of the post-war period.

Colonial state policing in Africa after 1945

Changes after the Second World War forced an increase in the expenditure on the police force and its expansion into rural areas, as most of the native authority police were either brought under the control of local councils or assimilated into the national force (Bouman, 1987:284). But the pace of change was slow. Even in 1952, the Deputy Under-Secretary of State for the Colonies acknowledged that native authorities were still active in policing. In The Gambia there were only three outposts of colonial policing outside the capital; for the rest it was 'some 200 "badge messengers" who aided the Chiefs and native authorities'. In the Gold Coast he observed that 'some of the native authorities have their own police forces [with] powers of arrest and search' and likewise in Nigeria there were unarmed Native Authority Police, 'maintained by the native administrations under the advice and supervision of Nigerian Police officers'. In Sierra Leone the police were confined to Freetown; beyond, the Protectorate was policed by the Court Messenger Force of the Chiefs and various Chiefdom Messengers. As for Kenya, he recounts that the Kenya Tribal Police still policed the native reserves. For Northern Rhodesia the police force was confined to the urban centres and mining compounds. For the most part, therefore, policing was the responsibility of 'the village policemen of the native authorities and the district messengers of the Administration' (Jeffries, 1952:92, 98, 100, 109).

The increased post-war expenditure was partly in response to increased criminal activity in the growing towns, 'illegal' strikes, ethnic political rivalry jockeying for position in the forthcoming independent state, secessionism, and above all growing political unrest associated with African nationalism. Yet everyday policing work still continued. A policeman's letters in Nigeria in the 1950s speak of tax collection enforcement, a murder investigation, the introduction of a one-way traffic system in the city, protection for the 'swollen shoot' [disease] cutting-out party, arrests of unlicensed market women (and controlling the subsequent demonstration), protecting visiting politicians, policing strikes, investigating robberies and ceremonial duties. In addition, there was the routine station work of consulting with trade union leaders and customary authorities, attending committees and interviewing (Clayton and Killingray, 1989:36). Most forces also had responsibility for fire brigade work, weights and measures inspection and civil bailiff's duties. But against this backdrop of the ordinary, nationalism was emerging as a potent force, leading to outbreaks of localised rioting against taxes, inter-party and inter-ethnic political violence, organised political movements and, in places, armed guerrilla struggle. Numbers were increased (in Ghana the 2,500 police of 1945 were raised to 5,360 by 1956; in Kenya the 6,000 police of 1950 were raised to 15,000 by 1953 with an additional 6,000 in the Police Reserve); equipment strengthened (e.g. water cannon, armoured vehicles); and riot control and co-operation with the armed forces became a major element in training. In addition, new police units (Special Branch, supplemented by MI5) were set up for handling labour unrest and riot control and for maintaining surveillance of nationalist, Marxist and foreign agitators (Clayton and Killingray, 1989:42–48). Everything in their power was done to carefully control political dissent. Laws fined, imprisoned or exiled political leaders, banned political parties, censored and restricted the press, and prosecuted trade unionism. Even membership of a political party, reading a banned newspaper and demanding improved labour conditions, became crimes. At times even these measures proved insufficient and the police had to seek military assistance, as occurred in Nyasaland (1959) and Nigeria. It sometimes even required the proclamation of states of emergency as colonial authorities attempted to reclaim public order. In Nyasaland the dissent was suppressed through: 'shootings, detention without trial, collective fines, burning of houses and seizure of possessions' (Killingray, 1997:181). In Nyeri district of Kenya before the Mau Mau rebellion there were just two police stations and 35 men; by 1954 there were 28 police stations and 500 men (Maloba, 1993:88). Tens of thousands of Mau Mau suspects were removed to the Reserves; 'villagization' resettled over one million Kikuyu; and troops and the Home Guard of Kikuyu 'loyalists' tortured to secure information, executed suspects, and looted and extorted goods.

Overall, despite the reorganisation of the colonial police, their efforts proved only a temporary holding operation. It was obvious that the colonial administrations would have to prepare for African self-government. Even as they did so, a number of armed liberation movements attempted to establish some rudimentary variant of crime control in the territory liberated from the control of the colonial state e.g. FRELIMO (Liberation Front of Mozambique; Frente de Libertação de Moçambique) in Mozambique (Honwana Welch, 1985; Isaacman and Isaacman, 1982; Sachs, 1984) and ZANLA (Zimbabwe African National Liberation Army) in Zimbabwe (Astrow, 1983). Such experiments in 'people's justice' were heavily influenced by their relationship to the political struggle. In South Africa they had their roots in what remained of customary courts in the rural areas, and from the dispute resolution structures of the anti-apartheid movement's alternative governance system. In the black townships, for instance, self-defence units, people's courts and street committees, in addition to the summary violent justice of the Comrades and kangaroo courts, became a major feature of community life (Burman and Schärf 1990; Pavlich 1992; Brogden and Shearing 1993; Seekings 1992). The main activity of the police and other South African criminal justice agencies was that of the enforcement of regulations criminalizing whole communities. In 1972 it was calculated that one in four black people was arrested each year by the police for such violations, which were officially defined as criminal (Brogden and Shearing 1993:66). In the context of resistance it was inevitable that these alternative policing arrangements were more than attempts at making up for the deficiencies of the authoritarian colonial state and providing crime control activities. They targeted political crimes such as collaboration with the regime, whilst at the same time there was a certain degree of tolerance towards petty crimes committed by those risking their lives to oppose the regime.

There were always areas of the colonies where even indirect rule was tenuous. One such region was the grassland of the Ethiopian–Sudan–Ugandan–Kenyan border. The colonial authorities of Uganda, Kenya and Tanganyika saw the pastoralists as not only difficult to administer, owing to their mobility and decentralised and fragmented political systems, but also as resistant to change and violent. They were reluctant to get involved in the disputes over cattle raids. One British colonial report of 1905 spoke of how they 'worried that banning raiding at a time of particular stress in the pastoral economy might drive young men into permanent poverty and alienation, since they would not be able to accumulate enough to marry and become adults' (Waller, 1999:36). In other words, the people had their own policing authorisers and providers and it was better left in their hands. With no settler pressure to worry about the authorities turned their back on the cattle raiding of Uganda's Karamoja district:

> Full occupation and control was not necessary; insulation of the area from outside, restricting the gun trade, preventing raiding into the administered neighbouring zones, and limiting conflict within the region to a manageable level sufficed. A minimal presence within the area would serve, mainly of police (Mirzeler and Young, 2000:412).

In Kenya, however, where there was European interest in the grazing lands, the self-policing was not acceptable. The white settlers put pressure on the colonial authorities from the 1920s to take stern action. Severe sentences against cattle rustling were introduced of 1–5 years imprisonment or heavy individual and community fines. As these began to bite in the 1920s, the large scale raids in the Kalenjin and Maasai areas began to slacken off.

Indirect rule was not only weak in the rural margins, but in the townships of the cities not many miles from the centres of direct rule of the colonial masters. Here the Native System Administration could exist, but more often didn't. Thus significant sections of the towns were not formally policed at all. Instead they were policed informally, perhaps by vigilante anti-crime groups (Turner, 1955) or often by the voluntary associations such as ethnic or hometown associations that provided welfare services (e.g. the Ga Shifimo Kpee in Ghana aimed, 'to protect the interests of the Ga people'). What sort of law and order they maintained is not clear, although Killingray suspects that, 'a closer look might reveal that this involved protection rackets, kangaroo courts, job allocation schemes, and also measures to protect ethnic "purity" through the control of prostitution and preventing marriages outside the community'. He goes on to observe that some of these ethnic and ethnic-political associations 'were groups who mafia-like, organized, manipulated, exploited, intimidated, conned, and also "policed" the community' (Killingray 1986:418).

Policing of a different order can appear anything but policing to outsiders. Thus the various cults and secret societies of Nigeria were viewed as 'criminal fraternities' and 'killing squads' by colonial authorities. This was because of their murder of warrant chiefs and persons friendly to missionaries and the colonial government, and their destruction of property associated with these 'traitors'. Yet these cults were seen by their own members as protecting local values and enforcing sanctions on those deemed to be disregarding customary authority. It is evident that these Nigerian cults and societies, such as Ekpe (Leopard Society), performed not just religious functions, but a wide range of administrative and judicial ones. Each priest/priestess possessed a body of part-time personnel who enforced their decisions as well as customary law. Their attempts to deter 'traitors' by harsh punishments were really little different from the colonial police's efforts to uphold their own version of right order by military expeditions and imprisonments (Ahire, 1991:125–27).

The variety and fluctuations of non-state policing of this period only reflected what Shaw calls, the 'ever-changing spectrum of moral codes'. The 1940s and 50s were a time when social relations, networks and cultures were:

Reshaped again and again, through rapid population growth, migration to and from rural areas, changes in employment patterns and income levels, the expansion of secondary education, removals and resettlement, shack demolition, house-building and infrastructural development, administrative and local government reform, as well as the ebb and flow of overt political organisation and struggle (Seekings, 2001:72).

The changes meant that in some areas, the most striking differences in moral codes and policing forms were between rural-based 'traditional' groups and the more settled urban residents. However, increasingly 'the contrasting experiences of successive generations gave rise to inter-generational differences in notions of morality and justice' (Seekings, 2001:72).

Some have characterised the whole period of European (and apartheid) rule, as one where policing changed from militarisation through de-militarisation to re-militarisation, over a short period of time. Yet in fact the shift to civilian police duties was never complete, with military reserves always standing by. In overall organisation, if not in activity, state policing first and foremost was armed control, even if that control could only be exercised over a very small area. To preserve European domination police forces had to engage in military and political activities of surveillance, penetration and oppression of suspect groups (Killingray, 1986). Thus colonial policing in Africa never followed the idealised European model of a civilian force, living in the community, under local control and engaged in upholding the law, irrespective of the government. It certainly undertook civilian duties for much of its time, but it was there above all to uphold the authority of Resident and District Commissioners and their allies the customary rulers. It was not locally authorised and controlled policing that was impartial and politically neutral. It was centrally controlled regime policing; and regime policing necessitates a very distinct relationship between those policing and those policed, one that some believe has endured to the present:

> By far the most crucial factor in understanding the existence in Nigeria of semi-military police lay in the nature of Nigerian opposition to British jurisdiction and rule ... These sources of friction ... emphasized the need for troops and police as the ready instrument of enforcing government orders when peaceful overtures failed ... In the circumstances, the police formed the front line of defence in Britain's attempts to maintain law and order while soldiers afforded the last – at least in theory. Where however the Constabulary housed, as it were, both the soldiers and the police, the distinction was meaningless (Tamuno, 1970:39).

It was an unfortunate legacy for the new African states. The colonial powers' half-century of rule was characterised by state repression and the ever-present threat of violence. Their rule was devoted to the maintenance of cheap labour and the exclusion of the population from effective political organisation. Crowder summarises the colonial state as one that:

> Was conceived in violence rather than in negotiation ... it was maintained by the free use of it ... It must be remembered too that the colonial rulers set the example of dealing with ... opponents by jailing or exiling them, as not a few of those who eventually inherited power knew from personal experience (Crowder, 1978:11–13).

The employment of uniformed aliens housed in barracks and police lines only confirmed to the people the coercive nature of the forces of law and order and their foreign-ness (Killingray, 1986; Alemika, 1988; Ahire, 1991). Special powers and declarations of emergency could always legitimise setting aside the law if it was thought necessary, or *de facto* immunity from prosecution could always be established.

> The colonial government organised the police as instruments of riot, opposition and suppression. They were not established as agents for promoting the rule of law, human rights, community safety or for delivering social services ... This marked the beginning of police-community disconnection in Nigeria (Chukwuma, 2001:128).

Secondly, though colonial states were authoritarian regimes, they were often weak structures. They were weak in size and in coverage outside the towns (as of course in the metropoles up to the early part of the nineteenth century). Jeffries gives total force size in 1951 (with population in brackets) as: The Gambia 218 (268,000); Gold Coast 3,917 (4,118,000); Nigeria 7,585 (25,000,000); Sierra Leone 620 (1,880,000); Kenya 6,050 (9,406,000); Northern Rhodesia 1,970 (1,866,000); Nyasaland 751 (2,349,000); Tanganyika 3,055 (7,478,000); and Uganda 2,797 (5,050,000) (Jeffries 1952:224). They were also weak in legitimacy, having to depend on force or else on native authorities, who themselves lacked legitimacy where they had been artificially created. Rarely were they popular, though they were at times respected. They were led by foreign oppressors, supported by 'martial races', and enforced laws that criminalized typical African behaviour. And certainly some were not averse to using severity, corruption and discrimination.

But in addition to its repressive role, colonial state policing attempted, thirdly, to fulfil a 'civilising' role. This meant that the police were called to be what Storch (1975) calls, a 'domestic missionary' of the modern 'civilized' order. Though they had little success in this role, the attempt nevertheless was made to bring about social and moral control. Their mission was the shaping and educating of the people to the ethical and moral values of the new order, whether environmental sanitation, moral hygiene, or the avoidance of anti-social behaviour and cultic practices. Indeed such was their concern on these issues that Ahire goes so far as to argue that social control of the dominated was the centre-piece of police activity in colonial Nigeria. Thus he sees parallels with Europe and America's experience a century before, when the police forces likewise sought to contain forces hostile to the emerging social order. He notes, for instance, that their relative lack of concern about criminal activity is evidenced by the fact that the average police officer in the nineteenth century made less than one arrest per week and then usually for disorderly conduct. In his view, a similar situation existed in the North of Nigeria where, despite the accentuation of the crimes of robbery, burglary, theft and impersonation that took place in the confusion and panic created by the conquest, crime prevention was not the primary duty of the police. Rather, according to the Resident of Muri province 1909 (in a letter to the Secretary of Northern Province): 'the detection of crime, the arrest of criminals and the carrying out of the orders of the court are not the main functions of the police by any means. Their main functions are guarding goods; provincial gaol guard, and escort to convicts whilst working; and escorting Residents whilst on district tours' (quoted in Ahire, 1991:129). But beyond these functions Ahire demonstrates how colonial state law:

> Opened up aspects of the private lives of the indigenous people to official regulation. Through legislation, the state criminalized a wide range of activities, some of them clearly customary, and others less so. The criminalization of desertion from contract work, squatting in labour camps, trading across boundaries, brewing of liquor and so on are a few examples in the economic realm. In the realm of public order, other activities like public gatherings, drumming, dancing and 'nuisances' were criminalized; while in the sphere of the environment, morality and culture, the targets of criminal sanctions ranged from stray cattle to witchcraft, ordeals and cults (Ahire, 1991:129–30).

Fourthly the colonial state by no means had a monopoly of policing. Despite its authoritarian nature, it allowed and even encouraged alternative providers of policing (commercial and customary), recognising that it did not have the resources or legitimacy to effectively control the territories they claimed. Further, the colonial state was in no position to eradicate alternative authorisers and providers (vigilantes). Policing was still multiple in terms of providers (the colonial state, customary authorities) and authorisers (state, customary authorities and liberation movements).

Finally, for the average African, colonialism did little to relieve them from the prevailing violence, fear of violence from criminal elements, ethnic disputes and religious conflicts. In the rural areas and the townships they were offered no protection or crime prevention from the colonial authorities and very little from the customary authorities. Rather, the two formal police forces in the bifurcated colonial state threatened institutional violence. Indeed, policing (and penal policy) was disciplinarian in nature, for its rules were enforced through harsh punishment, particularly corporal punishment (Baker, 2002b). Humanist ideas and influences in Europe were only very slowly impacting on colonialists' views of the suitability of harsh systems of penal policy, such as torture and capital punishment. Self-policing for most Africans in the colonial period was their only hope, for as Killingray admits, 'Colonial rulers rarely got to grips with African societies; colonial institutions, the panoply of alien laws and the forces of law and order, barely touched village Africa' (Killingray 1986:437). In fact to some degree they made matters worse.

> One of the key projects of colonial rule [was] to ensure that security derived, and was seen to derive, explicitly from the central state, and that any mechanism through which African communities might seek to maintain 'their own' security was systematically destroyed, or strictly subordinated to the colonial authorities. Wilfred Thesiger, describing his time as a British colonial administrator in Sudan, has an illustrative vignette: having deprived their Sudanese subjects of arms with which to defend themselves, the government had left them prey to lions, and one of the obligations of a district official was then to exterminate any of these vermin who posed a threat to livestock; an activity previously carried out by local people on their own was thus taken over by the agents of government (Clapham, 1999:23).

African state policing

Independence did not resolve the inherent problem of African statehood. As Clapham points out, this had serious implications for internal security:

> If there is no agreed 'idea of the state', as must almost necessarily be the case where states themselves are artificial amalgamations of peoples lacking shared

identities, then there is no public basis on which a security structure can be built; and whatever system for maintaining security is constructed, it cannot help but be privatised, in that it must be drawn from, and reflect the interests of, some domestic (or even external) groups rather than others (Clapham, 1999:23).

Therefore, despite the expectations that the police at independence would be reorganised and re-orientated from regime policing to a force committed to serving the people, little changed. True, decolonisation had seen an expansion and the belated Africanisation and training of police forces. Nevertheless there was no change in their role: they were there, as before, primarily to secure the new regime, which meant they were used for repression rather than protection of citizens (Goldsmith, 2003). Continuity also prevailed in the methods of crime control and detection; the urban focus; the political intelligence work; and in some cases, the ethnic recruiting patterns (e.g. Chad; Côte d'Ivoire) and senior white officers (in Malawi there were still 26 European officers in 1971). Only in post-revolutionary contexts like Mozambique were there experiments with new approaches. Popular justice that had evolved in liberated zones during the conflict and the transition period was turned into popular tribunals under chosen members of the community rather than the discredited customary leaders (Honwana Welch, 1985; Isaacman and Isaacman, 1982; Sachs, 1984).

In a short time, almost all the independent states abandoned formal democracy for some form of authoritarian regime. Commonly the change began with moves to one-party rule and, typically, one-man rule. Mistakenly, political leaders imagined that firm personal rule could keep ethnically divided nations together and secure their own legitimacy. Surely Mazrui is right when he observes of the African state that, 'it is sometimes excessively authoritarian in order to disguise the fact that it is inadequately authoritative' (quoted by Chazan, 1988:120). Under authoritarian regimes the police forces were poorly financed and poorly trained and, says Hills, subject to 'insecurity, political interference and economic depression' (2000:33). Officers were paid irregularly which, along with inflation, made for an unreliable force open to corrupt practices. Even more than in the past, policemen became predators on their own account or in the pay of whoever offered the best price. Meek's account of the Sierra Leone Police could be applied to many more, that from the late 1960s to the 1990s the story was: 'a litany of oppressive policing, nepotism and corruption that undermined public confidence in the police... skills were not sought after and officers were illiterate. The police were not given uniforms, training or equipment' (Meek, 2003:2).

The police relationship with the army was strained from the beginning. They both fought over scarce resources and the police resented the way armies usurped their internal role in disciplining the population. In Uganda, for instance, President Obote formed his own intelligence unit, rather than trust the CID. After Amin's military coup there was a rapid decline in policing and police investigating military corruption disappeared. When a former colonial inspector general visited Uganda in 1971 he found: 'the police despoiled – no transport, stores, workshops, no boats for the marine section, and all furniture and even books from the college and the training school removed' (Clayton and Killingray 1989:104). The conflict with the army was only exacerbated as military coups swept through Africa in the early 1970s. Without external armies to call on, the new rulers wanted to be sure their armed forces could defend their regimes; and yet not be so powerful as to threaten them. The fragility of civil order and the nature of political power had a profound effect on the police forces.

First, they were brought under tighter central control, that is, they were made accountable to the president rather than to the law. Ties with local and provincial authorities were broken and generally chiefs lost their powers of arrest, mediation, judgment and general responsibility for law and order in the rural areas. Ekeh gives the example of Nigeria:

> Unlike colonial times, the Nigeria Police Force under the military was the sole policing authority in Nigeria. During colonial times, there were multiple police jurisdictions, at least in Western and Northern Nigeria, in which local police were responsible to regional and local governments. It was the military that sacked other policing elements whose authority it vested in the huge and centralized Nigeria Police Force, at the onset of military rule in the late 1960s (Ekeh, 2002).

Second, policing was militarised. The military governments did not, by and large, understand what civilian policing meant and so harnessed the police alongside the army to fulfil the regime's aim of repressing and eliminating political opposition. Being militarised and housed in barracks, however, meant the police were separated from their communities and encouraged to cultivate a 'tough and intimidating' attitude to civilians. Their role, as opposed to their formal functions, was determined by what the regime saw as the best way of ensuring its survival. Inevitably the spheres of activity for the police and military became blurred.

Most military are ambivalent about domestic security or enforcement operations – even if such operations play to their vanity. Some are involved because military action appears to be the only way to control seemingly out-of-control violence/crime. Thus Nigeria's President Obasanjo approved the deployment of soldiers to a special police unit to combat crime in Lagos last year [1999] (Hills, 2001:10).

Third, the insecurity of the military regimes led to the fragmentation of state policing. Fragmentation of internal security ensured that power was not concentrated in potentially dangerous rivals. The more fragile the state, the more specialised internal security units were created (President Charles Taylor of Liberia had 12 internal security agencies at the time of his departure in 2003). Policing provision to the state came from a multiplicity of sources: the army or special units of the army, such as presidential guards and the state police or its special units, such as heavily armed paramilitary units, rapid reaction forces and elite units. Then there were officially approved state militia or provincial state militia and co-opted vigilantes.

> In Nigeria, for instance, policing must be understood in relation to the activities of the Nigeria Police Force, the military (some of whom may be deployed as special police units), some eight or more paramilitary units, various palace guards, numerous quasi-official units in various states, and miscellaneous thugs associated with strongmen. Notorious groups such as the Bakassi Boys, who drive around in police vehicles and are financed by a state governor, provide vigilante-style policing. As a result it is difficult to decide whether operations such as the Nigerian military's Operation Sweep in Lagos during 1996–1998, described as an anti-crime measure, should be understood as a policing or a military action (Hills, 2001:9).

Fourth, mistrust concerning the reliability and loyalty of security units leads to them being kept weak, dependent and with an uncertain future, through under-funding, low salaries and non-payment of salaries. This does little to increase efficiency and effectiveness. The almost total reliance on foot patrols as a means of saving money reduces the space and intensity of patrols. In addition, their use in regulatory duties that would be given to other agencies in the West, overburdens them. For instance, police have frequently been involved in licensing commercial enterprises, supervising trade, protecting currency, and given responsibility for refugee settlements and migrant labour (Igbinovia, 1981). Symptomatic of the process of keeping them insecure is what Hills calls, 'the cycle of recruitment and retrenchment so clearly discernible in post-colonial policing'. She illustrates her point from Lagos, a city of 10 million, where in 2000 the police numbered no more than 120,000 (they had been 145,000 in 1995). Unpaid for several months, she found them understaffed, under-equipped and demoralised (Hills, 2001).

Fifth, the customary justice system and its associated policing of society have inevitably had to remain largely untouched. In most countries in Africa the largest manifestation of non-state justice has remained the customary law administered by chiefs. This is because urbanisation is low in most African countries and the state justice system has little penetration outside the towns. The state system is for the minority. With independence some countries, such as South Africa and Botswana, maintained a small formal judicial role for chiefs, especially in the rural areas. Most countries, however, stripped them of their judicial powers and placed their former powers in the hands of lay magistrates, who were little more than poorly trained civil servants. Codification of customary law and its nationwide standardisation rarely took root and were usually abandoned (though Tanzania came close). In practice, though customary leaders have still presided over many disputes, they have not had formal jurisdiction and so their judgments have had no force in law. They have functioned mainly as mediators or as referrers to the police, the District Commissioners and the state courts. Yet their formal powerlessness has not robbed them of authority. Any resident living under their jurisdiction would think very carefully as to the full cost of appealing against their decisions. After all, they and their extended family may need the chief's goodwill for a future decision in relation to the allocation of land, inclusion in a development project or referral to a government service.

Yet the police of independent Africa have not just been the pawns of the regimes they represent. Though they are the product of political decisions and political events, they have also been actors themselves in their development. Hills identifies this quality as resilience, the ability of an institution to survive change largely unaltered. Regimes have come and gone, but the state police have been able to adapt to them all, whilst at the same time preserving their own interests. How have they succeeded?

> Many police characteristics result from the nature of policing, rather than the institution as such, but it is likely that significant attributes include the centralisation of decision making and recognition of the importance of intelligence and secrecy, as well as the fact that the police provide skills useful to governments. None of these characteristics are sufficient in themselves to ensure resilience, but the key appears to be the usefulness of the police ... It

is clear that the state police are too useful, and too potentially dangerous, for governments to ignore them (Hills, 2001).

The concern of the new rulers to defend themselves from internal dissent proved justified. Defective boundary demarcation during the colonial period, un-rectified at independence, left young states with a contested inheritance. Many had to face insurgency and civil war because certain populations within them did not accept that they were part of that country.[2] The option of securing national unity across the fracture lines of ethnicity, religion and language through economic prosperity was not available to the impoverished states. Consequently, to safeguard their nations' very existence, state leaders resorted to coercive internal security. Ironically they found that colonial emergency provisions and paramilitary police could serve their interests as well as those of their former masters. Similarly, the internal security forces were all too willing to commit abuses in their quest for success against the 'rebels' and 'bandits' or because the very success of the rebels means that state supervision and provision decline sharply (Amnesty International, 1998). However, in the face of insurgency, state policing often ceased to function or was superseded by the military in rebel held zones and contested zones.

With the police distracted by security affairs, concentrated in central urban areas, understaffed, under-resourced and under-skilled, criminal activity prospered. Frustrated by the difficulty of securing witnesses and convincing forensic evidence, police resorted to confessions made under duress or even to handing out summary punishment. But the problems went beyond training and resources. Those who held weapons and had information on security provision (or the lack of it) were in a unique position to exploit their advantage during times when pay was low and irregular. Their corruption became as endemic as their incompetence in the eyes of most populations. In African states law ceased to function in many areas.

In summary, the context of policing in the independent African state was one of a personalised and fragile political order, often accompanied by conflict, repression and corruption. This meant that the role of the state police depended more on how the government defined national security and

---

2. Insurgency and civil war have occurred for much of the independent existence of Angola, Burundi, Chad, Congo-Brazzaville, Democratic Republic of Congo, Ethiopia (since the fall of Haile Selassie), Mozambique, Rwanda, Senegal, Sierra Leone, Somalia, Sudan and Uganda. And it has featured over a number of years in the Central African Republic, Comoros, Côte d'Ivoire, Equatorial Guinea, Guinea-Bissau, Liberia, Mali, Mauritania, Niger and Nigeria.

how fragile public order was, rather than on the formal functions laid down in the constitution. Yet though the police have been weak in resources and often sidelined by the army or by special units, governments have been unable to ignore them. The state police have usually been the most obvious enforcers of political order. It is because the nature and purpose of power hardly changed between the 1960s and 1980s that policing remained the same. The persistence of weak and uncertain power elites meant that the chief function of the police was primarily to protect the regime. Only regime change that made governments accountable to the people would ever change this. Hence when democratisation swept across Africa from the late 1980s there was widespread anticipation that policing would change dramatically. The degree to which those hopes were realised is examined in the next chapter on contemporary policing in Africa.

CHAPTER 5

Contemporary African Policing

I think that people feel security is the most important concern, even before food, and before anything else, because you must be safe and alive before you can pursue your goals. If you do not make an extra arrangement for security beyond what the state provides, then you are vulnerable to attacks. (Nairobi citizen, reported in Leach, 2003)

Not much is known about this world of non-state institutions. (Vera Institute of Justice, 2003).

Self-policing of African communities can be said to be the historical norm, with state policing in some cases having been introduced alongside or even obscuring it, but never eradicating it. At independence many anticipated a national state police force that would provide a universal, effective and just protection, but after several decades of independence it had become apparent to African populations that their governments were not willing or able to provide the level of service promised. The explanation was partly financial, although weak states often chose to privilege 'regime stability and narrow sectional interests over public safety considerations' or at times were simply guilty of 'malevolent indifference' (Goldsmith, 2003:4, 7). As regards offering protection for citizens, state police were widely perceived as indifferent, inept, inefficient and corrupt (Adu-Mireku, 2002; Chukwuma, 2001; Shaw, 2002; Wood, 2000). They were also concentrated in urban and high-income areas. For instance in South Africa in 1998, 74 per cent of the police stations were situated in the white suburbs or business districts (Government of National Unity, 1998).

Worse, there have been many occasions when the police, pursuing their own or regime interests, have committed extra-judicial killings, used excessive force, arbitrarily arrested and detained persons, and acted in collusion with criminals. Given their regime-determined agenda, it is little surprise that police who have committed such abuses have rarely been investigated or punished. Sadly the onset of liberal democracy in the 1990s has done little to alter this, such that in 2001 the Kenya police were described as follows:

> Members of the police, the General Service Unit, and the CID, continued to use lethal force and committed a number of extrajudicial killings. The Kenya

Human Rights Commission, reported that it has documented more than a thousand cases of extrajudicial killings in the last decade ... Security forces continued to use torture and physical violence during interrogation and to punish both pretrial detainees and convicted prisoners ... Common methods of torture practiced by police included hanging persons upside down for long periods, genital mutilation, electric shocks, and deprivation of air by submersion of the head in water. There were numerous allegations of police use of excessive force and torture ... Security forces continued to commit numerous human rights abuses, often with impunity ... According to organizations that work with street children, police also beat and abused street children ... Police continued to arrest and detain citizens arbitrarily ... Citizens frequently accused police officers of soliciting bribes during searches or falsely arresting individuals to extract bribes (US State Department, 2002).

This negative report is confirmed by research in 2002 that showed that on average each Kenyan had been forced to bribe the police 4.5 times a month, paying them on average US$16 per month. Over 95 per cent of dealings with the police had resulted in a bribe (*Transparency International,* 24 January 2002).

Desperate to control crime, police across Africa have resorted increasingly to force and in particular have adopted 'shoot to kill' practices towards armed robbers. Tanzania's Prime Minister said: 'The government will go on fighting gangsters without mercy and whenever possible, excessive force will be used' (*African Church Information Service,* 21 July, 2003). 'Shoot to kill' operations have also been used in Burkina Faso, Uganda, Kenya, Nigeria, CAR and Cameroon. According to the Nigeria Police, between 2000 and February 2004 their officers killed 7,198 suspected armed robbers.[1] Kenyan government responses to violent crime have involved the use of special squads with the sole aim of killing off suspects rather than investigating and preventing crime. The chief Kenyan government pathologist claimed that police had been responsible for 90 per cent of people shot dead in 2001.

For those living in rural areas and the townships on the margins of the cities, it is not just that the state police are inefficient, predatory and potentially violent; they are absent and appeals for protection fall on deaf ears (Pelser et al., 2000).[2] Political scientist Peter Ekeh reports:

---

1. *New Vision,* 3 April, 2004.

2. *Times of Zambia,* 1 August, 2003.

Nigerian governments have virtually told Nigerians to fend for their own protection. My hometown of Okpara with its environs has a population that is more than 20,000 people in Delta State. It has no police station. Indeed, there is no presence of government in the daily lives of its people. That is, the Nigerian state and its governmental agencies are absent from their daily lives. Crimes will be committed in any community and are being committed in my hometown. How are they resolved?: Clearly, without the help of any governmental agencies (Ekeh, 2002).

Yet the failure of the state police cannot be said to be the cause of the emergence of self-policing since, as argued before, it predated state policing and was never totally displaced by it (Waller, 1999; Turner, 1955; Killingray, 1986; Ahire, 1991) because the two were not policing the same order (Buur, 2003). The police are agents of a state that for many is following alien values concerning how crime is defined (e.g. Does it include witchcraft, adultery, teenage pregnancy, disrespect to parents and 'unwarranted' evictions?) and how it is punished (e.g. Does it include corporal punishment? And does it include reparation for damages?). Even if the police had been effective in their role, there would still have arisen policing of alternative orders (Nina and Schärf, 2001). It has been, therefore, a profound dissatisfaction with the state police official remit, as well as police effectiveness, that has encouraged others to authorise and provide policing.

But if the state police failure has not caused self-policing, it has certainly reinvigorated self-policing. It has also ensured that it has taken new forms, since the post-independent state typically weakened the powers of local chiefs to authorise policing that could fill the security vacuum. Also promoting the rejuvenation of self-policing has been the real or perceived increase in crime, following the political and economic liberalisation of the last 15 years. A fear of crime and disorder prevails, especially among those with the fewest resources to defend themselves, such as females and the poor (Alvazzi del Frate, 1998). 34 per cent of people in Accra, Ghana, reported that they or someone they knew had been a victim of crime in a twelve-month period prior to the survey (Adu-Mireku, 2002:160). Whether rising crime is merely the product of more extensive reporting and recording of crime or whether there is a genuine rise associated with the weakening of customary forms of social control, the fact is that it has provoked fear (Adu-Mireku, 2002). It is hardly surprising, therefore, that there has been a rapid growth of private forms of policing. When individuals or a community are faced with a criminal or order problem with no state help on offer, then inevitably they will both authorise policing and provide it according to their own values. Currently communities and commercial interests authorise policing, besides the government. There is the same variety amongst those who provide policing. In other words, what has emerged is a plethora of non-state policing groups, some adhering to the law and having state police support, some being lawless and violent in their assault on crime; some spontaneous, short lived or evolving; some more permanent commercial enterprises.

But it would be incorrect to imagine that the expansion of non-state policing simply represents a shift from the public to the private or even only a reinvigoration of the private. In fact there is considerable interpenetration and overlap between the two. For instance, state police have been recruited by private security firms, autonomous residential security organisations and vigilante groups. In addition, community anti-crime groups have been absorbed into the public police reservists. Also blurring the boundaries is the use by countries like Uganda and Rwanda of the lowest levels of local authority to provide policing. These unpaid personnel undertake patrols, investigations, arrests, courts and suitable punishments for a wide range of lower level crimes. Though officially part of the local government structure, they have in practice considerable autonomy (the case of Uganda is discussed in the next chapter. For Rwanda see Baker, 2007a). Then there is an increasing exchange of information about the patterns of crime, policing techniques, anti-crime technology and (at least covertly) the disclosure of public criminal records to private police groups (Shaw, 1995:79). There are cases of commercial security and even of vigilante groups working with state police in dividing the work according to whose *modus operandi* was best suited for the required task (Buur, 2003:33; Buur and Jensen, 2004).

Beyond this interpenetration or even co-operation of policing groups, there is the geographical overlapping of policing agencies that means that Africans commonly move into and out of spheres of policing authorisers and providers or may be in a position to choose between providers where there is multiple provision. This of course may mean that for all the interpenetration of personnel and techniques between groups, the relationship is often as likely to be one of competition as of co-operation. Yet their very existence and variety demonstrates that policing emerges to fill the vacuum of unavailable or inadequate state provision.

Many Africans, whether in rural areas or in the urban informal settlements, rely on the presence of family members in and around their homes to act as guards. With large numbers engaged in the care of children, working from home or simply unemployed, property is rarely left unattended and even then the eyes and ears of neighbours act as a second line of defence. This informal network partly explains the low incidence of burglary in the tightly packed slums of the cities (Anderson and Bennett, 1996). Leach found that in Nairobi neighbourhoods: 'the scope and intensity of surveillance can be quite high. Participants confirm the density of surveillance penetration that makes even children informants' (Leach, 2003). Since, however, policing was defined in Chapter 1, as any *organised* activity that seeks to ensure the maintenance of communal order, security and peace, extended families should strictly be excluded from this review. Instead this chapter focuses on 11 other examples as evidence of Africa's contemporary fragmented policing (see Figure 1 for summary).

In the rest of this chapter policing structures common in contemporary Africa other than the state police are examined.

The mob

Mob violence is common throughout Africa in response to high crime rates and lack of public confidence in the state police and the judicial process. The victims are severely punished or even killed by stabbing, beating, stoning or burning. The spontaneous nature may appear to exclude them from the definition of policing as 'organised'. Yet 'The influence of particular individuals in planning, initiating and conducting vigilante actions is important to understanding its many manifestations – organised as well as spontaneous' (Harris, 2001b). A report on vigilante violence at the Amplats Platinum Mines in the North West Province, South Africa (NIM, 1997) highlighted the centrality of specific influential and charismatic individuals to the violence. These figures had a history of violent actions and held key positions within political organisations and the mining structures. In the following account it appears that a man who initially accused a woman of degrading her neighbourhood, later instigated a 'mob-attack'.

> Gugu Dlamini, 36, of KwaMancinza, near Durban, died after being assaulted by a mob who accused her of degrading her neighbourhood by disclosing that she [was HIV positive] ... on the day of the attack, Dlamini had been slapped and punched by a man who had asked her why she had gone public about her status when there were a lot of others like her in the area who kept quiet about it. ...Dlamini returned home. The mob attacked her at night. They stoned,

Figure 1. Typology of Policing Groups

CATEGORY	AUTHORISER	PROVIDER	OPERAT-IONAL RANGE	CON-STRAINED BY LAW	CO-OP. WITH POLICE	FOR PROFIT	SURVEILL-ANCE SECURITY	PUNISHMENT SECURITY
Extended family	family	family	very local	mainly	no	no	yes	rarely
Mob violence	community	community	very local	no	no	no	no	beating/death
Informal organised security group	community	community	local	no	rarely	no	no	censure beating/death
Religious police	religious organisations or sub-national units	usually unarmed groups	local	no	no	no	yes	censure beating
Ethnic/clan militia	tribe/clan or local strongmen	armed groups	tribal/clan area	no	no	no	yes	censure beating
Political party militia	political party	armed groups	regional/national	no	no unless ruling party	no	yes	beating
Civil defence forces	community	armed groups	regional	no	no	no	yes	beating/death
Informal commercial security group	business and political leaders	armed groups	local/regional	no	rarely	yes	no	beating/death
Formal commercial security group	business	trained guards	local to global	mainly	yes	yes	yes	exclusion
State approved civil guarding	citizen group or sub-national units	trained guards	local/regional	mainly	yes	no	yes	exclusion
Customary courts and police	tribe	tribal elders	local/district	mainly	yes	mini-mal	no	financial/corporal
Restorative justice committees	community	community	local	mainly	often	no/token	no	financial or service
State police, national, local	state	trained personnel	national/local i.e. urban	mainly	n/a	no	yes	court sentencing

kicked and beat her with sticks [so that she died the following day as a consequence of her injuries].[3]

Victims of mob violence are typically suspected of crimes such as murder, theft, cattle stealing, child abuse and rape. There are regular reports in the city townships of the stabbing and 'necklacing' of thieves in mob assaults. In South Africa one report from Johannesburg read:

> In the past fortnight, seven people have been killed by vigilantes. Last week a suspected thief was murdered by a mob in Johannesburg. And three young men were killed in Primville, Soweto, for stealing 20 chairs from a church … Primville's people are unrepentant. They say they will necklace all criminals they catch. On Tuesday, a mob in Indanda, Durban, killed two of four men they said tried to rob a woman … The sister [of the robber] heard people shouting 'Die you dog, die', and found several men and a woman leaning over her brother stabbing him in the throat and stomach. The killers ran past her, laughing, as police arrived. Paramedics had to be protected by police and soldiers when stones and bottles were thrown by locals wanting to finish off all the suspected robbers.[4]

In South Africa 'mob justice' in response to criminal activity appears to be particularly prevalent in the area of large taxi ranks and bus terminals where petty theft abounds (Meyer, 1998).

The crimes may also be defined by the mob in contradiction to the state, and include membership of criminal gangs, domestic disputes, adultery and sexuality. And there were 300 witchcraft related murders between 1990 and 1999 in the Northern Province (now Limpopo), South Africa (Hills, 2000:61).

The scale of the activity can be measured by the report of the Kenyan Human Rights Commission. They recorded 719 deaths from mob violence 1995–2001. In one example in March 2001, a mob killed three brothers for allegedly being involved in multiple incidents of theft and robbery on the outskirts of Nairobi. Apparently a mob-operated court, convened earlier in the day at a shopping centre, found the brothers guilty of several crimes. The brothers were beaten unconscious, doused with petrol, and burnt alive (US State Department, 2002). On one occasion in Nigeria the victims were the police themselves, when a mob in Lagos 'lynched' three policemen who killed a bus driver who had refused to pay extortion money.[5]

---

3. *Sunday Times*, 27 December, 1998.

4. *The Star*, 2000.

5. BBC, 30 January, 2002.

As with the extended family, this is a very localised form of policing, but unlike the extended family, is not constrained by state law. Its emphasis is on responsive security rather than surveillance. Being a very localised form of policing it enjoys widespread support, which makes the police reluctant to investigate and, if they do, makes it very difficult for them to obtain evidence.

Informal organised security groups (vigilantes)

Mobs are short lived but there are more permanent organised informal security groups that act in a similar way in terms of their emphasis on punishment security by the community. Commonly known as vigilantes, or what Johnston (1996) calls autonomous citizen responses, these groups not only act independently of the state police, but often do not co-operate with it and are prepared to break the law to achieve their goals of protection and investigation (or sometimes trials and sentencing). They are characterised by reactive, *ad hoc* and often violent methods of control. According to Daniel Nina, vigilantism:

> Will adopt either a crime or social order approach. In either case, it is linked directly to the use of physical force and intimidation at levels not normally used by the state. In the denial of the state as the guarantor of the social order, vigilantism will invoke an 'imagined order' that either existed in the past (in its decadent mode), or never existed but is desired (in its idealized mode) ... Vigilantism appropriates state functions in a way that creates a parallel sovereign power that is unregulated (Nina, 2001).

These informal security groups involve some degree of organised action by private citizens. Invariably they use or threaten the use of force in order to control crime or other social disorder. Whether or not vigilante acts are extra-legal or involve the infliction of punishment or simply censure, varies from group to group (Johnston, 2001; Harris, 2001a). Though volunteers run them, this doesn't mean that vigilantes may not profit materially from their actions. Some charge for their 'services' and others force their victims into 'paying up', not just to the complainant (if at all) but to the vigilantes as well (Harris, 2001b).

Rising crime in the cities of Africa has seen innumerable initiatives by communities to tackle it with a degree of ruthlessness. Only half of black respondents in South Africa 'could say with certainty that no act of vigilantism had taken place in their community, with 20 per cent saying there had and 31 per cent being unsure' (Schonteich, 2000:50). In a typical example from Grahamstown, Eastern Cape, an alleged rapist of a 15-year-old girl was summoned to a community committee to defend the charge and face the likelihood of a whipping. On twice failing to attend, the angry community members tore down his wattle and daub house.[6] Further south in Port Elizabeth, an organisation called Amadlozi serves, as they themselves put it, 'the local community of law-abiding people'. It can draw 400 people of all ages and backgrounds three times a week at a community hall on the outskirts of the city to discuss policing problems and to conduct quasi-court sessions that hand out sentences of corporal punishment (sensitive issues and physical punishment are conducted *in camera*).

> Separate from, but still integrated into the public meetings are 'working groups' conducting what are called 'raids'. These … formally investigate the cases brought to their attention in the public sessions … They consist of groups of 'residents' usually one or two older members and five to eight younger members … They conduct raids that resemble ordinary police investigations or operations. At times they will gather a group of 'residents', arrange rallies [in their hundreds outside the accused's home], summon people or enter premises for investigative purposes (Buur, 2003:19).

Their success rate in tracking criminals and getting them to speak so that stolen goods can be traced is so high that police crime statistics are said to show a reduction of 90 per cent since the group began their operations.

In some parts of South Africa these groups have become large and ruthless, for instance the 'People against Gangsterism and Drugs' (PAGAD) in Western Province (Kinnes, 2000; Nina, 2001). From its inception in 1996 PAGAD felt no constraint to work within the law. It began with a series of widely publicised punishments and assassinations of drug dealers. Within two years they had executed 30 gang leaders and drug dealers and had seriously decimated the gangs, although not without precipitating reprisals from the newly allied gangs (Kinnes, 2000:37). Over time, however, PAGAD attacks shifted to police officers, police stations (for weapons) and businesses that refused to make 'donations'. Between 1998 and 2000 they appeared to adopt an Islamist anti-Western agenda and switched to a bombing campaign against Western capitalist targets.

In Zambia's urban areas, vigilante groups (commonly called Neighbourhood Watches) of 20–30 people undertake regular armed patrols. They have widespread support because they are considered to be very effective in crime prevention. Yet for all their illegal and brutal methods, 'they

---

6. *Eastern Province Herald*, 25 August, 2000.

are registered organizations and in addition are acknowledged by the police with whom many work very closely' and by whom they may be armed (Schärf, 2003). In Lusaka's main bus terminal, violence, theft, and disorder prevailed until the early 1990s, when 'the young men trying to squeeze out a living by showing people to their seats and carrying their luggage (monopolising the right to seats and to luggage services in the process) organised into vigilante groups'. To popular acclaim they created an effective order, ensuring a fair and efficient way of allocating seats and physically punishing (to the point of severe injury, sometimes death), luggage thieves and those trying to travel without a ticket (van Binsbergen, 1997). Zambian vigilante groups also work in association with the local chief. They will arrest people on behalf of the chief and together with the chief's assistant will hear and deal with lower order criminal issues. Similar groups arose in Malawi during the famine of 2002. The theft of foodstuffs and crops became such a threat to survival that 'perpetrators would be lucky to get away with a serious beating' and in some areas 'chop-chop' groups literally chopped off the fingers or even the hands of those that had stolen quantities of food (Schärf, 2003).

In some lower middle class communities of Nairobi, Kenya, neighbours organise a neighbourhood security scheme and impose the association on all residents under threat of eviction. The security associations employ watchmen with dogs to sound an alarm if they detect anything unusual. They told Leach (2003) that:

> Whenever we are attacked, and we storm out to defend ourselves, what comes to mind is not the human rights of the people attacking us. What comes to mind is that we are in danger... that is why we come out with weapons. If you are an intruder, we will beat you up, we will not try to arrest you and take you to the police ... If you are arrestable, that's OK, but not until those guys will have really been beaten up. The neighbourhood will beat the intruder before they consider calling the police because of the sense of danger. We are feeling these guys have come here to kill us ... they can kill him, if the person is also trying to kill them. If you try to observe rules, then you will be the one to die.

Among the cattle herders of East Africa informal security groups have a long tradition. Cattle raiding is dealt with by pursuit and recapture by posses, together with the summary killing of those deemed responsible. Since state policing has never been capable of preventing cattle raiding or of bringing the perpetrators to justice, the old violent retaliatory raids have continued. Detailed accounts of rural vigilante groups' responses to cattle rustling and other crimes (including witchcraft) in Uganda and Tanzania have been published (Heald, 1998; 2003; Abrahams, 1987; Bukurura, 1994). The organisation in Tanzania was reported as simple but effective:

> Every man, young or old, had to be equipped with bow and arrows and with a gourd-stem whistle which was to be blown in emergencies. If a theft was committed, a hue and cry was raised and the thieves were to be followed by the young men of the village concerned. The whistles would alert the members of neighbouring villages who would in turn alert others in the same way (Abrahams, 1987:181–82).

In response to stock theft, people in Lesotho have formed 'stock theft associations' to retrieve stock and mete out brutal punishment when the culprits are found. They pay membership fees as an insurance to pay for bail and court fines for those members of the association that have committed assault/murder in the process of retrieving stock (Schärf, 2003:22). What muddies the water is that, according to some, chiefs and corrupt police are an essential component in this activity (Kynoch and Ulicki, 2000; Tsebo Mats, 1999). It appears that thieves and killers work very closely with young chiefs and police. Hence chiefs have been receiving bribes for sale-permits of stolen goods and police have given false evidence in court cases for the acquittal of their collaborators who use their licensed guns. It has even been suggested that chiefs and stock theft committees, in addition to being police, judge, jury and executioners, may be the perpetrators of stock theft. The Lesotho government has sought to dissuade people from participating in stock theft associations whilst exhorting them to form Crime Prevention Committees that operate in partnership with the authorities and operate within the framework of the law.[7]

Religious police

Religious police have much in common with informal organised security groups. They are community based, and use censure and beating to enforce their order with little regard for the state law. Also, despite their rhetoric, they have minimal co-operation with the police. Where they differ is that they are organised typically by community religious leaders and exercise surveillance as well as responsive roles.

Since Nigeria's independence, Shari'a has regulated family and personal law, but the newer versions, introduced from the Middle East, are far more

---

7. *New People*, May 1999, available at users.peacelink.it/npeople/may99.

restrictive and wider in scope. For instance, since 1999, a dozen states in northern and central Nigeria have required 'Islamic' dress and sexually segregated public transportation. They have banned alcohol, prostitution, gambling and co-ed public transport and closed churches and non-Muslim schools. The Nigeria Police are neither trained nor willing to enforce the locally enacted Shari'a Penal Codes, hence there emerged security groups called hisba (named after both the Qur'anic duty to 'enjoin what is right and forbid what is wrong' and the office of hisba, or market inspector, who, in classical times would enforce honest trade). Their members come from Islamic aid groups, the police, road safety marshals, officers of the national Drug Law Enforcement Agency, and the representatives of local councils.

In Zamfara State hisba (Shari'a Implementation Monitoring Committees, including The Zamfara State Vigilante Service) wear red uniforms and berets, arm themselves with homemade machetes, pistols and whips, and patrol the streets in six-man teams. They have powers granted by the state to arrest suspected lawbreakers and bring them to Shari'a courts, though they often hand out on-the-spot beatings. In one case they brought a 17-year-old girl to the Shari'a court when she was found pregnant. She was sentenced to flogging 100 times for having premarital sex, though the flogging was delayed to allow her to give birth to her child.[8] The hisba have also violently attacked places said to be used by prostitutes and where alcohol is sold:

> Recognising that these *hisba* groups must be curbed if law and order were to be maintained and also aware of the slackness of the police in enforcing the Shari'a, some state governments (e.g. Kano), decided to establish their own, government-controlled *hisba* groups. The rules and regulations of the Kano *hisba* committee list mainly religious duties, such as counselling and guiding Muslims who are negligent in their religious duties or do not behave as a good Muslim should. They are not authorised to deal with crime, except in co-operation with the police. In order to make them recognisable to the public, they wear a uniform (Peters, 2001:28).

Since the governor of Zamfara has said that Shari'a supersedes the Nigerian constitution and indicated that Islam requires Muslims to kill any apostate, the new laws are virtually irreversible – anyone trying to change them could be charged with attacking Islam. And from a communiqué issued by the Supreme Council for Shari'a in Nigeria, it is clear that it regards the provincial states as the legitimate authorisers of policing:

8. *San Francisco Chronicle*, 23 January, 2001.

The Hisbah group are an indispensable vehicle for the proper implementation of Shari'a as its indomitable vanguard. The Hisbah is to Shari'a what the police is to any government. The Nigerian Police Force as constituted today cannot by any stretch of imagination be a substitute for Hisbah. The police force has to be exorcised of its image of corruption and poor motivation. The Hisbah groups already established are meant to complement the police in their statutory duties and are not its rivals ... But this can only be achieved if the mentality and orientation of the police force is refocused to one of service away from extortion and tyranny ... we hereby wish to make it clear to the federal government and similar interested bodies who intend to interfere with the effective implementation of the Shari'a in Nigeria, that we are fully aware of our fundamental constitutional rights in a free democratic society to pursue our activities as Muslims in the attainment of our rights as free citizens of this country. We therefore call on the federal government to stop trying to subvert the institution of Hisbah in its effort to sabotage the Shari'a.[9]

In Ghana the predominantly Islamic communities of Nima 441 and Mamobi, suburbs of Accra, have seen the emergence of 'Shari'a police' known locally as Isakaba, (a name adopted from the title of a Nigerian film with similar characters). Members of hunting groups have constituted themselves into a volunteer group to enforce law and order. Critics accuse them of prejudging cases before inviting suspects for questioning and of subjecting people to corporal punishment if the person resists arrest. Apart from dealing with those who engage in un-Islamic behaviour such as pre-marital sex, they act as debt collectors and intimidate people reported to them to pay their debt instantly or face the consequences. The Isakaba also act as land guards in various locations in and outside Accra and are often hired at a fee to perform such assignments.[10] Some religious policing, however, is much more mild and eschews coercion and violence. There are many examples of faith-based organisations such as churches and mosques that handle primary justice complaints. These are dealt with under the category of Restorative Justice Committees below.

Ethnic/clan militias

Ethnic or clan militias share with religious police the use of both surveillance and punishment security with little regard for the state law or state

9. *Vanguard*, 2 July, 2001.

10. *Accra Mail*, Accra, 19 July, 2001.

police. Of course the order they are concerned to preserve is wider than religious matters and concerns the whole cultural web that constitutes what makes the clan or ethnic group distinct. The clan/ethnic basis also means that it has a wider geographical remit than the other informal groups so far mentioned. Unlike the customary courts of elders and chiefs, militias favour violence rather than negotiation and restoration.

Ethnic militias are often thought of as mobilised against other ethnic groups. For instance, ethnically motivated mass killings have been a feature of the conflict in eastern DRC since 1999. The conflict sucked in ethnic groups, spawning ever increasing numbers of ethnic and clan militias, as well as civilian vigilante groups to defend their own people. These paramilitary groups have also gone on the offensive and killed on a mass scale regardless of the presence of the small UN peacekeeping force.[11]

In Nigeria, however, there are examples of ethnic associations, founded to protect and promote the interests of their peoples, being turned against crime rather than other ethnic groups e.g. Arewa People's Congress APC (Hausa and Fulani); Movement for the Actualization of the Sovereign State of Biafra, MASSOB (Igbo); Egbesu Boys of Africa EBA (Ijaw); and The O'odua People's Congress OPC (Yoruba). The OPC, founded in 1994, has used violence as a tool of both its ethnic militancy and its vigilantism. Despite the programme outlined by the leadership, their activity is often in the hands of undisciplined members. OPC has had powerful backers, including the explicit support of state governors. Hence OPC members have provided security at official and public functions (Human Rights Watch, 2003). The federal government, on the other hand, has sought to outlaw them:

> In 1999, the federal government announced a ban on the OPC and gave the police orders to deal with the organization ruthlessly. Instructions to the police to 'shoot on sight', combined with the OPC's defiance of the ban, provoked a heavy-handed and brutal response from the police. The police regularly raided and broke up OPC meetings; scores of OPC members were killed by the police and hundreds arrested … Despite this crackdown, the OPC has continued to function, sometimes underground, but more often boldly and openly challenging the federal government's and the police's attempts to crush it (Human Rights Watch, 2003).

Not surprisingly for a stateless society, a common feature of Somalia is armed mobile groups operating under the leadership of factional or clan

---

11. www.oxfamamerica.org/emergency/art5351.

heads. 'Warlords' are most plausibly regarded as commercial operators, each with a private military force recruited largely on a clan basis. They deal in straightforward looting, the arms trade, qat (a locally grown narcotic shrub), profiteering out of humanitarian relief and, most ironically of all, international 'peace-keeping' operations (Clapham 1999:23–45). Farah and Lewis identified 40 militia-manned checkpoints (divided between more than 10 lineage groups) along two trade routes commonly used by qat trucks (1993:61). Though the armed groups evidently function as personal armies, they also enforce social order within the area claimed by their lineage.

Political party militia groups

Operating in the interests of modern political parties rather than customary tribes, but using similar methods to the ethnic militias, are the party militias. Yet whereas ethnic militias tend to have a regional basis, party militias may well have a larger range if they serve a national party. These groups are convenient bodies for national or local strongmen to enforce their will without the encumbrances of the law. Typically, young unemployed men are recruited and their dependency on the patron instils a fierce loyalty and willingness to use extreme violence. Conveniently any abuses can always be put down to the excesses of supporters. President Mugabe in Zimbabwe has put party militias to effective use to prevent electoral success by the opposition. 50,000 young people are said to have been trained in camps in how to torture and kill.[12]

President Banda of Malawi had set up a similar organisation in 1963, when he founded The Malawi Young Pioneers (MYP). This elite wing of the League of Malawi Youth, a division of the Malawi Congress Party, was charged with mobilising the youth for national development. Up to 1967, they were mainly concerned with rural development work and in promoting adulation for Dr Banda, his party and his government. Over time, however, the MYP added a security role. Trained in the use of small arms and the gathering and analysis of intelligence reports, they were deployed not just on rural development schemes, but as a 'third security force'. They forced people to buy the party membership card and to attend party meetings. They also served as Banda's private army to detain, torture and send into forced exile his opponents. Following an abortive invasion of the coun-

---

12. BBC, Panorama, 29 February, 2004.

try in 1967, they were given additional military training and were equipped with automatic weapons and even helicopter gunships. Thus by the 1980s they overlapped or even overshadowed the police and army in their security operations and had 6,000 members, plus a reserve force of about 45,000 previously trained Young Pioneers (Phiri, 2000). Their demise came in 1993 when the army, with enthusiastic support from the public, attacked MYP establishments and disarmed and dismantled the organisation. Interestingly within six months concerns began to be raised about the gap left in grassroots policing at community level:

> The disappearance of the Young Pioneers was followed by a considerable breakdown of public security. This took the form of such things as armed robberies in townships; the terrorising of school children as they returned from school; and of women as they returned from meetings. In reaction to such a deterioration of public security, some urban communities began to take the law into their own hands, by devising their own way of apprehending and punishing offenders or would-be offenders (Phiri, 2000).

When the militia is that of the ruling party, it works closely with the police, who refuse to take action against members when they commit human rights abuses. But opposition parties have militias as well. Renamo in Mozambique has an armed force of rebel fighters who, in violation of the 1992 peace agreement, were never demobilised. Contrary to their claim, most of them are not protecting any Renamo leaders. They are living in old Renamo bases, mostly in the central province of Sofala. They have been accused of beating and kidnapping government officials and FRELIMO members. Recent promises by the government to remove them have been strongly resisted. One such 'security force' severely beat a local FRELIMO official in August 2004. When two were arrested, 25 Renamo armed men broke into the Cheringoma district police station and freed them. When recaptured, an angry crowd gathered and as police fired tear gas some responded with gun shots.[13]

Not all political party militias are so violent. In Cameroon most political parties have long trained militants as security men. The 'vanguards' of the Social Democratic Front (SDF), according to the coordinator, are those who protect the party. They are seen as supplementing the police during large political events, particularly in maintaining order during rallies. They are not armed, but wear uniforms. The 'party police' of the National Union for Democracy and Progress (NUDP) are also uniformed. The 200

---

13. Agencia de Informaçao de Moçambique, 16 June and 13 August, 2004.

members, ranging from lower grades to the rank of 'General', guard party premises and officials. They are trained by retired policemen and those guarding top officials of the party are armed. The UPC (Cameroon People's Union) also has a non-uniformed security unit whose role is said to be to ensure peace within the party and to discreetly spy on their 'enemies', whether traitors within the party or other political parties.[14]

Civil defence forces

Civil defence forces (CDFs) typically emerge during a general breakdown of civil authority and law in the course of a civil war, when neither a depleted state army nor an ineffective police can offer state protection to citizens. In other words, they arise as substitutes for conventional defence forces. Thus, though they share the militia structure of ethnic and political party militias, they function in a different context and are concerned to provide general security for all within their region of operation.

For example, in Mali, the Patriotic Movement of Ganda Koy was formed to defend predominantly Songhoy communities against Tuareg/Arab rebels. Similarly, the CDFs in Sierra Leone – the Tamaboros (Koinadugu district), the Donsos (Kono district), the Kapras (Tonkolili district), and the Gbethis (Port Loko and Tonkolili districts) and the Kamajors, were formed to protect citizens from the Revolutionary United Front (RUF) and the Armed Force Revolutionary Council (AFRC). When, as in Sierra Leone, they have their roots in customary militia hunters and warriors, they are usually structured around the ethnic identity of their community and swear allegiance to their communal or tribal leaders (or civilian patrons). When the Sierra Leonean civil war began in 1991, they mobilised communal forces to support the army. But though they sought to maintain communal order, they were themselves guilty of atrocities against RUF/AFRC supporters. Like the rebels they fought, the CDFs participated in mineral extraction and fought for control of the clandestine trading networks around the mining regions (Ero, 2000). When peace finally came, they only reluctantly disbanded.

The long-running civil war in Angola saw similar developments in group self-protection. A study in rural Huambo shows that internally displaced persons and villagers established civil defence groups to handle potential security threats in rural areas during the civil war:

---

14. *Cameroon Tribune*, Yaoundé, 4 September, 2003.

Civil defence groups, composed of both men and women, have been organised both by the local population and the authorities. Men carry the weapons, women patrol the paths and roads. Some members of the civil defence teams carry light weapons to protect settlements and markets. On the roads into towns, members of the civil defence regularly check that people are not carrying weapons and bombs hidden in their bags and baskets. Sometimes, a small civil defence group is left to protect houses and crops in villages from which most of the population has already fled (Birkeland and Gomes, 2001).

As might be expected, there is a wide variety of overlapping local organisations providing defence and security in Somalia in the absence of a central state. In addition to the already mentioned lineage heads and gangs that run protection rackets, authorisers include local councils, mosques and neighbourhood watch schemes that alert neighbours to armed outsiders by whistles. In almost every case the providers were local armed young men (Hills, 1997; Menkhaus and Prendergast, 1995).

Informal commercial security groups

Earlier, informal organised security groups were described, but typically they involve action by private citizens on a non-commercial basis. However, the financial side that lurks among some 'voluntary' groups can become dominant. Self-gain is commonly cited as a central motive behind informal groups. One respondent in South Africa told a researcher of a group of about 10 or 20 people involved in kangaroo courts: 'they're benefiting because they are intimidating the people they are living amongst. They will go into a shebeen, demand free liquor, you know, maybe offer protection or demand protection fees'. Another told that kangaroo court members, 'only make money for themselves. And it's true and clear that they were only interested in making money, for instance, they fined me R450 in a short space of time without even listening to my side of the story' (Harris, 2001a). Under the patronage of local political or economic agents, such groups can grow into significant commercial operations. In other words, they commodify the violence they wield. Political agents may see informal commercial security groups as the solution to the crime wave in an area that threatens their legitimacy and popularity. In such a situation these security groups may assume a public or community role, rather than (or as well as) one intended for the benefit of a group or persons.

At the provincial level in Nigeria, a number of State Governors have employed informal security groups to be, in effect, regional police forces under their command. In South East Nigeria there was such a demand for a successful security group called the Bakassi Boys that three State Governors adopted them as state policing agencies (Baker, 2002c; Human Rights Watch/CLEEN, 2002). In Imo State, for instance, villages without any police presence had initially set up local vigilance units with the co-operation of the police to combat armed bandits. Following violent attacks on the members of the units, they discovered that information given to the police about suspected bandits was passed on to the gangs. They turned to the Bakassi Boys. One villager recorded:

> They went to work immediately … suddenly things began to happen. Well known hoodlums who were friends of the police gradually took notice and either fled or stayed at their peril. In a short time, locking and bolting gates and doors in my village became only a matter of habit; nobody needed to. Home was becoming haven again and evening parties and outside engagements returned to the community. It was such a great relief. Asked thereafter to choose between the Bakassi Boys and the police, the village folks preferred the former.[15]

Informal security groups have also been co-opted by national governments. In Uganda, Tanzania and Kenya the state has sought to control the vigilantes through incorporating them into state recognised people's militias (Baker, 2002b; for Nairobi see Anderson, 2002).

Elsewhere it is business interests that have funded commercial informal security groups. The largest such group in South Africa is 'Mapogo a Matamaga', formed in 1996 in the Northern Province to protect rural businesses. The group has become infamous for its sjambokking (whipping) and brutal assaults of alleged criminals. Initially concerned with protecting rural communities, it now also patrols the suburbs of Johannesburg and Pretoria. Its leaders claim 10,000 members in Gauteng and 40,000 in Limpopo (formerly Northern Province) and Mpumalanga (von Schnitzler et al., 2001; Oomen, 1999). Its president says:

> Naturally, as crime is escalating in all places, almost everyone wants to join Mapogo. They feel protected by us because of our approach to crime. The main thing that attracts members … is that we know how to deal with criminals. We believe in corporal punishment and that really works.[16]

---

15. www.waado.org/NigerDelta/Documents.

16. *Africa Research Bulletin*, 1, 2000.

They say their investigations are effective because they work with the community members, then 'arrest' the alleged criminal. Before handing them over to the police, members mete out their own brand of 'medicine' to the suspects to 'cure them of their bad ways'.[17]

In the southern Niger city of Zinder, it was taxi and lorry owners who in 1991 called on two vigilante leaders from the neighbouring city of Maradi to establish a group to protect their businesses. Clothed in new uniforms, they were presented to the prefect of Zinder department and the mayor of Zinder.

> The mayor provided torch lights for night patrol and the police commissioner was pressurised into furnishing the leader of the *m'banga* with a pair of handcuffs. Henceforth the m'banga was known as the *police traditionelle du Sultan* as well as the security service of the businessmen of the town (Lund, 2001:860).

Armed with sabres and spiked mace they preferred to beat suspected thieves and parade them dressed in women's clothes before the crowds dancing like a monkey, to handing them over to the police. The latter would only take place if the family refused to pay for their release. After the 1996 coup, when the police started obstructing the group's collection of money from businesses, they expanded into the realm of providing personal security guarding for politicians (for South African taxi vigilantism see, Dugard, 2001; Bruce and Komane, 1999).

Both political and economic interests have been at work in promoting informal commercial security in Côte d'Ivoire. During the 1990s the success of hunter associations (*donzo ton*) in reducing crime in northern rural areas led to their expansion at the national level as private security guards in the country's major cities. The government and political parties also employed *donzow* to complement the police and gendarmes in maintaining order during the 1995 presidential elections. Yet fearing that the *donzo ton* might become a politically destabilising force, successive governments have attempted to restrict its activities to the northern savannah region (Bassett, 2003; Hellweg, 2004).

Formal commerial security groups

So far groups that ignore the law and the state police have been considered. Formal commercial security, however, is essentially operating within the

---

17. *Africa Research Bulletin*, 1, 2000; *Mail & Guardian*, 28 January, 2000; on The Peninsular Anti Crime Agency, PEACA, see Tshehla, 2001: 38–41.

law and in co-operation with the police, using trained guards. It covers protecting a person or property; providing a rapid response service; protecting public spaces such as premises used for sporting, recreational, entertainment purposes; private investigation. Though their emphasis is on surveillance, they also use punishment security, usually in terms of exclusion and/or handing people over to the state police. Another striking contrast to the majority of the groups so far considered is their operational range. Though some are local, operating in a single town, many commercial security groups operating in Africa are now part of global companies headquartered in the West, for example, Group4Falck and ArmorGroup.

The origins of commercial policing in Africa are largely to be found in the mining industry and the desire of mine owners and their managers to exercise total control over their compound migrant workforce (Van Onselen, 1976). No economic sector took more trouble than mining to organise, train and arm company police of its own. Philip quotes from a leaked confidential report of *Gold Fields*, outlining the role of its security service in South Africa. It was to cater for 'prevention and detection of crime; protection of company assets; control of vulnerable and vital areas; screening of personnel; combating of labour unrest; combating subversive activities; training, supervision and administration of the security force; and liaison at a local level with the South African Defence Force (SADF), South African Police (SAP) and civil defence' (Philip, 1989:214). Mine security has long been equipped with anti-riot vehicles, riot dogs, tear gas, sjamboks, guns and pistols, and has used them, amongst other things, to break strikes (e.g. the miners' strike 1987) and disrupt union meetings (Philip, 1989:215).

In South Africa, with the increasing security problems of the 1970s and 1980s, and the SAP focus on this, non-state policing came into its own. White neighbourhoods sought protection from commercial security firms. Brogden and Shearing call the expansion, 'the major "hidden" supplement to the state policing' (1993:71). The expansion of this commercial security, unlike in most other countries, was actively encouraged by the government to relieve pressure on the overstretched SAP (Philip, 1989:213–14; Irish, 1999:12). In 1980 the government required 'key' strategic installations and factories to seek commercial protection, at the same time granting greater powers to such security guards. This, together with the privatisation of the railway police in 1987, 'placed vast areas of public domain under the policing agency of private security' (Brogden and Shearing, 1993:72). With this context it is not surprising that commercial policing took off in South Africa before any other Africa country (Irish, 1999). In 1986–87 it is estimated that 300,000 to 400,000 were employed as security guards, compared with 60,000 in the SAP (Brogden and Shearing, 1993:72). Between September 1997 and March 2000 the number of active security officers registered with South Africa's Security Officers' Interim Board increased from 115,000 to 166,000. It is estimated that there are an additional 50,000 in-house security officers in South Africa. Compared to the 216,000 security officers, there are approximately 90,000 uniformed police officers employed by the South African Police Service (SAPS). This figure contrasts with other African countries where the ratio is often about 50:50. Uniformed and equipped to a similar or better standard than the state police, commercial policing by the late 1980s rapidly assumed much of the day-to-day policing of white suburbs of South Africa's towns (Baker, 2002a). From guarding buildings, it grew to include patrolling, armed response and electronic systems and now undertakes all state police roles.

One aspect of commercial policing that is often overlooked is debt collection. The sector has a bad reputation for violence. In a recent paper on extra-judicial debt collectors, the Law Development Commission of Zimbabwe said their growth was due to 'declining standards in the Zimbabwean judicial process' and the desire to avoid lengthy and costly trials, and to maintain privacy in financial matters. To remain in business, the debt collector must get debtors to pay, which encourages coercion and intimidation. Their tactics typically include threatened or actual violence, abusive and offensive letters, frequent personal visits and unlawful dispossession of property. Among the biggest complaints is that collectors over-charge debtors, often demanding interest as high as 900 per cent.[18] The drive to regulate the activities of debt collectors in Zimbabwe follows South Africa's establishment in 1998 of a Council for Debt Collectors that exercises control over the occupation of debt collector.

In the 1990s across Africa the commercial security sector expanded rapidly, with governments, commercial corporations, aid agencies and private citizens increasingly using private security companies for their protection. The total number of private security personnel in Ghana was 400 in 1968, 1,250 in 1990, 3,400 in 2000 and 50,000 in 2001 (Appiahene-Gyamfi, 2003; for Nigeria see, Igbinovia, 2000; Akingbade, 2003). The private security industry flourishes where the state is weakest, such as in Angola, Liberia, Sierra Leone and DRC. In Luanda, for example, the number of security companies grew from two in 1992, to over 70 in 1996. Faced with

---

18. Inter Press Service, 20 January, 2004.

governments unwilling or unable to provide protection, even aid agencies and embassies are using private security companies for their risk analysis and protection of staff and sites (Spearin, 2001). In some instances, where government protection has not been available, private security companies have been involved in armed escorts for the transfer of emergency relief to war-affected communities (e.g. by CARE and World Food Programme, Vaux, 2003).

State approved civil guarding

Also working within the law and with the approval and co-operation of the state police, but not for profit, are a range of security groups authorised by citizen groups and sub-national political units and provided by small groups of trained guards. Johnston tries to capture something of their ethos by calling them responsible citizen groups. Take for example South Africa, particularly amongst the middle classes. There, some security units are based on city residents' groups, who operate vehicle patrols with the co-operation of the South African Police Service and private security firms. Elsewhere, city residents have formed non-profit companies and hire police reservists for armed foot patrols. Others are based on city businesses within a city centre block, which are protected and patrolled by security guards (Shaw, 1995:77). Still others are based on farms, which co-operate to engage security firms to patrol the farms.[19] In Kenya, the Nairobi Central Business District Association, following the Johannesburg example, has established a public-private partnership with the police, in which communities define their security needs and provide the state police with the means needed to satisfy them (Ruteere and Pommerolle, 2003:595). There are many examples, too, of forums where police and citizens meet and where this sometimes leads to citizens' patrols. In Malawi some Community Police Forums in rural areas with no police officers have formed their own patrols and have carried out arrests (sometimes with beatings). Civilian members of Lesotho's Crime Prevention Committees are allowed to undertake some policing work, including patrols. Although they are not supposed to confront suspects without a police officer, they generally lack supervision. In Swaziland, 'community policing' refers to civilians who police local crime, though they are said to have often treated suspects brutally.

---

19. *Africa Research Bulletin*, 9, 1998.

Their status, mandate and powers are unclear and they do not appear to have received very thorough training.

For all that these are private initiatives, they share the acknowledgement of the state as performing a valuable service for community order and safety. Yet the relationship between these citizen groups and the state police is often strained by suspicion and rivalry, in part because in some areas the neighbourhood watches outnumber the police. Nor do they have universal local support. Neighbourhood watches in South Africa are groups of 10–15 men armed with their council-issued batons as well as their own handguns. They patrol their streets and confront anyone they deem suspicious. This can easily degenerate into assaults that cause civilians to challenge the right of these groups to stop and search them (Schärf, 2003).

An example of a specific sub-national political unit that has authorised and provided its own policing, with state approval, although without it being national policy, is the Douala city council in Cameroon. In 2002 they set up their own traffic police in the face of what they deemed insufficient state policing in the commercial centre of the city. The uniformed Douala IV Urban Council police are divided into four teams of 10 persons. They are posted along the congested main roads to control vehicles, prevent illegal parking and to intervene when an accident occurs. According to the Chief of these municipal police, they only work with the gendarmerie or police, 'to reduce the traffic anarchy'. Sanctions are meted out for traffic offences, ranging from verbal warnings to large fines and the seizure of documents.[20] But the agenda of city police groups is not always so banal. Nairobi City Council *askaris* (patrol security guards) are viewed as brutal. Mitullah's 1988 survey of 425 street traders claimed that there were about 25,000 hawkers who were constantly in conflict with them. In October 1990, at Machakos bus depot, 300 NCC police took on hawkers with teargas and batons and were met with active resistance, including stone throwing and barricades. The following week Gikomba market was bulldozed and other 'illegal' markets were destroyed.

Customary courts and police

The chiefs' courts and their associated Native Authority police, for all their recent decline, are still the predominant administrators of justice in rural Africa (Schärf, 2003). The figure cited in Malawi is that they handle 80–90

---

20. *Cameroon Tribune*, Yaoundé, 26 June, 2003.

per cent of all disputes (Schärf, 2003), with about 24,000 customary justice forums (that is, roughly the number of villages). In Southwest Nigeria also it is estimated that some 80–90 per cent of disputes are taken to customary rulers (Anderson, 2002). Nor is it just in rural areas that they are important. A study in Nairobi province found that chiefs handle more reports of domestic violence than the police (Coalition on Violence against Women, 2002).

The extent to which the Native Authority police are organised, equipped or even active varies considerably. Some are no more than court messengers, others collect market dues and local tax, still others (such as in Sierra Leone and Liberia) are involved in community safety and security. As for the customary courts, they operate on the basis of customary law. Since they typically work within national constitutions they usually have state police approval. The courts have a conciliatory character, aiming to restore peace between members and social order, following such matters as petty theft, fights, out of wedlock pregnancies, adultery and civil disputes (Zwane, 1994; Stack, 1997; Kwame, 1985; Bekker, 1989; Carlston, 1968; Schapera, 1957; Seymour, 1970). The courts do not distinguish between civil and criminal matters, but rather deal with what they consider to be community problems. There are no formalised evidentiary rules, nor is there legal representation, instead people tell their stories in narrative form. Arrests can be made by native authority police, but more often litigants press the case themselves when every effort to resolve the matter informally has failed. The chief's court is a public affair, in which all adult men can freely participate. The men present have the right to cross-question the parties and to express an opinion as to what the decision or verdict should be. When the chief formally pronounces the verdict of the court, he is merely reflecting the consensus of opinion expressed by the tribal members present. Unfortunately, customary law is often even more discriminatory against women than the state. Many courts also frequently abuse their powers by illegally detaining persons, imposing excessive fines and adjudicating criminal cases.

Since most courts do not have formal jurisdiction (except in South Africa and Botswana, which still have a small formal judicial role for chiefs, predominantly in the rural areas), their judgments do not hold the weight of law. Nevertheless few would be willing to openly defy them. Punishment may include compensation to the other party in the dispute, a fine to the chief, and the guilty party may have to pay the full costs of the case. The party who wins the case may also be asked to give the chief a portion of the compensation received as a token of gratitude for a fair hearing. Some sentences include corporal punishment.

Dispute resolution forums

Informal dispute resolution mechanisms have long existed in African communities. Organisers include elders and clan leaders, religious leaders, friends, and customary doctors. To these informal spontaneous mechanisms have been added in the last 20 years more formal structures that have been formed outside of the locality where they operate and are based on Western mediation principles. NGO human rights and legal awareness groups are now shifting their focus from helping people find their way around the formal court system, to training paralegals in community-based justice forums (for Sierra Leone see Baker, 2006). Churches and mosques are also involved in handling complaints about domestic violence, labour disputes, land and property grabbing and land encroachment.

As one example, peace committees have been formed in some 10 South African townships under the Community Peace Programme (CPP) (Roche, 2002; Johnston and Shearing, 2003; see also www.ideaswork.org). The main work of committee members, for which they are paid a very small remuneration, is to provide local and accessible peacemaking facilitation to resolve specific conflicts. CPP 'gatherings', in the informality of committee members' homes, gather all the parties affected by the dispute. Together, the victim, offender and their supporters attempt to negotiate on a consensual basis the resolution of the injustice. Typically they deal with disputes over debt repayment and shack inheritance, but they also cover a range from strictly non-illegal matters such as noise complaints, infidelity and insulting language, to acts of domestic violence and rape. Negotiated settlements might include a promise to return stolen goods, to help repair material damage, to repay money owed, or to desist from offending behaviour. Most of the gatherings are held within five days of the offence. They provide, therefore, an alternative to formal conviction and sentencing in the criminal justice system, although there is always the threat in the background that if the issue is not resolved in the peace committee it may well be taken to the state courts. The peace committees, in contrast to other informal justice systems in the townships, abide by a strict code of conduct that pledges to work within the South African law, to eschew force and to follow transparent procedures.

An example of state-run alternative dispute resolution is found in Tanzania. Essentially it is a system of formalised village-based customary arbitration. The origins of Ward Tribunals can be traced back to 1969. They are under the overall control of the district-based local government authorities. Their purpose is to achieve justice at the local level through amicable settlement of disputes. They are intended to be reconciliatory, flexible, informal and sensitive to local culture. Lawi found them to be popular and performing well in the actual handling of disputes (Lawi, 2000). However, he noted some shortfalls: slowness in concluding cases; irregularity in the use of witness accounts in arriving at decisions; and inadequate guidance for Tribunal leaders in terms of court procedures. Further, despite the intention, the principle of reconciliation was not always adhered to. The Tribunals tended to be 'more compulsive than conciliatory in their conduct'.

Conclusion

By looking at non-state policing this chapter has shown that there is a clear trend in Africa away from the state police. The subsequent case studies on policing in Uganda and Sierra Leone will show that this is not necessarily towards non-state policing, as sometimes the authoriser and provider is another branch of the state. Nevertheless the overall pattern is clear. Policing is not a monopoly of the state police but is increasingly diversified to formal and informal agencies outside of the police and usually outside the state. Non-state policing is engrained in every community of Africa with the specific form of non-state protection adopted being determined by local historical, social, economic and political circumstances. It is ubiquitous to the point that few challenge its legitimacy, even if they criticise some of its practices.

Other emerging patterns that will be traced through the case studies of chapters five and six are first, the separation of those who authorise policing from those who provide it and second, a tendency, particularly for informal groups, to transform over time.

CHAPTER 6

Who Is Policing Uganda?

A key to building the legitimacy of the Police is to ensure effective forms of local control and accountability ... Here all transitional societies have had to balance the requirement of ensuring local accountability (which remains weak in all cases) with centralised control – the desire to manage change from the centre to ensure both that it occurs uniformly and that local groups (who may oppose the central state) do not obtain control of the police in their area .(Shaw, 2000)

Uganda makes a fascinating case study of contemporary African policing having passed through so many different eras in so short a time. Customary chiefs, ruthless dictators, revolutionary rebels and elected presidents have all played a part in the history of policing in the last 40 years. The civil war, 1981–86, was clearly a major turning point. The National Resistance Army (NRA), led by Yoweri Museveni against the Obote regime, was determined to bring in a new order. Fresh from the FRELIMO training camps of Mozambique, the NRA leadership was enthralled with the possibilities of 'popular' justice: a justice that was said to be popular in form because its language was open and accessible; popular in functioning because its proceedings involved active community participation; and popular in substance because judges were drawn from the people and gave judgment in the interests of the people (Museveni, 1997:30). Popular justice, they believed, could become a school of self-governance which taught people the social habits of co-operation. The vision was to put an end to security forces being above the law; to judges being politicised and corrupted; and to customary chiefs exercising their judicial powers in a self-serving manner. Just how much that radical vision persisted or was altered by processes of institutionalisation is the theme of this chapter.

Historical background to policing in Uganda

The indigenous kingdoms of Buganda, Bunyoro, Toro, Ankole (Nkore), Busoga and others arose around the 14th–16th centuries. They knew very little external intervention until the mid-19th century, when contacts were made with Arab traders in search of ivory and slaves, and with European explorers. The Treaty of Berlin in 1890 placed Uganda in the British sphere of influence and British politician Frederick Lugard, acting as an agent of the IBEACO (Imperial British East Africa Company), entered Buganda and established a military force in Kampala to guard the trade routes. However, with conflicts such as those between the Protestant and Catholic factions making administration burdensome, IBEACO transferred its rights in 1893 to the British Government. A protectorate was proclaimed the following year. It began with an armed constabulary of 1,400 men known as the Ugandan Rifles, recruited locally but under British officers. They had a dual role: to defend the protectorate against both external and internal threats. In practice the main task proved to be quelling riots and revolts against British rule, as well as suppressing the inter-tribal wars. In 1897 they were involved in military campaigns against the local Baganda and Banyoro rulers, which led to these 'troublesome elements' being deported to the Seychelles. The British then proceeded to install their own selected rulers and negotiated a comprehensive political arrangement in 1900 with the indigenous rulers. Given anxieties over Buganda resurgence, this made it illegal for its ruler, the Kabaka, to raise an army and all 'natives' were forbidden to possess any weapons. It was not until 1906 that civilian responsibilities were given to a reorganised protectorate police. Essentially they were under the control of the chiefs. Yet police posts were so few that self-policing was the norm in the villages. Internal conflict continued during the early part of the twentieth century, so to assist the overstretched British force, local chiefs were allowed to maintain police forces of their own.

Discipline was harsh in the police and only in 1913 was corporal punishment for misconduct abolished. On the other hand, privileges included housing and an exemption from tax. Slowly they were given extra resources. A Finger Print Bureau was established in 1908, bicycles were provided by 1912 and a small detective force was formed in 1913.

During the First World War the police focussed on defending the southern border with German East Africa. Yet following the war there was a fresh drive towards both the civilianisation and Africanisation of the force (from 1920 Ugandans were allowed to hold office up to the level of sub-Inspector). There was still occasional communal violence in the 1930s, but the day-to-day work of the police concerned poll tax collection, traffic control, vehicle licences, railway supervision and murder investigations. Yet the poor financial standing of the protectorate government meant that the expansion could not be maintained and nine officers and 275 other ranks were made redundant in 1931. Neglect also characterised the Second World War period as police were posted abroad.

The post-war period saw the police confronted with growing disorder, including serious riots in Buganda in 1945 and 1949. The riots were directed against colonial political rule and the Asian-European monopoly in crop marketing and processing. There were calls for independence using strikes, labour disturbances on sugar plantations, riots and 'agitatory publications'. This necessitated fresh colonial resources and hence the police force was expanded to 2,813 other ranks and 134 officers. Initially they used their powers under a State of Emergency 1953–54. However, from 1959 an area could be designated a 'disturbed area', where it was illegal to carry weapons and where curfews, roadblocks and deportations could be used. Other colonial responses to the increasing political activity included the formation of a Special Branch and an anti-riot unit in 1951. The latter were given training in handling urban riots, patrolling rural areas and preventing cattle theft. The latter drew them into inter-ethnic violence in Karamoja.[1]

As for the Local Administration Police, these were widely regarded as ineffective. This was not necessarily a matter of their small size, for the Buganda Government Police had 700 in its force and was equipped with vehicles. Overall, however, the Police Commissioner regarded them in the mid-1950s as 'an embarrassment'. 'Elsewhere, the local police appear to have been little more than the chief's henchmen' (Clayton and Killingray, 1989:82).

Since the Banyoro and Baganda had actively resisted the establishment of colonial rule, British policy was to mainly recruit police and soldiers from northern Uganda. In the 1960s a third of its police force was from the northern Acholi, Lango and Iteso. The resulting ethnic imbalance characterised the Ugandan Police and Army long after independence. Gender imbalance began to be addressed when female recruitment began in 1961. Likewise there were moves towards the Africanisation of the force. It began with Assistant Superintendents of Police by 1957 and led to over 100 of the executive command posts being African by independence.

Milton Obote, who led Uganda to independence in 1962, oversaw a rapid Africanisation of the state police. Unsure of their loyalty he also

---

1. In one of the joint operations of police and King's African Rifles (KAR) in 1961, a Lt. Amin tied two Turkana to a tree and let them die in the sun. For political reasons, however, the Governors of Kenya and Uganda decided not to press charges of murder.

formed his own intelligence unit, but it did not prevent Amin's coup in 1969. Under Amin, police investigating military corruption simply disappeared. When a former British Inspector General visited Uganda in 1971 he found the police facilities 'despoiled' (Clayton and Killingray, 1989:104). Over the next eight years an estimated 300,000 lost their lives, particularly the Acholi and Lango and the professional classes.

Like many dictators, Amin deliberately created four rival agencies, the Military Police, the Presidential Guard, the Public Safety Unit and the Bureau of State Research, to elicit intelligence on his enemies through detention and torture and to carry out his mass killings (Kasozi, 1994:114). Amin's Presidential Guard, drawn from his own Kakwa tribe, was both a death squad and his personal guard. Though Amin survived seven assassination attempts between 1972 and 1979, his political end came when he chose a border conflict with Tanzania. The Tanzanians pushed back the Ugandan army and pressed on to Kampala to institute regime change. When Amin fled, Obote returned from exile and won the presidential vote in a rigged election.

Like Amin, Obote favoured certain tribes. Large numbers of civil servants and army and police commanders belonging to southern tribes were replaced with Obote supporters belonging to northern tribes. Tragically murder, torture, looting, rape, terrorism and imprisonment of opponents began again under the army, the secret police (the National Security Agency) and party officials.

Under both Amin and Obote the head of state and the security forces were above the law and those able to call them to account, the judiciary, were themselves politicised and corrupted. The process also contaminated the police:

> ... who could not bring suspects to justice for fear of victimisation. Cases which involved the army against the people could not be investigated by the police in case evidence was obtained to convict army personnel ... The fear of consequences was aggravated by corruption. The Police were demoralised by the treatment they received, especially from the Minister of Internal Affairs during the second Obote regime. Promotion was based on party affiliation (Kabwegyere, 1995:228).

If the police were reluctant to investigate abuses by the state security forces and powerful political figures, the public were equally reluctant to report crimes by them. Serious crimes were thus committed with impunity, which encouraged some to seek revolution. When in mid-1985 Obote was over-

Figure 1. Policing Structures in Uganda

POLICING BODY	AUTHORISER	POWERS	KEY FUNCTION	LINKS WITH OTHER POLICING BODIES	FUNDING
State structures					
Local Councils Level 1 (LC1)	Central Gov. Locally elected	Local law and order. Courts	Courts; Night patrols	Criminal cases to Uganda Police and magistrate's courts	Local taxes contributions + volunteers
Uganda Police	Central Gov.	Standard police powers	Serious crime	Work with LCs, Crime prevention panels and Security Cos	State
Violent Crime Crack Unit (VCCU)	Military	Unclear	Organised violent crime	Independent	State
State approved					
Crime Prevention Panels (CPP)	Uganda Police	Citizen	Intelligence to police; peer pressure	Work with police and LCs	Volunteers
Traders' associations	Elected leaders of association	Citizen	Security of trading area	Work with police and LCs	Members' contributions
Commercial security	Private companies	Licensed by police	Guarding	Joint ops with, and inspected by, police	Commercial
Illegal					
Mob justice			Assaults on alleged criminals	None	

thrown in an army coup, it was only a stop gap measure, for already a guerrilla army, the National Resistance Army (NRA) led by Yoweri Museveni, controlled a large area of western Uganda. By January 1986 the NRA had taken Kampala.

The account that follows of how people in Uganda currently experience policing is based on field research undertaken in 2004. It records the various policing agencies available and how Ugandans evaluate them. A summary of the structures to be examined and their key features is given in Figure 1.

It reveals a fragmented pattern of policing, but one that, for historical reasons, is still heavily influenced, if not controlled, by state institutions. There may have been a diversification away from the state police, but it has not been a straightforward move to non-state formal and informal agencies. Rather, for the most part, the state has maintained a strong influence over most of the diversification. The diversification, therefore, is more a matter of choice than of ownership.

Contemporary crime and insecurity

In Uganda's villages most people reported that 'crime' was not a serious issue and that they enjoyed a sense of security. This, however, is not the whole story. Police statistics show increased numbers of reported crime across the country, particularly cases of theft, rape and defilement (sexual intercourse with someone under 18). In addition, a serious cause of disorder and tension in rural areas that is not apparent from the crime figures alone, is land. In areas where there is pressure for land from an increasing population, where land is being sold to outsiders, and where land has been transferred to estates or declared a national park, land has become a contentious issue. Local Councils (LCs), magistrates and the Land Tribunal face continuous civil disputes over boundaries, tenants rights, squatting, evictions, inheritance, and the sale of land that was not the vendor's to sell. These frequently spill over into criminal cases of criminal trespass and assault.[2]

As in most developing countries, both fear of crime and victimisation rates remain high in Uganda's towns. Crime committed in the capital, Kampala, is rising. Some 24 people were shot dead in 2002, compared to 80 in 2003. Also, between 2002 and 2003, defilement cases rose from 649 to 999; aggravated assault cases from 311 to 647; vehicle theft cases from 296 to 319; burglary and theft cases from 454 to 543; robbery cases from 461 to 606; while general theft cases rose from 3,504 to 5,073.[3] My own research showed that of 38 shopkeepers (22 men, 16 women) interviewed in Kampala, 25 felt safe or very safe; seven felt nervous or anxious at times;

---

2. Interviews with OC Mityana Uganda Police, 31 March, 2004; RDC Kabarole District, Ndiwa Chemasuet, 1 April, 2004; Administrative Secretary of Land Tribunal for Kabarole District, Eva Bira Ngeme, 1 April, 2004; LC3 Chairman, Karambi sub-county, Mr Mwiraumubi Eli, 2 April, 2004; LC3 Vice Chairman, Mugusu sub-county, Mrs Mbabazi Margaret, 2 April, 2004; Kiko Tea Estate manager, Mr Kiiroya Lameck, 2 April, 2004.

3. *The Monitor*, 6 January, 2004.

six felt unsafe. Concerning victimisation rates, it was found that 28 had been a victim of theft in the last 12 months or had known someone who had been; seven had been a victim of physical assault in the last 12 months or had known someone who had been; four had been a victim of damage to property in the last 12 months or had known someone who had been.

It is important, however, to disaggregate the reports of crime and disorder on a gender basis. Crime figures very much reflect a male definition of order, but do not always capture the female perspective. As will be shown later, Ugandan women often define law and order as more than the absence of crime. Instead, they commonly see it in terms of responsible behaviour, especially by men and youths; or 'they want to feel comfortable and secure'.[4] Some of those grievances may be prohibited in the legal code, but that does not necessarily mean that state policing will attend to it. There are those who say that police officers confronted, for instance, with an accusation of wife beating may not feel it is their business to get involved in another man's 'personal affairs'. And there are, of course, those issues that are not illegal in the formal sense, but are nevertheless unacceptable to women, such as harassment, abusive language, drunkenness and neglect of family responsibilities. This gendered perspective reminds us that for a very large number of citizens, the security they are looking for is the provision of care as much as protection. Though legal aid centres handle thousands of cases brought by women each year of domestic violence, inheritance disputes and failure to pay maintenance, there is no knowledge of just how large these problems are. Crime statistics may also fail to capture generational differences. Older persons, especially in rural areas, spoke with concern about young people not in terms of formal crime, but of the disorder associated with their promiscuity, drunkenness, drug taking, dropping out of school and general 'idleness' because of unemployment.

The Uganda Police

The Uganda Police, according to their Mission Statement, are to: 'secure life and property in partnership with the public in a committed and professional manner in order to promote development'. No one doubts, however, that they are seriously overstretched, with only 13,000 personnel, well

---

4. Interview, Keith Kibirango, Head of Information, The Uganda Association of Women Lawyers, 24 March, 2004.

below their goal of 40,000 to provide 1 police officer per 600 citizens.[5] Despite donor help from Britain, France, North Korea, Egypt, and Germany in the form of equipment and training, they are still under-resourced. One sub-district of over two million had just 184 personnel and one motor bike,[6] whilst in Fort Portal the police had no vehicles or motorbikes to cover a town of 45,000 (although the mobile patrol vehicle for Kabarole District was based there).[7]

Yet in the last ten years they have undergone a number of positive reforms that have enhanced their effectiveness e.g. the introduction of a Research and Planning Department (1992); a separate Inspectorate (1997) to evaluate performance; a Community Affairs Department (1998); a Legal Department (1989), which in 1999 took on a Human Rights Desk and a Complaints Desk; a Private Security and Police Firearms Department (2001); and a Police Marine Department (2002). Management units have been established at the level of the directorate, department, region, district and station, whilst discipline has improved following an independent judicial commission of inquiry into corruption in the police in 2000.[8] Their role has also been redefined, with their withdrawal from guarding and escort duties in favour of private security companies. The recent incorporation of Local Authority Police (LAP) into the Uganda Police was also intended to address the problems experienced with this locally controlled force, which in the past handled crimes too serious for it and was at times starved of funding by Local Councils that did not pass on all central government funds allocated to them.[9]

---

5. The police as an organisation has one of the highest rates of HIV/AIDS in Uganda. For example, it was found that 13 percent of police officers in Kampala are HIV positive – more than double the national average of six percent. The reasons given are; job transfers split police officers from their spouses, with male officers taking in a woman to cook and wash and have sex; living situations mean several adults live in extremely close quarters; the demand by officers for sex from female detainees and prostitutes and from younger officers seeking promotion; high alcoholism and associated rape in the barracks; refusal to test for fear of dismissal or discrimination (currently, police do not take on HIV positive recruits). *The Monitor*, September 27, 2005.

6. Interview, OC, Mityana, Uganda Police, 31 March, 2004.

7. Interview, CLO, Fort Portal, Uganda Police, 1 April, 2004.

8. Interview, Julius Odwe, Deputy Inspector General of Police, 3 March, 2004.

9. Interview, David Taitika, Assistant Commissioner of Police, Local Administration Police, 26 February, 2004.

Perhaps the biggest change, however, has been the relationship between the public and the police. Until relatively recently the police were still regarded with suspicion and fear. This is understandable given the abuses under Amin and Obote prior to the National Resistance Movement (NRM). Yet now, whatever the criticisms, the almost universal response was that the police were now friendly, approachable and showed respect to all citizens. Police may not always be close at hand to many citizens, but generally Ugandans would not hesitate to call upon them if they needed their assistance. This is a remarkable turn around, the more so given that across much of Africa the police are often held in contempt and fear. There was even an example (Naguru, Kampala) where the community paid Sh80,000 per month per home to provide for extra police to patrol their area.

Yet even the improvement in public perception is relative. Many Ugandans complain about the slowness of the police to respond; mass arrests during police sweeps for criminals (such as tax evaders) continue; and there were persistent claims by the majority of those interviewed of bribe seeking (confirmed by the Inspector General of Government's assertion of the police as the most corrupt institution in the country).[10] For those who cross the law the experience is more abusive. Deaths still occur in police custody, some due to torture. Suspected criminals are still shot and killed while being pursued resulting in deaths. And it is not always clear that any action has been taken against those concerned. Even the police's own Human Rights Desk, received 330 allegations of police abuse in 2005; and the Uganda Human Rights Commission reports 541 complaints of police torture 2000–2004.

The police are also repeatedly charged with political partisanship in the increasingly heated political atmosphere of emerging multi-partyism. In March 2005, for instance, police allowed a demonstration in Kampala in favour of Museveni running again as president, but banned one that was to be held in opposition. When the rally took place they used water cannon, tear gas and pepper spray to break it up. The evidence suggests a concerted campaign to use the police, CMI, and VCCU personnel against the political opposition. Though political policing may not affect directly the majority of the population, it is still prevalent and violent. Opponents continue to be arrested arbitrarily, later to be released without charge. Opposition parties say 60 supporters were arrested in 2005 for political reasons, and the ICRC registered 200 detainees held for offences against the security of the state.

---

10. *The Monitor*, 22 March, 2004.

Other opponents have 'disappeared' or suffered physical abuse, including caning, severe beating, and inflicting pain to the genitals. Treason suspects were subject to numerous abuses, such as detention without charge, detention in unregistered and unofficial locations, and mistreatment, including torture. Parallel with this is the use of the police to repress the opposition press, with journalists locked out of the High Court premises and arrested for sedition (based on their criticism of President Museveni). It is evident that for all the improvements in everyday policing this is not a democratic police service.

Other state policing

Violent crime units

One of the issues the government has had to address is the balance between a centralisation that offers the benefits of tighter control and better funding, and local control that offers greater accountability and specific responses to local needs. Centralisation is not only apparent in the bringing of the LAP under the Uganda Police, but also with the creation of central military units to address serious crime matters.[11] For instance, the response to armed robbery on an organised scale by Operation Wembley/Violent Crime Crack Unit (VCCU) under the Internal Security Organisation (ISO), which itself is part of the Chieftaincy of Military Intelligence (CMI). With its recruitment of informers, Operation Wembley was very successful in breaking up the crime groups or driving them away. Yet the cost was a loss of accountability and, perhaps inevitably, accusations that criminal elements had corrupted personnel. Further, the military style 'shoot to kill' policy against armed robbers and use of military courts to try suspects clearly weakens judicial procedures. Most people are indeed glad that organised crime has been driven from Kampala. One prosperous Asian businessman in Kampala claimed: 'Operation Wembley had a big impact; it was 100 per cent successful'. A rural Local Council [level] 3 chair said, 'they did a good job; they got seven armed robbers the police had failed to get; but their method was not good'. However, some traders criticise the VCCU for arrogance, seizing goods with no evidence and 'framing' people. There are also question marks over the increasing involvement of the VCCU and ISO

---

11. Museveni's first Minister of Internal Affairs claims that Museveni had such a low regard for the police that he wanted to replace them with military police when he took power in 1986. *The Monitor*, 5 April, 2004.

in investigating what might be termed 'ordinary' crime. Although there is a police CID, criminal investigation at the sub-county level is increasingly being undertaken by ISO operatives.[12] ISO has exposed 'ghost' payments by the Ministry of Finance for procurements and 'ghost' schools that were taking government money. Said ISO Director-General, Col. Elly Kayanja, upon unearthing 20 'ghost schools': 'anyone who subverts or aids and abets subversion of delivery of quality education to our people is a legitimate security target and we shall move on them with the vigour we moved with on the thugs'.[13] In other words, ISO has developed an investigative capability against serious crimes and fraud that in a civilian government is normally a role for police CID.

Anti-rustling units

In Karamoja in the northeast, serious and violent stock theft (often cross border) is rampant (Knighton, 2003; Mirzeler and Young, 2000; Hendrickson et al., 1996). The task of policing this activity is primarily left to a special unit under the army known as the Anti-Stock Theft Unit. Until 2004 it worked alongside local groups ('vigilantes'), who had been armed by the Ugandan government to enable the population to defend itself against the raids. The Anti-Stock Theft Unit's abuses, however, led Museveni to direct Ugandan Peoples Defence Force (UPDF) commanders to take charge of them: 'The vigilantes in Karamoja are misbehaving because they are not being controlled'.[14] In February 2004 it was announced that a 300 man strong local defence unit force would be trained to fight rustling by the UPDF third division.[15]

Anti-rebel units

In areas of rebel conflict with the Lord's Resistance Army (LRA), former Local Defence Units (LDUs) and new recruits have been assembled by the UPDF as militias, such as the Frontier Guards in Kitgum, the Elephant Brigade in Gulu, the Amuka in Lango and the Arrow Group in Teso. The intention is that they be the 'eyes and ears of the people' on local security

---

12. Interview, ISO operative, 16 March, 2004.

13. *The Monitor*, 3 March, 2004.

14. IRIN, 24 September, 2001.v

15. *The Monitor*, 20 February, 2004.

issues. However they have not always been up to the task of defending the IDP camps, hence their failure to withstand the LRA in the massacre of 200 in Barlonyo IDP camp in February 2004. Further, they have even been implicated in armed robberies (e.g. Arrows in Kumi district).[16] Museveni's approach to internal rebels has been to use militias alongside the army:

> When there are no security threats, we only maintain the small standing army, Police and intelligence services. When there are security threats, then, we call up a militia force to expand the capacity of the national defence ... In the last 17 years, we have trained two million fighters through mchakamchaka [political education and military science courses]. Therefore, the Arrow groups, the Anti-Stock Theft Unit of Karamoja, the LDUs in all parts of the country, are all part of the vast national defence capacity ... Mobilising the reserve militias is, partly, addressing the question of mobilisation. ... The solution of [LRA] "massacres" is for the National Defence system to mobilise – call up more manpower and buy better equipment. ... However, massacres never happen where the people are empowered with the gun. It is only the innocent, unarmed that are massacred.[17]

Ill armed and ill trained militias, however, cannot (by themselves) provide quality security, whilst to arm civilian militias in a region with a high level of ethnic polarisation can cause the conflict to be ethnicised. Once rebel or criminal activity is perceived in terms of ethnic antagonism, it can lead to discrimination and violence against civilians for no other reason than their ethnic identity.

Local Defence Units (LDU)

Local paramilitary units have been available to LCs since 1986. Some say that villagers were only too happy to send their 'problem kids' away to the LDU, resulting in their reputation for being 'trigger happy' and prone to human rights abuses. Elsewhere the problem was one of inactivity where they had ceased to function. Recently, the army has taken over some as militias and others have been put under police command as Special Constables (SPC). A few however remain as yet unplaced.

Despite the fact that LDUs are supposed now to be disarmed, there is clearly some confusion over their status, role and the legal framework guiding them. It appears that unplaced LDUs were involved in an incident in

---

16. *New Vision*, 17 March, 2004.

17. *The Monitor*, 8 September, 2003.

the western district of Kasese in January, 2004. LDUs shot dead a man and a child on suspicion the man was carrying a stolen goat. Residents, however, said he had bought the goat from thieves. They said stray bullets hit the child. The police had to be deployed to stop residents from lynching the LDU members involved.[18]

Militarisation

Military policing has proliferated under Museveni, reflecting the insecurity of the regime in the face of rebels, terrorists, organised crime and regional states with intent to destabilise Uganda. Co-ordinating the operations against 'terrorist organisations' (such as the ADF; Alliance of Democratic Forces) is the Joint Anti-Terrorism Task Force (JAFT). There is also the Chieftaincy of Military Intelligence (CMI), of which the ISO is part and doing similar work. Finally there is the 10,000 strong Presidential Protection Unit. This not only offers Museveni personal security, but acts as an elite unit for armed conflict. At election times it has engaged in intimidation of opposition candidates through searching homes without warrants, denial of permission to hold public rallies, forcibly dispersing 'unauthorised' rallies and detaining and beating officials of opposition parties and supporters. An unpublished Parliamentary Report on election violence in 2001 said that the small number of police officers and their lack of training in controlling demonstrations was used as an excuse for bringing into the elections the UPDF, Internal Security Organisation, Local Defence Units, District Internal Security Organisation, Gombola Internal Security Organisation, Kalangala Action Party, the Presidential Guards and the Chieftaincy of Military Intelligence. The report claimed that it was these paramilitary forces that were behind the violence, which 'led to violations of human rights, rigging, violence and loss of lives as soldiers and state security became agents of particular interests'.[19]

This pattern of centralisation and militarisation of policing in new democracies in the face of rising crime has been noted before: 'The growth of crime itself in transitional societies has in many cases undercut the growth of local forms of policing by ensuring more centralised and militarised responses to disorder' (Shaw, 2000:11). Unfortunately it works against the very legitimacy that states are trying to create for their forces after years of abuse under authoritarian regimes. This requires effective forms of local

---

18. *New Vision*, 13 January, 2004.

19. *The East African* (Kenya), 24 November, 2005.

control and accountability. On the other hand, transitional societies favour managing change from the centre to ensure both uniformity of provision and the denial of space to local groups to gain control of forces of coercion (Shaw, 2000:11).[20]

Municipal Law Enforcers

Not all the other state policing agents are paramilitary, however. The municipal law enforcers of the sub-counties supervise bye laws on public health of food outlets, building standards, street parking, vendors, markets, children attending school, licences, hawking on behalf of the municipalities (LC3). They are best, however, with problems of authority, mobility and finance. In Fort Portal they had 14 staff and one vehicle covering the town of 45,000 and the Town Clerk reported a high level of non-compliance with the payment of fines, market ducs, taxes and directives.[21] In Mbale it was reported that the municipal law enforcement department had run out of cash in March 2004 and was said by the Chief Law Enforcement Officer to be 'depending on good will from other security organs'.[21]

Policing at the local level: the local council security structures

The process by which the Uganda state has configured itself, following the National Resistance Movement's (NRM) assumption of power in 1986,

---

20. Gunmen who attempted to enter the High Court chambers in November 2005 to arrest opposition leaders were members of a previously unknown military group, apparently related to the Presidential Guard. 'The appearance last week of the "Black Mamba", an Urban Hit Squad, has raised concern in Uganda about the increasing militarisation of politics and the police force. The group besieged the High Court in Kampala and demanded to re-arrest 14 suspects who had been granted bail. The 14 were accused along with opposition leader Dr Kizza Besigye of treason. Sources say that since 2001, the army has infiltrated the police force, to the extent that professional police officers now have only minimal say in the affairs of the force. Conservative estimates put the number of UPDF men in the force between 1,000 and 1,200. One source said: "They are not appointed officers-in-charge or district police commanders because then they would have to sign documents and state their names and ranks." He added: "They don't sign arrest warrants. They are appointed as deputies. They stay in the background but they are the ones in charge" ... Opposition politicians believe the army is being sent to the police to help the regime rig the 2006 elections. But they say that the government is breaking the law in the creation of shadow forces' (*The East African*, 24 November, 2005).

21. Interview, Fort Portal town clerk, Mr Mugaraura, 1 April, 2004.

has been crucial in determining the nature of justice in the country and the relative absence of informal justice. Perhaps no single institution has been so influential on law and order as the Local Council (LC) structure at the lowest local government levels.

From the beginning, the lower local government levels of the tiered structure of LCs (originally known as RCs – Resistance Councils), that is the village (LC1), parish (LC2) and sub-county (LC3), were given responsibility amongst other things for law and order. Their progressive introduction into the liberated territory ensured that the sweeping away of the old order of appointed local chiefs left no vacuum. The effect of this speedy transition to local democracy makes an interesting qualification to what Schärf believes is the more standard pattern for democratising an initial power vacuum. He believes there is normally a time gap between the discrediting and dismantling of old forms of social control and policing, and the introduction of new substitutes (Schärf, 2003:14). It is precisely the absence of this law-enforcement vacuum that has ensured the failure, by and large, of non-state policing agencies to emerge in Uganda (as also Rwanda, Baker, 2007a). The LCs took hold at the local level even before the state had fully established itself.

LC duties include: the mobilisation of the local community in law and order matters; law enforcement through the LC funded Local Administrative Police (LAP); the gathering of criminal data; the service provision not only of courts but of psycho-social care of the victims of crime; the establishment of bye-laws that reflect local needs; and LC Courts.[22] It appears that most participants have treated membership of LCs seriously and have acted effectively. The LC Courts are popular since they offer accessible justice when there are issues that cannot be resolved by the family or clan:

> Most of the cases that come to the LC courts are those that forums like the family, the clan, or friends have failed to resolve. In Gulu for instance, it was stated that where the dispute involves members of one clan, the clan is the first forum to be approached for settlement. In case more than one clan is involved, then elders from these clans are invited to settle the dispute under the chairmanship of "Rwot Moo". There is also the "Rwot Kweri" (Head of Agriculture) who settles issues related to agriculture. It was agreed by all, that people always approached these other institutions before going to LC courts (DANIDA, 1998).

---

22. *The Monitor*, 4 March, 2004.

LCs have had a remarkable ordering effect on social life and have acted as the first line of protection against serious disorder and crime and the first point of call when it does occur. Commonly people say that they turn first to the LC1 for protection from disorder and crime (often in terms of night patrols, although these are sometimes only activated during periods of insecurity and some question their effectiveness). When surveyed as to where people go to solve a problem, 85 per cent said the LC alone or first and when asked 'how has the LC made life better' 35 per cent mentioned 'peace and security' and 22 per cent 'problem solving (Wunsch and Otte-moeller, 2004:188). Likewise they turn first to the LC1 in cases of breaches of law and order.

It is justice in their own language, from a body that respects local traditions and is in turn respected, since leaders have been chosen that are known, experienced and stand for the new values of the NRM popular revolution (Barya and Oloka-Onyango, 1994). In addition, the LC1 patrols or LC3 home guards, plus the LC courts, offer a framework of justice that is not financially burdensome on the state.

This is not to say that there are not problems. Justice Professor Kanyeihamba admits that 'records show that the exercise of judicial powers by some of the local councils and councillors and officials has been inadequate, illegal and in some instances, corrupt' (Kanyeihamba, 2002:262). There are the problems, too, of widespread popular ignorance of the law (e.g. understanding that 'marriage' to and sex with an under 18 is 'defilement'; or that begging can be classified as the offence of 'idleness'), and of LC courts exceeding their authority by hearing criminal cases (DANIDA, 1998). Anecdotal evidence suggests that the LC courts are at times sources of injustice, due to bribery and male dominance. They are also thought to hand out sentences that are beyond their powers, such as corporal punishment and banishment from the village (DANIDA, 1998). One police inspector commented, perhaps with a certain amount of understandable exaggeration and frustration, that LC Courts 'don't know anything' as regards the law and that they 'lack training'. There are also complaints from the LCs that local revenues and LC5 district assistance are insufficient to run the service adequately.[23] Yet the main point is that the difficulties experienced are primarily ones of implementation, training and resources that can be remedied. The fundamentals of a local law and order system are in place. Uganda is not faced, as are many African countries, with a local sys-

---

23. Interview, General Secretary, Uganda Local Authorities Association, 26 February, 2004.

tem of customary courts functioning outside of the state and with different values and procedures that awaits incorporation into the state system.

To examine the detailed effect of the LC1s on law and order in rural and urban areas four examples are examined.

LC1 provision in rural villages

The fishing village of Busaabala beside Lake Victoria has a diverse ethnic mix. Given that the nearest police post is 8 km away, the LC1 naturally see themselves as the principal law enforcers in the village. They operate a night patrol, charging all households Sh500 per month (about 30 US cents). The LC1 court is ready to meet immediately for vital cases or on a regular weekly basis for less urgent matters, though often there are not enough cases to warrant a meeting for a month. Typical cases handled include fighting and stealing. More than 40 villagers have been trained by the local Crime Prevention Panel as 'crime preventers' (see more below). This has raised awareness of what the law requires and given the 'crime preventers' confidence to contact the police for help.[24]

The fact that none of the men could remember a case of mob justice in recent years proved, in their eyes, the success of the LC1 leadership in preserving law and order in the village. For women, who defined law and order more in terms of responsible behaviour, especially by men and youths, there was less certainty. One of their greatest concerns was husbands who spent their income from fishing on alcohol. It meant that, instead of the men spending time with their families in the day or their money on their families, they were inclined to disregard their duties. It led, in the women's view, to 'immoral tendencies' and 'made it a difficult place to raise children'. Women also had concerns with the LC1. Some believed it was 'not functional'. In their eyes those born in the village dominated the later migrants and got their way more with the LC1; access was difficult because they feared the men might not listen to them and would give more weight to those with money; and the village council (of all villagers) met only if there was a serious mater, but did not keep to regular set dates.[25]

Mugusu is a market village of 640 persons, 9 km south of Fort Portal, in the west. Since the rebel ADF crisis 1998–2002, the area is described as 'safe, with only minor problems'; 'we are really sleeping'. No one could

---

24. Interviews with LC1 Chairmen.v

25. Focus group with LC1 executive members and other village leaders, 10 March, 2004.

remember a case of mob justice in the last four years. The LC1 do not run a patrol (the LC3 run a voluntary 20-strong home guard) and see little of the police, except for the police mobile patrol on the main road going through the village. For the LC1 the overall prevalence of law and order was due to their close knowledge of one another. Others, however, reported fairly regular occurrences of petty theft, drunken fights, rape/defilement and domestic violence. Perhaps the fact that many of these were not reported or were related to the weekly market's visitors explains the fact that the LC1 court had few problems to attend to. For those market traders that were caught stealing, there was a prohibition from returning. The overall success in preserving law and order in the village was qualified, however, by older persons, who defined law and order to include morality, particularly sexual morality. They expressed serious concern about young people from their village and those who were attracted to the market and the disco that followed it. They spoke of unemployed school drop outs drinking too much, being promiscuous, taking drugs and resorting to theft and therefore saw them as a negative and destabilising factor in the village and surrounding sub-counties.[26]

LC1 provision in urban zones

Two LC1s were examined in the high density areas of Kampala. The first was Luziga Zone. This is home for people from a wide variety of ethnic groups from Uganda and from Rwanda and Congo. Despite the heterogeneity and short-term residence, inhabitants report that it is '98 per cent safe' and has grown much safer over the last few years as 'pickpocketting' by street children has been largely eradicated. The improvement is largely attributed to the work of the LC1, which itself is multi-racial. To tackle crime the LC1 instigated a patrol (charging 'every door' Sh500 per month) that arrested pickpockets and others, and took them to the LC1 Court or police. The LC1 Court meets twice a week, but sometimes they can go 'three weeks without a case'. They deal with domestic violence, fighting and illegal buildings and claim a decrease in their occurrence. And given that four of the ten LC1 executive are women, it is said women are freer to bring issues forward. The LC1 also encourages others to report matters that individual women might be afraid to report themselves. Their success has meant that there have been no incidents of mob justice 'in the last few years'. Though problems with law and order are first taken to the LC1 by

---

26. Focus group with 20 women, 15 March, 2004.

the community, there is said now to be a good relationship with the police. They go to them regularly (their police post is only 500m away) and find them co-operative and respectful.[27]

Mbiro Zone adjoins Luziga Zone and is similarly diverse ethnically, having many Congolese. Residents report that law and order has changed dramatically since 1986. Then there was a high crime rate, including murder, kidnapping of children, rape, defilement and the illegal possession of weapons. Since then crime has been greatly reduced and this is attributed to the work of the LC1, though they do not operate a night patrol. 'We have power' said the councillors, 'As people together we fight the crime'. None could remember when the last incident of mob justice occurred, although it had been common in the 1980s. As with Luziga, the LC1 Court doesn't always have a case to try for months on end. Typical cases include domestic violence, theft, simple assaults, land issues and disputes between landlords and tenants. They readily admit that in the beginning the court was not fully aware of which cases came within their remit and which were the duty of the police. But following police training they now feel confident about what their legal powers are. In fact, they sometimes rebuke the police who come to deal with a case that it is too petty for them and should be left to the LC1. Like the other LC1s, they also report a marked improvement in their relationship with the police.[28] Though it might have been expected that the rural system of collective communal control would break down when it came to transient, mixed ethnic and unfamiliar populations, the supervisory and ordering functions of the LCs persists.

The LC structure at the local government level, both rural and urban, is largely successful in providing law and order in the community (a male-defined order, that is). It not only provides law and order itself, but significantly supports other policing structures, such as the Uganda Police, Interior Security Organisation (ISO) and, as will be shown below, Crime Prevention Panels. However, it should not be assumed that there are no matters for concern. Beyond the issues raised above, there is always a danger of declining enthusiasm and commitment when a system relies heavily on volunteers. The longer that system continues, the more pressing the question of sustainability without state resources becomes. Put differently, once revolutionary fervour has waned and volunteerism subsides,

27. LC1 Chairman, Mugusu, Sarapio Gafabusa, 1 April, 2004; LC3 Mugusu sub-county, Vice Chair, Mrs Mbabazi Margaret, 2 April, 2004; LC3 Karambi sub-county, Chair, Mr Mwiraumubi Eli, 2 April, 2004.

28. Interview, Secretary, LC1, Luziga, 12 March, 2004.

how much will it cost to set up and sustain local participation in the justice system? (Schärf, 2003; Baker, 2007a). There was evidence that already full LC1 Meetings are only being attended by activists or those with a pressing crisis, and that the meetings themselves are often not held unless there is an emergency. Likewise there was evidence of a disinclination by youth to work within its structures. With reported crimes still rising according to police statistics (even if this is a measure of greater willingness to come forward), there is no place for complacency that the local provision of law and order through LCs will always be adequate. Some inhabitants, even in poorer areas, have already decided that LC night patrols are not effective and have secured the services of commercial guards.

State approved self-policing initiated by the police

Given the limitations of state police forces across Africa, it is inevitable that citizens will mobilise to play a role in keeping law and order and in implementing anti-crime strategies. Of course this strategy will always produce the emergence of undesirable elements. Nevertheless, there is considerable potential in governments mobilising communal self-interest to join in the effort in an acceptable manner. Two types of citizen self-policing have emerged in Uganda; one initiated by the police themselves and one originating from commercial interests.

The Uganda Police introduced community policing in 1989. For many African countries this has meant little more than enhancing intelligence gathering for the police. In Uganda however, they have a more developed system. The main emphasis has been on education in the law and on crime prevention, using the media, schools work and local forums. Community Liaison Officers (CLOs) located at every police station have been instrumental in initiating police Dialogues with the community over security issues, Neighbourhood Watch schemes and Crime Prevention Panels.[29] The latter are planned for every sub-county or district, though currently they are only successfully operating in a few districts. They consist of local residents that are trained in crime prevention with a view, not only to empowering people about crime prevention and the requirements of the law, but also that citizens and communities will accept responsibility themselves for law and order in their locality. Two models of Crime Prevention Panels are

---

29. Focus group with 5 members of the LC executive committee, 12 March, 2004.
   Focus group with 5 members of the LC executive committee, 12 March, 2004.

emerging: one based on the community at large and one based on employ-ment groups. Their difference of emphasis can be appreciated by examining two successful Panels.

Community based crime prevention panels

Prior to Katwe Crime Prevention Panel, Kampala, being formed in 1993, the prevailing attitude was that the police only existed 'to arrest and to torture; they can never be friendly' and few criminals were handed over to them. Reinforcing the gulf was 'an initial resistance from the local police' to the community policing programme, for fear of empowering the people in the field of their own expertise and of exposing police corruption.[30] Since the Panel's formation a remarkable 30,000 have been trained as 'crime pre-venters'. Given that the Katwe Police Division only has 400 officers and a few LAPs (Local Administrative Police) scattered between four police sta-tions and 20 police posts, this is a considerable crime prevention resource. During the course of 30 two-hour evening sessions, these local volunteers are given training by the Panel and the police. Topics covered are: the na-ture of community policing and crime prevention; the differences between criminal and civil cases; the importance of preserving the evidence at the scene of the crime; the institution of criminal proceedings; the LC judicial structure and the cases that they should and should not handle; summons and warrants; road safety; community service; bomb threats; sexual of-fences; human rights; constitutional rights; domestic violence; laws as they relate to children; marriage and divorce; and mob justice. As each group passes the training, it forms a local team or sub-panel. To maintain their motivation, functions and competitions are held each year to see who is the best team. Though these 'crime preventers' are separate from the LC struc-ture, they are to a considerable extent under-girded by it, since the elected Crime Prevention Panel executive includes local LC1 and LC2 chairmen and others with experience of civic responsibility. The success of the scheme lies largely in the way people have been mobilised, so that the Crime Pre-vention Panel is now largely self-sufficient. As far as the Katwe police are concerned it has improved the public's perception of the police and is linked by them to the absence of mob justice in the last three years.[31]

---

30. Interview, Simeo Nsubuga, Crime Prevention Officer, Police Headquarters, 25 February, 2004.

31. Interviews with Katwe District Police Commander, Mugisha Bazil; Inspector Ali Amote, Police Liaison Officer, Katwe Division; Corporal Kyagulanyr, trainer of

Employment based community crime prevention panels

The second model is based more on work associations than neighbourhood panels and in practice is more dependent on police input for sustainability. It has been used by the Crime Prevention Panel in the Kawempe Division of Kampala. Because many local leaders 'looked at everything politically' and saw the new scheme as a 'Movement' project, it proved impossible to secure their interest. The approach, therefore, was to go over their heads to gain a rapport with the people. Beginning in 2000, distinct employment groups were singled out and given a sense of identity through bringing them together in associations. There then began the work of sensitising them regarding crime matters that affected their own interests. Only after that was complete was the offer made of training in crime prevention. Employment groups that were brought together in associations included milk sellers, timber merchants, boda bodas (motor cycle taxis), disco and video halls, teachers, probation officers, special hire companies, bars and lodges, and religious leaders. In the process of meeting with these groups, patterns of crime that particularly affected each one were identified and complaints by the public about any member's activities were directed to these associations. In time, as they began to see their role in policing their own members and community, association members volunteered to attend the crime preventers course. Upon completing the course they were given direct line phone numbers to the District Police Commissioner (DPC), CID, Human Rights Desk and others to assure accessibility. Being empowered in terms of knowing what the law required, the local panels of trained crime preventers or the work associations began reporting cases of unlawful activity (including police demanding bribes) and making recommendations for curbing crime. Between 2000 and February 2004, 860 completed the course with a further 500 expected to complete it in 2004. As in Katwe, groups of trained crime preventers form local panels with an elected leadership.[32]

'crime preventers', Katwe Division; Jamil Sebalu, Crime Prevention Panel Chair for Katwe; Hassan Muwamugzi, Crime Prevention Panel Secretary for Katwe, 5 March, 2004.

32. Interview with Inspector Ngako Abbey Moiti, Community Liaison Officer, Kawempe Division, 11 March, 2004.

Rural crime prevention panels

Crime Prevention Panels are far less common in rural districts, but Matugga Crime Prevention Panel is one such example, lying some 20 km north of Kampala. Its origins go back to 1994 when problems arose in the LC2 as regards police conduct. Accusations were made to the LC2 chairman of police beatings following arrest. At an ensuing public meeting, the DPC offered a training course for local people on crime prevention and legal rights. The Crime Prevention Panel has 300 members and operates throughout the sub-county, where there is just one police post with up to 12 personnel, three SPCs and five LAPs. Its male members gave as their reasons for joining: 'to help the police to help us and to eliminate crime'; 'in the [civil] war up to 1986 there were many violations of people's rights and this was an opportunity to protect people's rights. It was also an opportunity to learn about the law, of gaining legal advice and of avoiding costs'. Its female members added: 'before there was fighting; now the people are restrained because they know preventers are around; it reduces crime'; 'in the past there were lots of crimes like rape which especially affects us as young people'. Publicity is done through the LC (some 50 per cent of Panel executive members are LC members), posters, churches and through mention by the community police on the radio. They see their primary function as assisting the police and the LCs in crime prevention. However, they are not afraid, if they feel either organisation is ineffective, 'to report to other organs such as Kawempe police station, police HQ or non-police organs'. Each year they hold a 'Get Together', where sport, dance, music and drama take place along with a guest speaker (in 2003 it was the Inspector General of Police). Though the Panel and LC members attributed much of the order to their own committed work, there were others that placed the success elsewhere. Some shopkeepers attributed improvements to the dismantling of the LDUs, who had been 'bad people', they 'had guns' and 'co-operated with thieves'. Their dismissal and replacement by SPCs was seen as a turning point. Another point of view came from a member of the ISO. He thought that the police were 'hopeless' and 'corrupt' and that the crime preventers contributed little other than improving people's knowledge of the law. The real work of addressing serious issues of crime such as cattle thieves and marijuana growers was attributed to his own work. Perhaps the truth lies somewhere between the two. Everyday law and order is maintained by the police and Crime Preventers working with the LC, whereas more serious threats are tackled by the ISO on the basis of information from LCs and others.[33]

Why have these particular Panels been successful, whereas across the Kawempe District, Panels have only 'taken root' in four of the 16 sub-counties. The success is due to both structural and contingent factors. Structurally, as already noted, the support of the LC system through its executive personnel sitting on the Panel executive has been invaluable. But beyond that, some places have enjoyed high levels of commitment and enthusiasm by volunteers and individual CLOs. With that there is often a 'snowballing', as success breeds success.

State approved self-policing initiated by work-based associations

The Community Policing Programme with its Crime Prevention Panels represents one type of citizen self-policing – that initiated by the police themselves. The other originates from private and commercial interests. These are less common but still important among traders and services. Two examples can be given, one urban one rural; one large scale, one small. The Uganda Taxi Operators and Drivers Association (UTODA) was begun in 1986 as a forum for taxi (minibus) drivers and owners to express their views and grievances. The taxi drivers consist of about 60,000 members (30,000 in Kampala) with 10,000 taxis. The drivers themselves elect their management committee. Initially relations with the police were strained, as there had been a history of taxi drivers facing police roadblocks and demands for money. Over time, however, dialogue has produced a good working relationship with the police and a definition of respective roles. Given that taxis are the principal means of public transport, they have considerable leverage on local politics. They have used this to establish themselves as a managing and policing authority of taxis nationwide. They operate a contract with the Kampala City Council to run the taxi parks. Their traffic warden department is 100 strong and, working with the police, has responsibility for enforcing traffic regulations by taxi drivers and in directing traffic in rush-hour congestion. The department also provides help for children's crossings. A Law Enforcement Department, trained by the police and LC, arrests thieves and other criminals operating in the taxi park.[34] For

---

33. Focus group of seven Panel executive and members, 11 March, 2004.

34. Interview, Rev Atwiinine, Executive Secretary of UTODA, 27 February, 2004.

the state, allowing this self-policing clearly offers the benefits of increased resources and local knowledge. However, the disadvantage is that it loses some control. There is a political trade off, therefore, between loss of control and yet enhanced provision of policing to the benefit not just of customers, but of voters.

Market organisations also commonly organise their own security. A small rural example is Matugga town market. This busy market on the edge of the town is where stall-holders sell produce from local farmers to traders from Kampala. About 120 have stalls, 80 of them women. They have organised themselves into a traders association which has an elected committee of four women and five men. This committee is the policing agency of the market. It acts as arbitrator when there is conflict between stall-holders (perhaps over theft of produce) or between stall-holders and farmers (perhaps over non-payment). Their sanctions include a fine or exclusion from the market for two days. More serious problems are taken to the LC and the police. They also employ a local man to guard the stalls and produce at night. He is 'not trained, but he is trustworthy'. Through self-organisation, therefore, they have been able to enjoy security levels they call 'fine'. No one knew of any mob justice locally since 2002.[35]

Though this citizen self-policing by taxi drivers and market vendors was initiated by their own commercial considerations, its autonomy is not total. In that respect it does not fully represent that form of diversification that creates policing 'away from' and 'beyond' the state. Like a planet, it is still under the gravitational pull of the centre.

Commercial security groups

There are about 87 commercial security companies in Uganda, though perhaps half are 'shelf' companies. Their rapid growth since 1992 has been associated not just with rising crime, but with the strategic withdrawal of the police from guarding. Though concentrated in the towns, they are also found in rural areas guarding quarries and plantations. They are licensed and supervised by the police under the statutory instrument: The Control of Private Security Organisations Regulations, 1997. Operating licences have to be renewed each year and are subject to satisfactory inspection by the police of the company, including the armoury and the suitability of the guards. Though the regulations do require criminal vetting, and training

---

35. Focus groups of 35 men and women, Matugga market, 19 March, 2004.

and controls on the use of firearms, they are broad enough to allow wide discretion. For example, only 'appropriate' insurance cover of employees is required; personnel are simply to have 'proper and regular training'; and organisations may be deregistered if companies are 'below the acceptable standard'. Nevertheless, some firms have had their operational licences withdrawn.[36] More serious than organisational problems are accusations made by some that security guards aid criminal activity.[37]

There are two ends of the market. First, there are those larger (often foreign-owned) companies that offer a range of security services such as guarding, VIP protection, risk assessment and corporate protection to companies, banks and embassies. The largest two employ some 2,000 guards between them and operate fairly thorough training in social skills, guarding skills, weapon handling, public relations and personal hygiene and the like. Joint operations with the police have been undertaken (e.g. following a tip-off of armed robbery being imminent) and exchange of information occurs. Weapons are rented from the police.[38] Interestingly one of the companies gave applicants a polygraph test to determine their 'honesty' and 'integrity' and used the polygraph test to investigate crimes within companies.

At the other end of the market are smaller local companies that focus on providing guards for individual properties and businesses. They guard both public (e.g. hospitals, government ministries) and private property and offer cash escort. Training varies from non-existent through basic to thorough, but the most striking difference is recruitment policy. Some took recruits only from the army, police and prison service (it meant training was not necessary); others preferred to recruit from inexperienced candidates ('since the police are corrupt'). There was also considerable variation on how companies perceived their relationship with the police. Some companies (particularly one that also undertook private investigation) regretted that there was no co-operation from the police since they were seen as rivals; another said they offered information to the police, but information from the police only came on request; another said that there was an exchange of information both ways. One even that as a public service it worked with the police at public events.[39]

36. *The Monitor*, 19 February, 2004.

37. *New Vision*, 2 March, 2004.

38. Interviews, General Managers, *ArmorGroup Uganda* and *Securicor*, 25 February and 3 March, 2004.

39. Interviews with company managers of, *Home Guard Services, Ultimate Security, Alert Guards and Security Systems,* and *Elite Security*, 26 February, 18 March and 22

For those who used guards, such as traders to protect their stalls at night and shopkeepers in the day and/or at night, most of the comments from interviews were favourable: 'They do a good job at night', 'they show respect', 'they do good'. It was a matter of commercial reality that they did the job they were paid to do and treated clients well and that companies took complaints seriously.

Besides formal commercial security groups, there is also some evidence of informal commercial security groups. In the mid-1990s police CLOs conducted training in crime prevention and detection for the public in central Kampala. Many of those trained were taxi drivers. Though the intention was to educate the public and for information to be disseminated, these 'crime preventers' took on a life of their own. They assumed an authority in and sometimes outside of their neighbourhoods and began to exploit their knowledge for personal gain. As a result the police have been trying to 'discourage' their activities, though they admit they have 'failed'.[40]

Militias: party organisations

Few speak of it, but most are aware of the Kalangala Action Plan, which has acted as an armed political mobilisation organ for Museveni's Movement system (now a political party known as the NRM, National Resistance Movement). During the 2000 presidential election it attacked anti-Movement supporters and rallies. Its leader, Major Mutale has claimed that the original aim of its formation was to foil a coup attempt:

> I received information as early as 1993 that Besigye and Kategaya [two opposition figures; the former a presidential candidate in 2000] were planning to overthrow Museveni by using LC leaders and other people who supported the NRA bush war and were not thanked or rewarded by Museveni. So what I did was to collect thousands of them, took them to Kalangala and then I called the President to address them and promise to reward them, which he did very fast because I told him that his old supporters were not happy with him.[41]

Its current activities, beyond being an economic branch designed to help Movement supporters, remain obscure.

March, 2004.

40. Interview, John Kamya, Acting Assistant Commissioner of Police, Community Affairs, 25 February, 2004; see also Davis et al., 2003.

41. *New Vision*, 10 February, 2004.

Informal security: mob justice

The UN's Human Rights Committee asserts that the history of vigilant-ism in Uganda goes back to the 1970s when Amin enacted a policy to have all robbers shot on sight. 'This policy set the tone for public perceptions of criminal punishment to be not only harsh and quick, but meted out by members of the public as well' (Human Rights Committee, 2001:78). In addition it is often motivated by widespread distrust or misunderstanding of the justice system (especially police bail) and with dissatisfaction with state policing. Mob justice against alleged criminals is still present, if in-frequent, in Uganda. They engage in stonings, beatings, machete attacks and burning alive or stripping suspects of their clothes and parading them through the streets. In April 2001 the Inspector General of Police, Major General Wamala, estimated that more than 1,000 persons had been killed by mob violence since 1991 and called for an end to the practice. Likewise the National Political Commissar, Dr. Kiyonga, called mob justice, 'anoth-er type of insecurity'. Admitting that it was rampant in many parts of the country, he called for the use of dialogue through elders to resolve conflicts. Where that was beyond their powers, he called for issues to be forwarded to the courts.[42] Despite such appeals, the practice continues across all parts of the country and in both rural and town environments. For example, the press alone reported 11 incidents from January 2003 to March 2004 from every region of the country and many more went unreported. There were 'lynchings' (i.e. mob murders) for suspected murder, theft, personal injury, defilement and witchcraft. It is usually viewed as spontaneous and therefore not strictly policing, but in fact it is often led and organised by an aggrieved person. The BBC's Andrew Harding, caught up in a 'lynch mob' in Lira seeking revenge against Acholis for an LRA massacre, noted that there was a clear ringleader, a woman:

> I watched an elegant lady in a beautiful green and yellow dress go to hut after hut, directing the violence. 'Smash this bicycle' she ordered a group of teen-aged boys. 'Here, let's throw all this inside that hut. Now stand back – I'm going to set fire to it. OK. Let's go this way'.[43]

One particular concern is that the Uganda Police do not always act to stop mob justice. The Human Rights Committee accuses: 'the state response to mob justice has mainly been a policy of denial. Most cases of popular jus-

42. *New Vision*, 24 December, 2002.

43. BBC, broadcast, 28 February, 2004.

tice go unreported, however those that are reported usually go unchecked' (Human Rights Committee, 2001:79). For instance the police did nothing to stop the lynching of an Acholi in an anti-LRA rally in Lira in March 2004, arguing that to intervene in such an angered crowd would only have made matters worse.[44]

However the consistent testimony of LCs, the Uganda Police and the public during the course of the research was that mob justice was on the decrease, sometimes quite dramatically. One senior police officer said that when he took up his post in 2003 'mob justice was an almost daily occurrence'. When interviewed in 2004 he believed it had been reduced 'by 70 per cent'. He attributed the drop to active pursuit of the culprits and sensitisation of the public in the places where it had occurred.[45]

Conclusion

The limitations of the Uganda Police have meant that they have not been able to provide crime protection and crime investigation for all citizens. As a result, other policing agencies have been appointed by the state or have arisen from communities to fill those gaps. A situation exists in Uganda today, therefore, of diverse provision or what I have termed multi-choice policing. Ugandans are confronted with different policing agencies offering different or alternative services. The extended family may protect the home, but it is the LC1 that sorts out the minor disturbance at the village bar, the vendors' committee that mediates a settlement over theft in the market from a fellow trader, the illegal vigilante group or legal militia that pursues the cattle rustlers from a rival tribe in Karamoja, the UTODA marshal that handles the bus station pickpocket, the commercial security guard that secures the entrance to the city shop, the Uganda Police that are called if someone is shot at the bank, and the ISO or VCCU that tackles the sub-county gang that are stealing vanilla seedlings.

Yet though increasing diversification is the reality on the ground, for historical reasons it is not a clear-cut diversification away from the state. The new agencies are not predominantly non-state formal and informal agencies. Instead much of the diversification taking place is still within the boundaries of state initiation or at least state influence and approval (as is true in Rwanda, see Baker, 2007a). The legacy of the NRM revolution

---

44. *Economist*, 25 February, 2004.

45. Interview, OC, Mityana, Uganda Police, 31 March, 2004.

included a deeply rooted local democracy and a fear of national insecurity recurring. The democratic instinct meant that the LC system established to provide local law and order by the NRA during the course of the war has persisted. The fear of a return to war has led to a predilection for military solutions to insecurity or the militarisation of policing units. The extent of the provision of law and order by the LC system and the militarised units ensure the state has maintained a strong influence over most of the diversification of policing.

Because the LC structure has always had a law and order function, it has choked the space available for informal organisations to emerge. If organising law and order structures without its support is difficult, those that have its blessing, whether state initiated (such as Crime Prevention Panels) or commercially initiated (such as market policing), can expect to succeed. Even military style national security bodies such as ISO and VCCU are dependent to a degree on LC supply of intelligence. Likewise, because Museveni has always been doubtful of the loyalty and discipline of the police he has kept them constrained and allowed an array of military-style organisations more directly under his control to flourish at the national level.

— CHAPTER 7 —

Who Is Policing Sierra Leone?

*The establishment of public order and the rule of law is the missing
priority in establishing post-conflict security and initiating reconstruction.*
(Woodrow Wilson School of Public and International Affairs, 2003)

The violence and insecurity of civil war attacks the structures of law and
order, both state and non-state. Customary chiefs and their court and policing systems are driven out or flee; state police are targeted as defenders
of the regime under attack; the social control of family, neighbours and
clan dissolves in the anarchy of displacement and bereavement. Wars not
only disturb the old order, but bring in a new order and a new way of regulating that order. They cause change directly by decimating state police
forces, scattering customary police, destroying state police infrastructure
and burning customary courthouses. In addition, if they destroy autocratic
governments, they often destroy their regime policing and in the new democratic order allow in new doctrines of civilian policing and community
involvement. They also may open the way to economic liberalisation and
with it the growth of commercial security. Finally, post-war donor reconstruction may bring a policing agenda that includes new styles of policing,
new skills in management, new institutions to crackdown on the endemic
corruption and new capital resources.

Yet the history of policing in Sierra Leone is not identical to that of
Uganda. The two countries have responded quite differently to their post-
conflict circumstances. Part of the difference is related to the passage of
time. Uganda's civil war finished in 1986, whereas Sierra Leone did not
find peace until late 2001. Another striking difference is that, in the case
of Uganda, the new regime is that of the victorious rebels, whereas in the
case of Sierra Leone it is that of the victorious existing state. In other words
the ruling elite on the one hand has a military past, the other has a civilian
past. On account of these factors, and others beside, the following chapter
reveals a very different pattern of policing from that of Uganda.

Historical background to policing in Sierra Leone

Though the 'Province of Freedom' was established for freed slaves in 1787 on the Freetown Peninsula, it was not until 1808 that the Sierra Leone Frontier Police was founded. Its chief role was to protect the borders against hostile neighbours. Nearly a century passed before the British declared a Protectorate over the hinterland in 1895 and with it a court messenger force. But the security challenges were more concerned with keeping order than combating crime as rivalries arose between the Krio descendants of freed slaves and the ethnic groups of the Protectorate. The colonial policy for controlling the ethnic and communal conflict was, as elsewhere, coercion and indirect rule through loyal chiefs. However, there were several unsuccessful revolts against British rule and Creole domination. Perhaps the most notable was the 'Hut Tax' rebellion of 1898 against the Court Messengers who were collecting taxes on behalf of the colonial authorities.

In the 1920s the Court Messenger Force merged with Frontier Force and was renamed the Sierra Leone Police Force. Whilst the Sierra Leone Police enforced British law, the chiefs administered customary law (and commercial policing secured the diamond mines from the mid-1930s).[1] But the police were never simply a crime prevention and crime fighting force. As the coercive arm of the colonial state they had a political role as well, as indicated by the following secret memo of the Governor to MI5 referring to a recent railway strike in the colony:

> Possibly you may be able to arrange that the London Post Office should examine any correspondence from Germany or Belgium or France addressed to any of the following [various names] … In any case you will no doubt be able to arrange that any letters from the Colony to the address of the League should be censored and I should be very glad to be acquainted with any results (PRO CO 323/971/7. 'League against Cruelties and Oppression in the Colonies'. R. Slater, Gov. of Sierra Leone, to Col. Sir Vernon Kell (of M.I.5), secret, 25 April 1927. Quoted in Killingray, 1997:187).

From independence in 1961 until 1991 the country only knew authoritarian rule. The civilian rule, interrupted by military coups in 1967, finally degenerated in 1978 into Siaka Stevens' long-running one-party government.

---

1. The first security company was the Diamond Protection Force, formed by Sierra Leone Selection Trust Ltd in 1935 (Killingray 1997: 189).

Under Stevens the Sierra Leone Police (SLP) were tribalised and became an instrument of state oppression. Meek goes so far as to say that the force's history has been 'a litany of oppressive policing, nepotism and corruption' (Meek, 2003:1). Nor was it just corruption. 'With corruption and the appointment of friends and colleagues came the decline of the service – skills were not sought after and officers were illiterate' (Biddle et al., 1999:1). The Truth and Reconciliation Commission describes the police before the war as 'incompetent', 'corrupt', 'a ready tool for the perpetuation of state terror against political opponents', and as engaged in 'extortion of money' and 'the violation of basic human rights … All these factors served to widen the gulf between the public and the police' (Sierra Leone Truth and Reconciliation Commission, 2004, Vol.3a:77). Fearing a military coup, Stevens established, in addition to the SLP, a parallel security force of presidential guards, officially known as the Special Security Division (SSD), though popularly called 'Siaka Stevens' Dogs' (Howe, 2000). They were used as the armed wing of the ruling party.

Stevens' All People's Congress (APC) party also used militias to maintain control. In 1983 the Ndogboyosoi (bush devil) war between the ruling APC and opposition Sierra Leone People's Party (SLPP) supporters racked Pujehun District in the south. The localised rebellion was linked to electoral manipulation and rivalries over control of cross-border smuggling into Liberia. APC government supporters fought against supporters of the SLPP candidate. The conflict ended when the people surrendered to the Sierra Leone army.

The ten-year civil war broke out under the rule of Stevens' successor, Major-General Joseph Momoh. It began in March 1991 with 300 rebel RUF troops penetrating the east from neighbouring Liberia. Despite the backing of 1,500 Nigerian and Guinean troops, government forces were unable to contain them, owing to lack of training, equipment and low morale. The following year front-line soldiers, disgruntled with the lack of pay, took their grievances to Freetown. Fearing a coup, Momoh fled and the young officers seized power. The National Provisional Ruling Council (NPRC), as they called themselves, decided in 1994 to go to the streets of Freetown to increase the strength of the army. Youths, some only twelve years old, were trained in a few weeks and assigned to units in the provinces. Though the army grew rapidly, the new recruits adopted the RUF tactics of living off the civilian population.

As the RUF changed to guerrilla tactics, it moved into the centre and north of the country. Faced with the new terror, some 40 per cent of new recruits to the army are said to have defected. Those who remained scarcely had a better reputation. They were accused of drug abuse; of human rights atrocities against opponents and civilians; of exploiting the war-economy for personal gain; and of collusion with the RUF. By 1995 the NPRC turned for help to mercenaries. Executive Outcomes, a South African private security company, was hired for cash and diamond concessions. They quickly cleared the RUF from the environs of Freetown and the Kono diamond fields.

In 1996 a palace coup led to presidential elections being called, which Ahmad Tejan Kabbah won. After a short-lived peace agreement, the war resumed and within twelve months junior military officers, calling themselves the Armed Forces Revolutionary Council (AFRC), staged a coup, overwhelmed the Nigerian ECOMOG troops (Economic Community of West African States Cease-Fire Monitoring Group), forced Kabbah to flee and invited the RUF into Freetown. They were, however, resisted by civil disobedience, the ECOMOG force and in the provinces by civil defence units (CDF). When the AFRC/RUF was driven out of Freetown in 1998, Kabbah was able to return. However the rebels infiltrated the capital in 1999 and intense street fighting took place. Neighbourhood 'vigilante' or militia groups sprang up with the support of ECOMOG. 'We encourage that, but there should be orderliness. They should be organised enough to help ECOMOG in countering the movement of suspicious characters or likely rebels in the society,' said the ECOMOG spokesman (The Agence France-Presse). In fact, they killed not only rebels, but those thought to be their supporters.

The peace negotiations that followed saw a power-sharing arrangement between the Kabbah government and the rebels, and agreement to deploy a UN contingent of peacekeepers and military observers alongside ECOMOG. Yet the disarmament and demobilisation deadlines were not met, and the RUF blocked or seized the peacekeepers. Moreover, The RUF leader, Sankoh, who though found guilty of treason, had been pardoned as one of the conditions for signing the peace agreement, had been made vice-president. It may have been deemed politically expedient, but the population of Freetown saw him as a criminal. In May 2000 he was chased from his Freetown residence by an angry crowd of over 200,000 demonstrators after a string of major breaches of the ceasefire and disarmament terms of the Peace Agreement (he was subsequently recaptured and died in custody).

The UN/ECOMOG troops were struggling to contain rebel activity but the intervention of the British troops and their elimination of a militia group known as the West Side Boys, demonstrated that the UK was determined to resist any rebel revival. By 2001 the UN peacekeeping mission, UNAMSIL, began deployment into RUF held territory and RUF and CDF fighters began disarmament. The civil war was formally declared over by President Kabbah on 18 January 2002.

The war seriously disrupted formal policing. The history of police abuse plus their loyalty to the elected Kabbah government resulted in their being targeted in the rebel attack on Freetown in 1999 when more than 300 police officers were killed. During the ten-year war approximately 900 SLP officers were killed, and a considerable number suffered amputation. As a result, the size of the SLP was reduced from 9,317 to 6,600 (Malan et al., 2002:65). In addition, the native authorities lost some of their authority where chiefs failed to provide protection through flight or death. Yet as state and customary policing failed, armed militias, vigilante groups and mob power emerged in their place.

It was clearly going to be a long struggle to rebuild the forces of law and order, state and customary. The police, for their part, were in a very weak state after the war. One UNAMSIL official observed that just about the only positive aspect of the post-war SLP was that at least it existed, even if in name only – so at least there was a base to build on (Meek, 2003:1). But it was evident that the SLP needed help, not only to maintain law and order and internal security, but also to restructure and rebuild. The initial need for security personnel was largely provided through the support of UNAMSIL. The training and restructuring of the SLP came from both the UK and the UN. Even before the conflict was finally over, the UK in 1999 seconded Keith Biddle, a retired senior police officer, to Sierra Leone to become the Acting Inspector General of Police. It also funded the Commonwealth Community Safety and Security Project (CCSSP) to provide training and management support to the SLP. Likewise UNAMSIL, through its civilian police, CivPol, provided training and support until the end of 2005.

So what has been achieved in the short time since the war ended? The account that follows of how people in Sierra Leone currently experience policing is based on field research undertaken in 2005. It records the various policing agencies available and how Sierra Leoneans evaluate them. A summary of the policing structures to be examined and their key features is given in Figure 1.

Figure 1. Policing Structures in Sierra Leone

POLICING BODY	AUTHORISER	POWERS	KEY FUNCTION	LINKS WITH OTHER POLICING BODIES	FUNDING
State structures					
Sierra Leone Police (SLP)	Central Government	Standard police powers	Serious crime	Work with Partnership Boards	State
Mine Monitors, Beach Police, Traffic Wardens	Ministry of Mines; Tourist Board; Traffic Authority	Reduced police powers	Supervision of mining, and Freetown beaches and traffic	Work with police	State
State approved					
Police Local Partnership Boards	Sierra Leone Police	Citizen	Provide intelligence to police	Work with police	Volunteers
Work-Based Associations	Elected leaders of association	Citizen	Security of work place	Minimal contact with police	Members' contributions
Customary Structures	Chiefdoms	Judicial powers in civil matters	Civil and customary arbitration	Minimal contact with police	Chiefdoms and State
Commercial Security	Private companies	Licensed by police	Guarding	Joint patrols with armed police in high-risk situations	Commercial
Peace Monitors	Community Groups	Citizen	Civil arbitration	Minimal contact with police	Volunteers
Unauthorised					
Youth Groups	Youth Groups	Citizen	Guarding and rapid response	Minimal contact with police	Volunteers
Mob justice			Assaults on alleged criminals	None	

Like in Uganda, it reveals a fragmented pattern of policing, but it is one far less influenced by state institutions. A much weaker state has done little more than concentrate its efforts on rebuilding its own state police. In the social spaces where the rebuilt force has not been able to penetrate, diversification has largely been in the non-state sector. It is more accurate to say that this is not diversification away from the state, since state policing has never been strong in the history of Sierra Leone, but diversification outside of the state.

Contemporary crime and insecurity

Opinion is divided among the public, police, commercial security managers and journalists about crime rates. The conflicting views of 'high' and 'low' rates is not resolved by the Annual Crime Report published by the SLP. Inevitably there are problems of under-reporting to the police because of lack of access, alternative resolution systems, embarrassment, fear of the police and desire for speedy justice. But in addition, there is the problem, admitted by the report, that: 'most police officers in the provincial setting have yet to grasp the importance of crime statistics ... some crime officers do not send accurate crime figures' to police headquarters (Sierra Leone Police, 2005). The under-reporting is particularly evident as regards sexual offences and domestic violence. Reports from NGOs suggest that the incidence of these is very high (e.g. Campaign for Good Governance, CGG, field officers' reports), though reports to the police nationwide for the whole of 2004 were only 800 for sexual offences and 740 for domestic violence. Likewise 'loitering with intent' (usually prostitution offences) were only 345, despite widespread evidence of brisk activity in this area. And unlawful possession of diamonds at only 13 cases and of cannabis at only 244, suggest that these offences are scarcely being policed.

In the areas of assault, wounding with intent and robbery, there is much greater likelihood of reporting being commensurate with experience. The 19,468 cases of assault for 2004 and 4,183 cases of 'wounding with intent' are still a low figure for a population of 4.9 million. Robbery cases number 331 and 'robbery with violence', which is regularly splashed across the newspapers as if it was a nightly occurrence in Freetown, is only 91 cases nationwide. Meek is certainly right to assert that these are 'very low rates of fire-arm related crime' (Meek, 2003) and few of the police or public interviewed could recount such an incident in the previous few months. However the fear of crime is disproportionate to the incidence of crime. 25 per cent of the public do not feel safe, 26 per cent say they 'just trust in the Lord's protection', and only 3 per cent feel 'very safe' (Sierra Leone Police, 2004).

Contrary to those who argue that war and its aftermath causes a sudden growth in crime (UNDP, 1999; Shaw, 2002), and contrary to Uganda's experience, there is as yet no evidence of a post-conflict crime wave in Sierra

Leone. The top four crimes of assault, larceny, fraudulent conversion and wounding with intent have scarcely changed since the 2002 survey. Nor has robbery risen. Where there have been steep rises, such as child abuse, unlawful carnal knowledge and domestic violence, this is almost certainly the result of sensitisation programmes amongst the public and police and hence the greater willingness to report such cases.[2]

Court system

The formal justice system is still very limited and does not have the local back-up of Uganda's Local Council courts in every village and urban zone. Courts operate only in Freetown and the towns of Bo, Kenema, Port Loko and Makeni, and there are only 15 presiding magistrates and 18 judges. The paucity of court personnel, court records and legal reference materials, plus the inadequacy of the evidence provided by the police, contribute to the serious problems of lengthy delays of cases and imprisonment of suspects without formal charge. Sierra Leone's official legal system has only limited practical relevance for most people, not only because of its remoteness and slowness, but because few can afford lawyers.[3] Many defendants go entirely unrepresented and, knowing little about their rights, are seriously disadvantaged.

Magistrates themselves appear to be mixed in their effectiveness. Reports of CGG field officers detail some progress. For instance, 'the vigilance of the magistrate court has been a major factor in the reduction of crime' (Kono field officer, July 2004). In contrast others speak of widespread concerns: 'the people claim to have lost confidence in the magistrate court due to its corrupt ways of administering justice'; 'it is reported that the mag-

---

2. Police Commanders, Youth Group Leaders and Women's groups reported greater willingness of the police to treat sexual crimes and domestic violence seriously when reported to police stations. Interviews with Local Unit Commanders, A, B, D, S, T Divisions; Chairlady of The Women's Organisations in Kono; Youth Leaders, Makeni, February, 2005. Domestic violence is said to be rampant and certainly reports from field officers of CGG confirm this with many reports of severe beatings given to children and wives for what would be considered in the West as relatively minor offences.

3. Even wealthy criminals have problems, apparently. The Assistant Inspector General of Police for the Western Area, Mr Tamb Gbekie, says that arrested armed robbers have claimed that they were conducting robberies 'because of their desperation to bribe lawyers so that their cases [pending from previous arrests] could be killed or endlessly adjourned in court' (*Standard Times*, Freetown, 31 January, 2005).

istrate is in the habit of perpetually absenting himself from court sittings' (Koinadugu field officer, January 2004, July 2004). Likewise, 'ironically the resident magistrate is not staying in the district, but only appears in the court once a month. Most of the time two Justices of the Peace are left to preside over judicial matters in the Court' (Kailahun field officer, July 2004). There are widespread complaints about dubious discharges and long delays.

In this context of moderate crime rates but of a faltering formal court system, people must weigh their options as to the best police agency for their situation. They can choose from agencies authorised by the state, elected work committees, chiefdoms, commercial companies, community groups, youth or their own family.

The Sierra Leone Police

If the Ugandan leadership does not fully trust the abilities of the police but prefers to look to the army, the Sierra Leonean leadership has no such doubts about favouring the police when it comes to internal security. Nevertheless there are serious issues to tackle. Though the force, as it existed after the war, was 'contaminated' by past events and conduct, it was decided not to disband it, but to totally restructure it and to retrain the executive management team. That management team is now implementing a wide-ranging Change Management Plan and, with increased autonomy at divisional level, the SLP is at last losing its over-centralisation.

The main body of the SLP is comprised, unlike in Uganda and most of Africa,[4] of unarmed general duty officers, who are supported by specialist branches such as the Criminal Investigation Department (CID), Traffic Police and Family Support Unit. Also part of the SLP is the large Operational Support Division (OSD). The 2,500-strong armed element (though perhaps 1,000 are support staff) is kept from general duties. In addition to providing mobile armed support to the general duty officers, the OSD is responsible for riot control, VIP protection, providing static guards for government facilities and working with major commercial security companies when engaged in high risk areas or at diamond mines. Though taking a large proportion of the force's resources in vehicles and wages, the OSD justify their size in terms of a perceived high security threat, and regu-

---

4. The Gambia Police and Liberia Police are also unarmed.

lar and nationwide armed robbery.[5] There seems little evidence to support this.

The strength of the whole force at the end of 2005 was 9,300, although this includes at least 2,000 support staff. Infrastructure, such as police stations and holding cells are slowly being refurbished following war damage. Donors have supplied radios, weapons, uniforms and up to 800 vehicles, although maintaining the latter is not sustainable. At least three Local Unit Commanders (LUC) reported severe lack of fuel and two spoke of accommodation as one of their biggest problems.[6] The SLP request for 2005 for 60 billion Leones (regarded as reasonable by CCSSP advisers) received a response of 21 billion from the government.

There is an open policy of recruitment that does not discriminate against former soldiers or rebels. However, recruits have to undergo quite stringent testing and have to have a minimum education standard of four Ordinary Level Certificates (in fact, most of the initial 200 recruits were graduates from Foray Bay College). The government found expansion of the SLP to the pre-war figure of 9,500 difficult given the pay of 130,000 Leones (Le) per month ($45; cf. 60,000Le for a bag of rice) and with poor accommodation.

There was no training during the war years and little before that, hence there is still a legacy of illiteracy. This illiteracy 'is a major contributor to poor performance … it is commonly accepted that 15–20 per cent of the total force is illiterate' (Woodrow Wilson, 2003:39). The Police Training School in Hastings outside Freetown has a current capacity to train about 800 recruits a year.

Complaints are common of officers engaged in acts of corruption such as demanding bribes at illegal road checkpoints, falsely charging motorists with violations and impounding vehicles to extort money. 81 per cent claim that the traffic police demanded money from drivers (SLP, 2004). The practice also continues of charging complainants fees for papers and pens before obtaining statements from them. More seriously, police are said to be in collusion with criminals and to accept bribes from suspects in exchange for dropping charges. It was the current Inspector General himself who closed down the rump of the Special Constabulary that was not suit-

---

5. Interview, T.T. Kamara, Deputy Head, OSD, 28 February, 2005.
6. Interviews with Local Unit Commanders, A, B, D, S, T Divisions and CCSSP advisers spoke of fuel shortages and equipment/vehicles that were out of service since parts were too expensive.

able for inclusion in the SLP because it was 'working with criminals'.[7] The creation of the Complaints Discipline and Internal Investigation Department (CDIID) is one way that corruption has been addressed. They take public complaints about police bad practice (400 in 2005) and as a result more than 100 officers have been removed from the force since 2001. Yet as Keith Biddle, the former Inspector General, has stressed, reforming the police force is not just an operational problem, but a personnel management problem. It requires line managers to accept responsibility for those under them rather than the force leaving it to the HQ Department, the CDIID. Said Biddle: 'It's a massive culture we've got to change. It's not only stopping corruption. It's changing culture. And part of the culture that's changing for us is government providing the money to manage the force'.[8]

More serious than the corruption that still exists are the cases, though relatively few, of the police beating and raping persons in custody. Further, although the OSD have adequately handled many demonstrations since UNAMSIL departed, they did on two occasions use live ammunition to quell violence, with the tragic result that in two incidents in 2005 two bystanders were killed.[9]

The SLP has received more than £20 million from UK in the last five years (with £17 million more earmarked 2005–2010). Besides the equipment mentioned earlier, the focus has been on training, advice on strategic and operational planning, and senior personnel, through the CCSSP and UN CivPol programmes. Unfortunately many of the 170 CivPol officers that came lacked the appropriate background or skills to provide the required expertise and, coming from 17 different countries, had different standards and procedures. In addition, there were problems of co-ordination between the two programmes.

The biggest impact of the reform process since the war has, like in Uganda, been in the change of relationship between the public and the police. Despite the problems that still exist in the public mind as regards corruption, the slowness to respond and the use of excessive violence against political dissent, there is not the suspicion and fear of the police that there once was. Today the almost universal response in Sierra Leone as in Uganda is that the police are now more approachable. Police may not always be

7. Interview with Inspector General of Police, Brima Acha Kamara, 15 February, 2005. See also, 'Police Exhibit Blatant Corruption', *Standard Times*, 8 July, 2003.

8. Quoted in *Sierra Leone Web*, 17 June, 2001.

9. 'Police Used Excessive Force During the Student Demonstrations', *Standard Times*, 8 March, 2005.

close at hand to many citizens, but generally people would not hesitate to call upon them if there was something that needed their assistance. True, there are those who say it is 'better to take hurt' than to go to the SLP, but many more spoke like the youth leader who said: 'before the war we were afraid of the police ... [now] we should play our role with the police as partners'.[10] In 2004 the SLP commissioned a small public perception survey.[11] Carried out for four urban areas (Freetown, Makeni, Bo, Kenema) it gives a snapshot of urban perceptions. Importantly, only 15 per cent felt that there had been 'no improvement' in SLP behaviour, whilst 46 per cent thought there had been 'a great improvement in police attitude', particularly as regards human rights and 'rudeness'.

With Sierra Leone's population of 4.9 million people, the SLP can only provide an operational police/civilian ratio of about 1.5 per thousand citizens. This is not adequate to provide the crime prevention and crime investigation service that the public want. But the issue is not just of people wanting 'more police on the street'. Though it may be reassuring to them that the police are approachable if required, the everyday problems they confront are not taken to the police. There is little evidence that they have confidence in police willingness to protect their lives and property or in the police having the skills to investigate the crimes they experience. Most interviewed dismissed the idea of reporting anything other than major crimes to the police as futile. Even as the police sought funds to establish more police posts in rural areas where there was no police presence, people in those very areas were saying that they did not want one and had no need of one, since they had made alternative arrangements for their own protection.[12]

Other state policing

In addition to the 7,300 operational police, other government ministries and parastatals have also created policing agencies, but they scarcely have any impact on the public. This makes a strong contrast with Uganda with

---

10. Interview with Youth Leaders, Makeni, 20 February, 2005.

11. 300 structured self-administered questionnaires, with non-random sampling. 287 questionnaires were returned.

12. The villages of Massesse and Malong and Makundu in Bombali District had no police post, but when asked if they would like one it was universally declined. Interviews, 21 February, 2005.

its considerable array of militarised units that take such an active role in curbing serious crime.

Mines Monitoring Officers

To combat illicit diamond mining and smuggling, the Ministry of Mineral Resources has 210 Mines Monitoring Officers (MMOs), 60 of whom are in the diamond area of Kono District in the east. Their task is to check licences, inspect monthly sales of diamond dealers and to deter smuggling. With only 16 motorbikes for the Kono district, little training and low salary,[13] they are not a significant policing agency. One diamond dealer in Kono said that their poor training and pay put them at the mercy of the dealers: 'If I want to smuggle it is easy to bribe a man on $50 per month'.[14] Miners/diggers interviewed said they never saw them and local youth asserted that they were bribed.

The policing of the diamond mining and certification process is not thorough. A monthly report is sent to the Ministry of Mineral Resources, based on physical inspections of the diamond dealers' records of the values and caratage of each diamond sold. However, 'historically it is standard industry practice to only record a small percentage of goods bought, mostly lower value diamonds' (Global Witness, 2001). Another report is made for sales in Freetown. It is not clear what facilities there are to analyse the data, nor what happens to the information when it arrives at the Ministry. Indeed 'there appears to be very little coordination between the Ministry of Mineral Resources and the MMOs' (Global Witness, 2001).

Beach wardens

The National Tourist Board has long operated a beach warden scheme at the popular Lumley beach, Freetown. 10 uniformed wardens on two daytime shifts seek to provide some security from theft and to offer advice to users. But they have had no training and carry only a radio. Given that the beach is quiet during the day, except at holidays and the weekend, and that the main disturbances occur at night when large crowds frequent the bars, the effectiveness of this force has to be questioned.

---

13. Interview, J. Sharkah, Government Mining Engineer, 9 February, 2005.

14. Interview, Dealer, Koidu, 9 February, 2005.

Traffic wardens

The Road Transport Authority has created a corps of 34 traffic wardens for Freetown. The wardens control and regulate road traffic and are also empowered to issue tickets to enforce traffic laws. The wardens enjoy the same powers as the police in the control and regulation of traffic, but are only be able to exercise their functions when in uniform.

The most striking fact about these minor state policing agencies is the lack of co-ordination between them and the police that inevitably follows from the different ministerial responsibilities. That their responsibilities cover (lucrative) areas that the police could manage themselves does not endear them to all police officers.

Policing at the local level: customary structures

Almost everywhere in Sierra Leone, anti-social behaviour and its resolution are regulated by chiefs.[15] They either advise people to go to state courts, or using customary law, handle them within their own local courts. This system was the only form of legal system available before or during the war. Since the war there have been difficulties in re-establishing them, with many courthouses yet to be reconstructed after their destruction by rebels. Many chiefs have also had their authority undermined because of their failure to protect the people and some lost their 'mystique' when they were seen being tortured and killed by the rebels or queuing with the people for food handouts.[16] Yet for all their current weakness, the government is most unlikely to take Uganda's course of abolishing their judicial powers, since chiefs still play an important role in supporting the ruling party.

The courts are particularly focussed on cases involving family law, debt repayment, inheritance, and land tenure. Unfortunately, customary law is often discriminatory, particularly against women (Justice Initiative, 2003). The CGG have regularly reported cases of serious beatings of wives for

15. Despite being a predominantly Muslim country, there is no use of Shari'a law nor calls for it either.

16. Interviews February and March, 2005 with Native Authority Police in Kamara chiefdom; P.C. Sebora, Paramount Chief, Sebora chiefdom, Bombali; Joe Kamgeai-Macavoray, Paramount Chief, Tikonko chiefdom; Village Head, Massesse; R. Clarke, headman, Krootown; A. Wright, headman, Waterloo; Village Head, Malong; Kenneth Tommy, Town Chief, Yengema; Sahr Babonjo, Town Chief, Tombodou.

which customary courts handed out sentences of small fines or even took no action at all. The local courts also frequently abuse their powers by illegally detaining persons, charging excessively high fines for minor offences, and adjudicating criminal cases.[17] Juvenile crime is usually dealt with by customary law, even where judicial authorities are present. 'Where a child has been committing crime or causing mischief corporal punishment, usually flogging, is frequently administered to the child' (Harvey, 2000). Though it is a criminal offence for anybody other than a local court, magistrate or judge to perform an adjudicative function, chiefs and elders still do (Kane et al., 2002:15).

The Native Authority police are a shadow of their former selves. The numbers of Chiefdom police per Chiefdom currently range from 2–25.[18] They now face problems recruiting because of the lack of pay and few benefits available.

> The extent to which these police are organized, equipped or even active varies considerably. So too do their roles (and presumably their understanding of their roles). Some are basically court messengers. Others play a role in community safety and security (Kane, 2002:16).

This research found that their main job was to collect market dues and local tax. They have no uniforms, no weapons and only minimal training by the district office of the Native Authority. Their justification for their continuing role is that 'customary laws will always need policing'.

Having played the major role in crime prevention and protection for most people in Sierra Leone for more than a century, there is indeed a danger that this alternative policing structure may fail in the near future because of its evident limitations. What the next section shows, however, is that it may not necessarily be to the police that the people will turn to take the place of the Native Authorities, but to alternative community based organisations, whether approved by the police or not.

---

17. In Freetown headmen cannot adjudicate civil cases either.

18. In Kamara chiefdom there are 9 Native Authority police, 16 in Sebora chiefdom and 3 in Tikonko (the pre-war figure was 23). Interviews with chiefs in Yengema, Tomodou and with Native Authority police in Kamara chiefdom, 8 February 2005.

State approved self-policing initiated by the police: partnership boards

The Local Policing Partnership Boards were initiated by the police when they embraced the concept of Local Needs Policing after the war. This community based policing aims to give local communities a voice in how they want to be policed and has some similarities to Uganda's Crime Prevention Panels. They are chaired by civilians and include representatives of the significant groups and interests in the locality. The aim is to have at least one in each of the 26 police command units and under them to create neighbourhood watch groups. The Inspector General sees information-led policing, such as these groups provide, as 'the key to success in the future' for the control of crime.[19] In Makeni, Bo and Koidu there were complaints that the Partnership Boards were not effective and were failing to meet regularly. However one Freetown Partnership Board has already provided information that has led to the arrest of eight 'hard core' criminals and the seizure of their weapons and has begun to map 'ghettoes' (drug houses) with a view to the police using the information to make arrests and to knock down the premises. In addition to intelligence, they have improved communication between police and communities and provided investigation, intervention, arrest and dispute resolution. On the negative side, however, they are elite dominated and most of the activities, initiatives and even finance are coming from the community (for more see, Baker, 2007b).

Officially the prime aim of the Boards is to give local communities a say in how they want to be policed. Yet when 26 people attended a Partnership Board one Saturday morning to consider their Community Action Plan, they were handed a printed copy of the Plan drawn up by the SLP beforehand. The Board was simply required to confirm it.[20] The co-operation of the public in these newly formed Boards does point to a desire to see better state-provided policing and there is no doubt that, despite the difficulties, the Partnership Boards are universally valued and are not seen as unwelcome foreign imports. Yet if the police continue to exclude local voices from anything other than intelligence gathering and fail to maintain the regular meetings, they could be a mere temporary phenomenon.

---

19. Interview with Inspector General of Police, Brima Acha Kamara, 15 February, 2005.

20. B-Division Partnership Board meeting, 5 February, 2005. Interview with P. B. Williams, Chairman, B Division Police Partnership Board.

State approved self-policing initiated by the community: peace monitors

Like the Peace Committees of South Africa, this style of policing promotes and facilitates the resolution of disputes within very poor communities through the mobilisation of local capacity and knowledge. So far they are concentrated in a few communities in the Bo, Pujehun and Sulima areas in the South. Bo Peace and Reconciliation Movement (BPRM) is a coalition of 11 community groups working on peacebuilding, reconciliation and crime prevention in the Bo district. Its 20 local peace monitors have resolved many conflicts such as family matters, fighting, land cases and leadership issues, including some longstanding disputes (they handled 255 cases in 2004). Their work has reduced community conflict and litigation in the local courts, and helped many ex-combatants reintegrate into the communities. BPRM's success has earned it the recognition of the provincial administration in Bo.[21]

Further south, the Soro Gbema chiefdom, in Pujehun District, had a number of local problems, including disputes caused by the death of a paramount chief, lack of civil authority and the usurpation of this authority by CDF commanders. With help from the only community-based organisation working in the chiefdom, The Sulima Fishing Community Development Project, the community developed a peace monitoring system that promotes peacebuilding, development and access to justice. Each section of the chiefdom was provided with a Peace Monitor for early intervention in conflicts. The community also established grievance committees. Local conflicts are brought to this committee for arbitration or mediation. The twelve peace monitors (mainly respected Koranic teachers) work for a small stipend 10 days every month and cover 10 to 15 villages each.

When there are local grievances over property ownership; looting and unlawful claiming of property; drug abuse and trafficking; and disregard of local customs; the people call the peace monitors in preference to court actions. Hence one of the negative impacts of this alternative policing is that the district administration has been unable to generate revenue, so there is a growing official resentment. When the District Officer of Pujehun District sought to re-institute collection of local taxes and to re-establish the Native Authority court, the people refused to pay the taxes and rejected the reinstitution of the court because they saw it as ineffective. The people prefer the free assistance of peace monitors to settle their conflicts

---

21. Interviews, Peace Monitors, Bo, 3 March, 2005.

and differences in contrast to paying a summons fee of 10,000 Le (£2) to the Native Authority court (Massaquoi, 1999).

The peace monitors have only been introduced in a few places in Sierra Leone, but their potential to expand is obvious. Here is a policing system that is effective, accessible and cheap. Few will imagine that an enlarged SLP would necessarily provide them with such a service.

State approved self-policing initiated by work-based associations

Many of the economic activities in Sierra Leone's towns, from money changers to taxi drivers and market traders, have an association that disciplines and protects members. In this respect they are identical to Uganda. All town markets have a committee that is recognised by the city council. They act to control the conduct of vendors and customers. Low level misconduct, such as smoking cannabis, spitting and abusive language can result in a fine. More serious issues of debt and fighting are brought to mediation. If they cannot be resolved it may lead to the suspension of the trader for weeks or months in addition to the fine. The police are largely absent from the markets and the vendors prefer it that way. They regard going to the police as 'a waste of time' – either because they will not act or they release the thieves taken to them very quickly (a sign to many of collusion). Indeed, one chairlady of a large Freetown market said that she 'abhorred' their presence at the market since they would only appear if they were intent on extorting money. The overwhelming view was that traders were on their own as regards protection from and punishment of crime. 'Discipline is done by the market women [rather than the police] because we know their problems and know native customary law' said a Freetown market women's leader. It was acknowledged that pick-pocketing and petty theft were hard to prevent, but if a thief was caught he was usually beaten on the spot.[22]

The Motor Drivers and General Transport Workers Union/Association, with a membership of about 5,000, claim to control many of the commercial vehicle and mini-bus parking areas in the main towns. They provide various levels of policing activity. In Freetown they check owners' particulars, including driving licence and insurance and use car park attendants

22. Interviews with market executives at Freetown Big Market; Garrison Market; Congo Town Market; Koidu Market; Makeni Market; Bo Market.

to oversee loading and protect passengers. In Waterloo members take it in turn to be attendants. They have distinctive bibs and deal with problems relating to drivers, passengers and pick-pockets. They issue fines, ban drivers and exclude undesirable persons. In Bo the drivers claimed responsibility for all vehicles in the town and took offenders to the SLP. In Makeni the drivers alleged that dangerous driving by members was punished severely: 'We give them lashes'.[23] The Bo Bike Rental Association ran the motorbike transport in Bo, enforcing rules concerning speeding, reckless driving, carrying more than one passenger and carrying a woman with child. It also has a disciplinary Task Force which patrols at night and investigates and resolves disputes between drivers and the public.[24]

There is no evidence that these work-based policing associations are only accepted reluctantly or seen as of limited use. On the contrary, the demand for better security is being satisfied by non-state providers.

Commercial security groups

The principal work of commercial companies is to provide unarmed guards to commercial businesses, international organisations, NGOs and residential customers. The absence of weapons is due to the UN arms embargo. At the start of the war there were only two companies operating, but since the war there has been a rapid expansion, due to the prevailing sense of increasing crime, the weakness of the SLP and the presence of many International NGOs requiring security for their staff. There are now about 30 licensed companies, most of which are based in Freetown. Though licences are required for commercial security companies, there is no effective inspection on the Ugandan scale and no licence has been withdrawn.

Of the 20 more significant companies, the largest are Mount Everest (1,700 employees), Pentagon (900) and Hughes Security (800). There are also international companies, such as Group4Falck and SecuricorGray, which together employ about 1,000 guards, primarily in Freetown and the large mines (Abrahamsen and Williams, 2005:6).

At diamond mines, banks, some diplomatic missions and for some rapid response teams, commercial operators work alongside the OSD to provide a mix of armed and unarmed guards. In these situations the security companies pay a premium to the individual OSD officers above the standard

---

23. Interviews in Freetown, Waterloo, Koidu and Makeni, February, 2005.

24. Interview, Task Force Commander, Suliaman Silaah, 3 March, 2005.

wages. The irony does not go unnoticed that government revenue is spent sending SLP personnel to guard commercial rather than citizen interests.

Most companies employ ex-soldiers or retired police, with screening of recruits for criminal records by the CID. The screening does not, however, cover rebel background, for which there has been national forgiveness. Hence some companies are unwittingly employing ex-rebels, which they consider an unsatisfactory situation.[25] Only the larger companies offer training to the recruits. It includes human rights training at the request of the UN for its own contracts. Human rights, however, are not normally a priority. As one operations manager of a large firm insisted, human rights should only be considered *after* the suspect has been 'made' to tell the truth!

Most international organisations, larger commercial businesses, NGOs and the wealthier residential customers do not have confidence in the SLP to provided them with protection from crime and appear much more satisfied with the commercial alternative.

Informal security: youth groups

Youth in Sierra Leone (as in most of Africa) means, effectively, young males of 15 to 35 years. Many young men are unemployed and this, together with their history in the war as combatants, makes people wary of them and quick to label them as criminals at worst or untrustworthy at best.[26] The more violent certainly perpetuate mob justice or continued their combatant role in Liberia.[27] However, the vast majority of young people perceive themselves as 'guardians of security'. Indeed, though they recognise that 'youth are still struggling to gain acceptance' from the local communities, they assert that 'this is no longer a time of violence, though not every youth

25. Interviews with A. Sillah, Managing Director and Administrative Manager, Pentagon Security; J. Fofanah, General Operations Manager, Mount Everest Security Agency; E. Hudi Turay, Manager, C&C Security; A. Tunkara, Manager, Hughes Security, February, 2005.

26. For example the Annual Crime Report of the SLP attributes the increase in crime rates in the Western area to, inter alia, 'lots of idlers and unemployed youth roaming about'.

27. 3,000 Karamajor having gone to Liberia to fight, the government of Sierra Leone acknowledge that there is a threat of their imminent return. Interview, J. Sandy, Office of National Security, 27 January, 2005.

has got that understanding'.[28] Far from being criminal, they argue that 'security is in our hands'.[29] And in villages and poor townships it was found that this has been turned into a reality. In the absence of the SLP and sometimes in the failure of the customary structures to re-establish themselves after the war, there is a clear security gap and it is the youth that more often than not are filling it. It was they who initiated the Bo Peace Monitors and the Bo Bike Rental Association Task Force.

In the town of Yengema, in Kono, the youth stay alert at night and respond to fights and other problems. They are particularly opposed to drugs: 'we harass anybody who brings drugs ... we arrest them, destroy drugs and give them a beating'. In their view the drug problem 'is solved; no more drugs'.[30] The town chief concurred that the area was 'depending on youths to take care of us at night', though he added that 'youths are not always reliable'.[31] Similarly, in the nearby village of Tombodou, the chief spoke of youth controlling security: 'they see [that] things go on normally' and filled in for the inactive chiefdom police and absent SLP.[32] And according to the Tombodou women's leader, they 'ensure local policing where SLP don't go. They make arrest and take them to the SLP'.[33] In Makeni I saw youths dealing at night with a fight between two girls, one of whom had broken a bottle over the head of the other. Youth also frequently provide security for small diamond companies. In the alluvial mining area of Gbense chiefdom, a 12-man youth group secured Kariba Kono Ltd.'s holding on behalf of the elders, who had been promised development projects by the company. Though currently unpaid, the youth had been promised employment when mining began.[34]

In the town of Koidu in Kono, the Movement of Concerned Kono Youth (MOCKY) also claimed to deal with youth problems and to settle 'small cases'. In the past they have been accused of using violence. In particular, it is said that they have mobilised youth to resist the influx of fortune seekers in the alluvial diamond-mining sector, sometimes collaborating with local police units and the Civil Defence Force (CDF) (Reno, 2004). Other

28. Interview, youth leaders, Makeni, 20 February, 2005.

29. Ibid.

30. Interview, youth leader, 8 February, 2005.

31. Interview, Kenneth Tommy, Town Chief, Yengema, 8 February, 2005.

32. Interview, Sahr Babonjo, Town Chief, Tombodou, 9 February, 2005.

33. Interview, Women's Leader, Tombodou, 9 February, 2005.

34. Interviews, 9 February, 2005.

reports say that MOCKY and former CDF have held informal courts to settle disputes among area residents not satisfied with the results of the formal judicial system (State Department Country Report, 2003). There is no evidence of this currently. Whatever the past actions, MOCKY's 5,000 members' aims now seem focussed on advocacy (for 'just mining'), local development, the protection of the interests of youth and resolving youth problems. In this role it has a seat on the local Police Partnership Board ('though it is not very effective' in their view).[35]

In parts of Freetown youth groups have shown a serious concern for crime prevention and security provision. A considerable number of the participants in the Kissi Police Partnership Board were local youth and elsewhere the youth of Firestone Cultural and Community Organisation ran sensitisation programmes on drugs and for prostitutes.[36] Security provision has also emerged in some of the poorest settlements. By the port, in Krootown, Camp Divas Youth maintain a measure of order, especially among the youth. They fine cases of fighting and abusive language and 'flog' those who fail to pay the fine. Thieves, they say, they take to the SLP.[37] A local tribal headman concurred that youth often intervened to stop fighting when the police failed to respond. Though he also acknowledged that they stoned a police station when a man they wanted was taken there.[38] And outside a police divisional headquarters I watched 40 youth demonstrating loudly for compensation for a cow the youths had 'arrested' wandering down the main road. Inside the station the Local Unit Commander negotiated with the youth and the cow owner, until a financial settlement was reached and the crowd left in jubilation.

The wariness noted above in Kono district and in Freetown by the older population regarding youth was also found in Bombali district in the north. A paramount chief in Sebora chiefdom feared that if they were given a role in security there would be a return to political militias and the youth would 'make a living out of it'.[39] And a local police commander felt that the Neighbourhood Watch was not effective locally because the youth repre-

---

35. Interview General Secretary of MOCKY 9 February, 2005. The Assistant Superintendent of Police of Kono District concurs that they have 'much improved', interview, Clarkson Momoh, 8 February, 2005.

36. Interview, executive member, 1 March, 2005.

37. Interviews, 31 January, 2005.

38. Interview, R. Clarke, 31 January, 2005.

39. Interview, 20 February, 2005.

sentatives on it were 'criminals'.[40] Yet this unease has to be balanced by the almost universal village voices of Bombali. In the villages of Massesse and Malong and Makundu it was the youth alone who provided security. They were the ones who kept alert at night for trouble, so much so that neither the headmen or youth wanted a police post, for they saw no need for one.[41] There is a divide, when a choice has to be made between youth policing or state policing.

Informal security: militias/vigilantes

Sierra Leone's now defunct civilian militia, the CDF, was very active during the civil war, fighting along with the Sierra Leonean army. There was a large degree of 'factional fluidity' among the different militias and armed groups, however. Both overtly and covertly, fighters switched sides or established new 'units'. Indeed many of the early members of the RUF on its Southern Front in the Pujehun District reappeared as Kamajors under the banner of the CDF after 1997. Theirs was not so much a switching of sides as the identification of a new vehicle on which to conduct their notions of empowerment as militiamen (Sierra Leone Truth and Reconciliation Commission, 2004). Given this fluidity, it is little surprising that all sides are accused of dealing harshly with the civilian population. Forced recruitment, looting, rape and executions of suspected 'enemy' sympathisers were common tactics. And those caught for alleged criminal activities were 'militarily' punished and others received severe beatings.

Even as late as 2004 it was claimed that the CDF still existed as an organised group:

> ... despite a December 2002 agreement between the government and foreign donors to dismantle it. The CDF's offer to assist the Sierra Leone Army's efforts to stem incursions of Liberian fighters in 2003 and reports that it assisted insurgents in Liberia against Liberian president Charles Taylor suggest that it may have a greater capacity than the national army, at least in some parts of the country (Reno, 2004:8).

However, national intelligence agencies have concluded that they are not currently present in Sierra Leone. However they were anxious about the return of an estimated 3,000 Karamajor from Liberia.[42]

---

40. S Division LUC, 20 February, 2005.

41. Interviews, 21 February, 2005.

42. Interview, J. Sandy, Office of National Security, 27 January, 2005.

What does remain in Sierra Leone, however, is mob violence. The absence of a local security system like the Uganda LCs appears to explain its greater prevalence. Present reports suggest that beating or even the killing of criminals is widespread. One councillor reported that, 'where I live we give thieves a good hiding; we don't take them to the police for we won't get the exhibit [the stolen property] back'.

Conclusion

In Sierra Leone, as elsewhere in post-conflict countries, there has been much talk of SSR (security sector reform) (Fayemi, 2004; Gbla, 2006; Peake, 2006; Albrecht and Malan, 2006; Ginifer, 2006) but the focus has been very narrow and almost exclusively on state agencies. Yet in Sierra Leone, as Uganda, there is a wide choice of policing agencies – non-state and state, offering citizens crime protection and crime investigation. Far from it being the case that 'pluralization of security ... largely ignores the weakest members' of weak states (Goldsmith, 2003:18), the evidence from Sierra Leone is that it provides almost all that the weakest members know of policing.

What is particularly striking in Sierra Leone is the abundant evidence that youth are actually providing local security in areas where the SLP are rarely seen. In Uganda the same space has been filled by government sponsored Local Councils. But in Sierra Leone there has been no government initiative to provide security at the local level, only the promise of 'more police' in the distant future. So often demonised as bearing a large part of the blame for Sierra Leone's woes, and feared as 'the idle unemployed', the youth, in practice, are committed to playing a role in security and development.

CHAPTER 8

Patterns of Multi-Choice Policing

People make their own history, but they do not make it just as they please,
they do not make it under circumstances chosen by themselves, but in
circumstances directly found, given, and transmitted from the past.
(Karl Marx, 1978)

Once security ceases to be guaranteed to all citizens by a sovereign state,
it tends to become a commodity which like any other is distributed by
market forces rather than according to need. (Garland, 1996:463)

I have sought to establish that multi-choice policing is endemic in Africa. Alternatives to the state police are a feature of every community of Africa. Yet whilst policing choice is ubiquitous, it is not true that the available mix of auspices and providers of policing is identical everywhere. In general terms, the manifestations of policing in Africa today are societal responses to the flouting of norms, criminal activity, armed conflict and weak state security provision. Yet the specific patterns of policing vary according to the social context. In other words, the ingredients may be similar, but not how they are cooked. As with all social phenomena, the variation is a product of agency and structure: the one unique and unpredictable; the other more permanent and predictable. Like all social patterns they are more or less contingent outcomes of the interaction of different and possibly contradictory forces. Few have put it more clearly than Marx:

> [People] make their own history, but they do not make it just as they please; they do not make it under circumstances chosen by themselves, but in circumstances directly found, given, and transmitted from the past. The tradition of all dead generations weighs like a nightmare on the [minds] of the living. And just when they seem engaged in revolutionizing themselves and things, in creating something entirely new, precisely in such epochs of revolutionary crisis do they anxiously conjure up the spirits of the past in their service and borrow from them names, battle slogans and costumes in order to present the new scene of world history in this time-honoured disguise and with borrowed language (Karl Marx, 1978:595).

Agency, therefore, cannot occur outside existing social structures and practices, but only through them. At the same time, the social structures and practices that constrain agents are also the product of past agency.

Actors who authorise and provide policing

The wide variety of responses to insecurity and crime, therefore, is in part a reflection of the many categories of actors that authorise non-state policing in Africa. In the previous chapters I have recorded heads of households/ extended families; business persons; customary leaders; religious leaders; ethnic/clan leaders; political party bosses; local politicians; entrepreneurs; social activists; and non-government organisations as all being engaged. Most of them have resources of their own or access to them and carry some standing in the community policed, based on age, political power, economic power, custom, or possession of the means of coercion. The motives described have been as varied as their background. Some had altruistic motives (the 'concerned citizen'), others were seeking political or economic gain, still others were victims of crime or closely connected with those who were and wanted solutions or revenge. For all these reasons they have been willing to initiate enterprises that have supplemented/complemented or even challenged the state. Those described as providing policing in response to these authorisers have been just as varied. They have typically shared the identity of the authorisers and been in a position to gather together guards, investigators, posses, revenge groups, 'courts' or resolution forums and equip them for the task.

Together, then, authorisers and providers of policing offer a large range of the unique and unpredictable. The initiative of community leaders is a constant theme in policing patterns in Africa. It is local political, religious, ethnic and customary political figures that have most property to lose; who have the resources to plan, negotiate and finance a response; who are subject to pressure from poorer members of the community to take action; who may feel a community responsibility as part of their role; and who may be encouraged overtly or covertly by elements of the state. Yet just how their personal anxieties, communal concern, state connections, political calculus and entrepreneurship combine varies widely. Similarly, their levels of authority and influence within their communities differ and fluctuate. Hence there are very different responses from them in terms of the policing they initiate or support in their local communities.

As one would expect, business interests are active in defending their property and livelihoods against crime. Commonly they have turned to commercial security companies to provide at least a guard at the gate and sometimes more sophisticated armed response teams when an alarm is activated. But they have also been active in authorising policing themselves, with or without the co-operation and approval of the state police. Rural business has initiated commercial informal security groups; city traders have called on vigilante groups for protection. There are also many examples of initiatives in co-operation with the state police. Businesses within a city centre block have organised their own security patrols or have entered a public-private partnership with the police, in which they define their security needs and provide the state police with the resources to satisfy them (for Cape Town see Samara, 2005).

Political entrepreneurs, regional 'strongmen' and 'warlords' are also keen to preserve their 'turf' from political and commercial rivals and use armed groups. Their private military forces may be recruited either on a regional or a clan basis. Though the armed groups evidently function as personal armies, they also enforce social order within the area claimed by their patrons.

Religious leaders have a keen interest in order maintenance, though it is a different order from that of the state. Most are content to preach, cajole or verbally intimidate those they have influence over. Others resort to various forms of informal organised policing that exercises surveillance and responses such as beating to enforce their order. In Islamic communities 'Shari'a police' enforce religious duties, confront those who engage in un-Islamic behaviour such as premarital sex and attack unacceptable businesses like bars and brothels. Those who view the state police as corrupt and immoral are not inclined to work with them. Other religious policing, however, is much more mild and eschews coercion in favour of handling primary justice complaints in dispute resolution forums.

Ethnic and clan leaders are equally concerned to preserve an order that accords with their own culture. In rural areas of Africa the great majority of disputes are processed in customary courts. The cases are normally brought to the court by the disputants, although arrests may be made by native authority police. Hence customary leaders have a very great influence on local policing. Although in most African countries the judgments of such courts do not hold the weight of state law, few villagers idly dismiss the judgment of the one who is the administrative head of the village. The fact that many customary leaders, where they are employees of the state, are expected to inform intelligence agents about any opposition to the ruling party and that they hold unfavourable views toward women's rights, only enhances the fears of discrimination on the grounds of political adherence or gender. The customary courts overall have a conciliatory character, aiming to restore peace between members and social order. However, chiefs do not always follow conciliatory procedures. They may authorise posses to go after cattle thieves and kill the presumed culprits; they may send organised urban vigilantes out to 'catch criminals' with little concern if they are shot or beaten to the point of near death.

Such are the unpredictable elements that contribute to the specific multi-choice policing patterns that are emerging. But what of the significant structures that have constrained their decisions and through which they have had to operate? Under what circumstances, found or inherited, must they authorise the policing of their choice? Four key structures have emerged throughout the previous chapters as constraints on policing:

1. the state
2. internal conflict
3. development programmes
4. commercial opportunities

The constraint of the state

The state, in accordance with its political character, administrative organisation and capacity, and economic strength, is a major force in shaping the experience of policing throughout the country. Though it may not always be successful, it seeks domination over all other organisations within the national territory and is intent on establishing binding rules regarding the other organisations' activities. Besides claiming the authority to make binding laws, it also claims the right to use coercive means to punish those who disobey it. Indeed, it sees itself as the security guarantor for a populated territory. Yet rarely is there that inter-agency harmony to ensure an integrated internal security policy. After all the state is 'a contradictory, disunified set of structures, processes and discourses, the different parts of which often act at cross purposes' (Poulantzas, 1978). Nevertheless for all that the state is not monolithic, it does have a wide network of agencies designed to gather intelligence on persons and to enforce its will. Though many speak of its demise, none would deny that the policing policies and the action (or inaction) of state police agents shape the decisions of those authorising and providing policing across Africa. As for the configuration of the state, this has undergone a degree of transformation as a result of the political liberalisation processes that have swept the continent since 1990. There remain five variables that determine the impact of its policing policies. They are the degree of its penetration, centralisation, militarisation, supervision and facilitation.

Penetration

State penetration of society concerns the degree to which the state is present on the ground. It relates to state capability and capacity across society. Whilst governments on paper have been highly interventionist, overseeing a plethora of laws, controls and security services, in practice many governments are absent and irrelevant over large areas of their territory when it comes to preventing crime or responding to it. This lack of penetration is partly a reflection of the state's available resources for state policing and for supervising other policing agencies. It is also a reflection of its commitment (or lack of it) to areas outside those deemed significant to the regime in terms of regime preservation and revenue generation.

High levels of non-state policing typically arise in communities where the state offers no protection of its own. In other words, the mix of policing is closely related to state strength. Strong states 'that have high capabilities to complete the tasks of penetrating society, regulating social relationships, extracting resources and appropriating or using resources in determined ways' (Migdal, 1988:9) will be in a position to provide national policing themselves. Weak states, that have low capabilities to complete these tasks, will vacate the space of providing internal security to other authorisers and providers.

The effective reach of many African states and the rule of law have never been established nationwide since independence, despite their insistence that providing internal security is their legitimate function. Instead, state control has often resembled a domination of an archipelago of resources. It is in the 'sea' that lies between the state policed resources that alternatives thrive.

Some African states have had their functions so weakened that some commentators speak of collapse and anarchy (Zolberg, 1992; Zartman, 1995; Mbembe, 1992). Many have assumed that the end of a central political authority must mean the breakdown of law and order (Zartman, 1995; Samatar, 1994). They conflate the collapse of public services with the collapse of social order. In fact, when all central control evaporates, there are very often militia-run structures or more traditional kinship organisations that come to the fore to prevent total social disorder. Plunkett speaks of some customary lifestyles where the primacy of the state may not be known or recognised but where they, nevertheless, have micro-rule of law systems (Plunkett, 2005: 79). An example is Somalia. It has neither an institutional state nor a ruling regime, instead people rely on themselves and their small lineage unit for their everyday security needs (Simons, 1998). As Forrest notes:

> The loosening of state tentacles has not meant an end of politics but rather the removal of arcane administrative superstructures ... This has rendered more visible the social bases of power that exert real world influence over the lives of most Africans ... In the context of state disintegration ... rural society has the capacity to craft its own micro-level political frameworks (Forrest, 1998:54).

Yet though the weakness or even absence of the state does not mean that community security provision ceases, it does alter the nature of that provision. It allows space for non-state authorisers and providers, which may be more accessible, accountable and in tune with local values than the state policing.

Centralisation

The degree of centralisation of police powers is a product of the political settlement between the central state and local powers to share their power. The central state is often suspicious of any power holders not under its control, particularly if those actors control coercive forces. Hence, apart from Nigeria and Ethiopia (with possibly Sudan and DRC shortly), federal constitutions have not been popular. Most states oppose the local control of policing, whether motivated by a desire for equal service provision for all their citizens and local accountability or, more likely, from a reluctance to allow regional strongmen to secure a political power base that could threaten them. Through constitutional provision and legislation they seek to exclude or reduce any space for alternative policing and to create a monopoly for themselves. However, recognising their own inability to provide a national service, they do have to strike deals and alliances with local agents who are in a position to provide such security. These may be customary authorities or local political power brokers from provincial governors to town party bosses. Customary courts, anti-crime committees, village patrols and anti-cattle rustling militias will certainly relieve their own state police personnel and courts and deny the opposition the opportunity to say that the government is doing nothing to provide security. If they can be brought under some sort of state umbrella of legitimation, that is even better. However, these local actors can themselves be reluctant to hand over such a very visible feature of their power and a source of their legitimacy and support. There is more political support to be gained from running a local vigilante group than from subsuming the group under a central government initiative that gives the credit to the ruling party. The outcome of the negotiations and 'public consultations' by which policing responsibility is distributed between central and local authorities reflects the strengths of the parties. Customary authorities may have their powers to provide policing stripped from them (e.g. Uganda) or they may have their role recognised as legitimate (e.g. Sierra Leone, Liberia, Botswana). Security may be subcontracted out to the lowest levels of local authority (e.g. Uganda, Rwanda) or village 'self-reliance' may be harnessed. Regional state governors may be allowed local vigilance committees or the groups may be criminalized and forcibly closed down (a battle has raged over this issue in Nigeria). Successful non-state anti-rustling groups may be co-opted into government police structures (e.g. Tanzania) or replaced by centralised police and paramilitary units (e.g. Kenya's paramilitary police force, the General Service Unit).

Whatever the degree of centralisation inherent in the deal, it will determine the nature of the policing that arises or the degree to which it flourishes. No settlements are of course permanent. The current Nigerian constitution states: 'The Nigeria Police Force shall be under the command of the Inspector-General of Police and any contingents of the Nigeria Police Force stationed in a state shall, subject to the authority of the Inspector-General of Police, be under the command of the Commissioner of Police of that state'. However, the situation is contested and state governors, such as the one of Lagos state, are calling for each state to have its own police force.[1] Likewise the boundary between customary courts and formal state courts is currently being extensively reviewed (e.g. Malawi) as state provision is increasingly accused of being inaccessible, costly and detached from local values.

Militarisation

The worldwide trend toward paramilitary policing has been noted by several commentators (e.g. Kraska and Kappelar, 1997; Jefferson, 1990; Waddington, 1991). Militarisation is the state's response to social disorder or the fear of it. The disorder may arise from criminal or political groups. When governments feel that either are getting beyond control by normal civilian policing, or they feel politically insecure, they are inclined to re-

---

1. *This Day*, 24 June, 2004.

sort to military solutions or the militarisation of policing units. These may be directly controlled military and paramilitary units such as Presidential Guards, crack anti-crime units, special services units and internal security forces or indirectly controlled local militias and civil defence units. Often such groups have a history of using force of arms in an abusive and extra-judicial manner (e.g. Namibia's paramilitary police, The Special Field Forces, have regularly been implicated in beatings and 'disappearances' in the Caprivi Strip).

Part of the explanation for a militarised response may also lie in the nature of the regime. A regime that has a military or authoritarian background may have a greater confidence in military-type law enforcement initiatives (e.g. Nigeria, not only under military rulers but under democratically elected President Obasanjo). Alternatively, if there is a legacy of civil conflict, whether from insurgents, secessionists or terrorists, regimes may genuinely be fearful that the horrors of that period may return (e.g. Uganda).

Militarised responses can also be the product of public outcries against insecurity and insistence that the government 'comes down hard' on all forms of disorder and lawlessness. For example, South Africa's crack unit, the Scorpions, was set up in the face of the perceived failure of the SAPS. Partly in response to popular demands for more effective crime control, African governments have adopted 'shoot to kill' practices towards armed robbers (e.g. Tanzania; Burkina Faso, Uganda, Kenya, Nigeria, CAR and Cameroon). These have involved the use of special squads with the sole aim of killing off suspects rather than investigating and preventing crime. There may also be pressure from within the security establishment. Policing organisations that have undergone dramatic processes of transformation seek security in the sort of paramilitary operations with which they are familiar and confident. Such 'war' against crime is frequently urged upon the government:

> The lack of real policing structures in Africa, together with high levels of social disorder and conflict, mean that, in the interim, public order or paramilitary policing structures which are highly mobile, highly trained, and equipped with a knowledge of sophisticated weaponry may be a solution to the inappropriate use of the military in internal security issues (Marks, 1998).

Supervision

Governance, particularly the management systems of state police, has become a key area of policing reform in the last decade. States that fail to put in place effective executive management teams in their police forces face high levels of police corruption, inefficient practices and uncurbed crime rates. External Complaints Boards have their place (Etannibi, 2005; Lumina, 2006), but bad police practice is at heart a personnel management problem. Yet the degree to which states are prepared to tackle the necessary supervision of their police forces varies widely, despite the 'democratic' reforms. Several recent reports on the police in Southern Africa (e.g. Amnesty International, 2002; Klipin and Harrison, 2003) make it clear that in the majority of the Southern African Development Community (SADC) countries (South Africa, Botswana, Angola, Lesotho, Malawi, Mozambique, Swaziland, Tanzania, Zambia, Zimbabwe, Namibia, Mauritius, Seychelles and the Democratic Republic of Congo) police harass and disrupt the activities of opposition leaders, trade union officials, youth activists, human rights monitors and journalists. They also extort money from travellers and from suspects or even from those wanting an investigation to take place. They frequently use torture and coerce confessions during investigations and rarely, if ever, are punished for such abuses. In addition, there is widespread use of summary killings of suspects even prior to investigation.

The failure of governments to curb these abuses or to prosecute police has led to a widespread belief that the police are outside the law and enjoy immunity. Even more troubling is evidence to suggest that in some cases, police employees are complicit with criminal elements and therefore unlikely to challenge them. For instance, the 2002 State Department report on human rights said of the Angolan National Police:

> Police participated in extortion, robbery, and carjackings and were cited as the primary human rights abusers by local human rights organizations by year's end. It is believed widely that police resorted regularly to extrajudicial killings, especially of known criminal gang members, as an alternative to the country's ineffective judicial system. Other than those personnel assigned to elite units, the Government gave tacit permission for security personnel to supplement their income through the extortion of the civilian population. For example, independent media sources accused police in Lunda Norte of terrorizing and extorting money from citizens in the municipality of Nzagi during the year. Police commanders were accused of permitting such activity and killing market vendors who complained about the abuses. Impunity remained a serious problem.

Weakly supervised police are not natural allies of the citizen, the community leaders, development organisations or even some members of government itself. This situation, not surprisingly, makes many individuals conclude that they are on their own in the fight against crime and that if they want any progress they must take matters into their own hands. As for those who have authority, it presses them to consider setting up alternative arrangements. Thus decisions about self-policing are made against a background of state abandonment and police predation.

Facilitation

In many societies citizens have begun to take their own initiatives against crime. The degree to which this manifests itself in any society is dependent on its history and traditions. In countries in Africa where communities have, often in response to authoritarian rule, sought community responses to ensure local safety, self-policing has become reasonably common. And states focussed on repression of rebellions may see businesses turn to commercial policing. Yet the success of both informal and formal alternative policing in part depends on the favourable response of the state or at least the absence of repression. The government of Sierra Leone was only too happy to see the Civil Defence Forces assume responsibility for local policing when their own police force was withdrawing from areas contested by the rebels in the civil war. Initially the government of Côte d'Ivoire tried to take some of the credit for the success of hunter associations in reducing crime in northern rural areas.

The early growth of South Africa's commercial security industry was not just a factor of the size of the economy. It was partly the result of the government encouragement of commercial policing in the latter years of apartheid to relieve the hard-pressed SAP. Almost everywhere the state holds the power to grant licences to commercial security companies and the power to withdraw them; to grant contracts to protect economic resources such as mines and ports or to deny contracts; to provide arms to militias or disarm them. There is often an informal facilitation of such companies. In other words, it is the close and often personal relationship that policing agencies have with local governors, ministers and district police commissioners that ensures their prosperity and a breakdown in that relationship that causes failure. Indeed it is not unusual for commercial companies to be run by former ministers or senior police officers. For instance, in Cameroon a former Minister of Defence heads the Société d'Intervention Rapide; and a former Minister of Defence in Liberia owns Exsecon.

Most African states now increasingly look to various forms of community policing to assist their weak police forces. Community policing is based on the principle of co-ordination and consultation between the police and the policed, to provide intelligence, guide security agendas and solutions and supplement police patrols (Ruteere and Pommerolle, 2003). There has been much scepticism of community policing programmes as Western imposed and ineffective (Brogden, 2004), but there have been some successful partnerships between the police and the community (e.g. Uganda; Baker, 2005). The alienation felt by many local communities has inevitably starved the police in the past of information necessary to develop accurate criminal intelligence and denied them the civil cooperation needed to prevent and detect crime. And so their ineffectiveness is perpetuated.

State facilitation does not stop at what is legal. It may well be in the interest of the authorities to allow smuggling and trade in illicit goods to flourish because of the rents they can take from it. Roitman (2004:134–36) records that both the Nigerien and Chadian armies at times provide armed guards for the transport of illegal goods to border markets to ensure they are not waylaid by bandits or customs guards operating illegal road blocks.

Whatever characteristics apply to the state, it invariably constitutes a set of agencies with which other authorisers and providers of policing have to negotiate continually through formal or informal channels.

The constraint of internal conflict

Rebellion in Africa in the last twenty years has frequently had its roots in resistance to authoritarian regimes with failing economies and police forces that have used intimidation to maintain regime control and suppress opponents. What elites do, especially how they exercise state power and how they engage political opponents, conditions what non-elites consider permissible. The men of violence that elites once relied on to intimidate and eliminate their opponents came to realise that 'they can use the violence they produce not only to prop up their patrons but to usurp them, not only to eliminate opponents but to extort society, and not only to reproduce lumpen penury but to overcome it' (Kande, 1999:361). So they resorted to armed rebellion in Liberia, Ethiopia, Mozambique, Guinea Bissau, Angola, DRC, Congo Brazzaville, South Africa, Somalia, Sierra Leone, Uganda, Rwanda, Burundi, Nigeria, Chad and Niger.

The conflicts inevitably destroyed what rule of law existed. As they developed, regimes and rebels resorted more and more to financing their military efforts from the proceeds of organised crime (for diamond smuggling in Sierra Leone see, Report of the Panel of Experts, 2000; for natural resource exploitation in DRC see, Report of the Panel of Experts, 2002). The pre-existing state security and legal systems in the war zones disintegrated, police and court buildings were destroyed along with equipment, records, archives and law books. In addition, police, judges, prosecutors, lawyers, and many support staff fled or were killed.

The withdrawal of the state from conflict zones produces a public order vacuum that, if it is not filled by rebel-initiated policing, as with the NRA in Uganda, encourages organised crime. Aided also by the collapse of formal economies and unmet demand, criminal groups profit from illicit opportunities and consolidate power. During conflict there have been cases of rebel groups, the state military and government leaderships engaging in criminal enterprises, accruing wealth from trafficking and smuggling. Sometimes the proceeds finance military spending. In Côte d'Ivoire, according to the International Crisis Group: 'Today's political actors have found that war serves as an excellent means of enrichment, and they may be ill-served by the restoration of peace and security' (ICG, 2004). Large amounts of money are skimmed from the cocoa crop; in the north rebels monopolise the trade in cotton and weapons, and levy informal taxes; in the south, businessmen close to the government have their interests protected by it and security forces profit from illegal roadblocks.

The disruptive nature of rebellions and the violence that often accompanies them weakens old forms of social organisation, such as faith groups, community groups and the extended family. These no longer provide an attractive option for increasingly militarised and vocal sectors of the society such as the youth. The lack of effective state law enforcement on the ground, together with the breakdown of social and state controls, further stimulates the growth of crime. Communities, therefore, come under threat from armed rebels/criminals or even state security agencies (or state sponsored militias/vigilantes). People, community leaders, rebel/criminal groups and even governments have been forced to rely on local militias, civil defence forces or other ordering groups to provide protection of their interests, often through violent means. In other words, customary forms of internal social cohesion may be replaced by – or mutate into – a different set of organising principles, including militias, vigilantes, street gangs and criminal organisations. Faced with violence from the state police and state sponsored vigilantes, as well as from organised crime, South African townships under apartheid responded. Alternative forms of community cohesion and social control arose, such as the street committees and associated people's courts. In the process a tradition established itself of self-reliance and suspicion of state (and by association, chiefdom) structures. Rebel groups, too, establish policing systems in areas which they control, either their own as the NRA of Uganda; or, as the Renamo rebels of Mozambique, exercising informal control through a rudimentary form of civil administration and customary courts, with extensive use of customary authorities as judges.

Even after there has been a settlement of the conflict, public disorder, crime, and violence frequently constitute a major problem. Organised criminal activity thrives in the absence of political authority left by a failed or toppled regime, or as yet unfilled by the new regime. In some cases these informal power holders use their power and profits to undermine the legitimate government; in other cases, they eventually become part of the legitimate government through their associations with corrupt politicians (or directly in the case of Sierra Leonean rebel leader Foday Sankoh, who became Vice-President and responsible for the diamond industry!). A whole range of actors may emerge to fill the post-conflict power vacuum, claiming authority based on customary allegiances, such as ethnicity or religion and backed by armed groups formed during the conflict (e.g. the militias of DRC, Sierra Leone and Liberia). Whether they are perceived as criminal organisations or self-defence anti-criminal organisations, they are likely to act with impunity whilst the state struggles to establish a semblance of national policing and the rule of law.

Post-conflict situations present special policing problems at a time when the state police are invariably very weak in manpower and resources to handle them, and may be caught up in the disrupting processes of deactivation (for human rights abuses and the like) and reconstruction themselves. The police may be so weak that the government is forced to look to short-term help from self-defence groups comprising voluntary youths, as CAR did in its capital Bangui, the capital, after the conflict of 2002–04. The displacement of large numbers of people both within and across borders is a common aspect of conflict, but their resettlement, can become a con-flictual issue when it comes to land use and ownership. Another challenge to policing is the disarmament, demobilisation and reintegration of rebel forces and militias. They are likely to return to a life of violence if they find no legitimate livelihood. There is a need, therefore, for programmes to ensure that demobilised soldiers (and in Liberia's case, 3,855 deactivated internal security agency personnel) have opportunities for gainful employment. Failure to reintegrate IDPs and ex-combatants may lead to criminal activity by them and encourage local policing 'solutions'.

Where rebellion has had an ethnic base, the legacy can be one of ethnic tension or hostility. Ethnic groups that supported the authoritarian state or rebels who engaged in atrocities may be ostracised or discriminated against (some say this is true of the Hutu under the current regime in Rwanda). Discrimination may also apply to social class. Following Uganda's civil war, chiefs discredited by their compliance with Presidents Amin and Obote were stripped of their judicial powers. These were handed to the village and parish Resistance Councils that had first been introduced into the liberated territory during the progress of the civil war (Baker, 2004b).

Against a background of escalating crime, the call for law and order is paramount. 'The establishment of public order and the rule of law is the missing priority in establishing post-conflict security and initiating reconstruction' (Woodrow Wilson, 2003). Yet there are a multitude of reasons why the post-conflict state is slow in establishing an effective national police force. In most countries emerging from a long history of internal conflict, internal security has, as a rule, been transferred to the armed forces. When, therefore, the reconstruction of the police force includes integrating these military (or militarised police) elements and rebel fighters, it requires extensive vetting of candidates to remove the worst human rights offenders. This in the case of Liberia removed most of their senior and most experienced personnel. In addition, training programmes have to overcome casual attitudes to human rights developed during the course of the violent conflict; to instil attitudes of political neutrality for the police force; and to develop skills in civilian methods of controlling demonstrations. The success of the training of the new force will determine the quality of the state policing that follows for the next generation.

The impact of rebellion on policing lasts long after the direct fighting has ceased. Trust, predictability, and information suffer when violence is high, which is likely to prove harmful to security. So is the banality of violence. 'What is feared may be true – is that violence has become a norm within social and political behaviour, not an option and a last resort; that violence may now have become an end in itself, rather than an instrumental device; and that violence and warfare have become self-reproducing' (Allen, 1999:368–69).

Ten years after the end of apartheid in South Africa, street committees are still widely distributed in the townships, though they have now lost much of their support, whilst the courts no longer exist. A minority, however, persist in their vigilante style approach from a mixture of anti-state suspicion and commercial self-interest. More positively, nearly 20 years after Uganda's rebels established resistance councils in villages, they still continue to provide the basic system of ordering and policing at the local level, though now under the auspices of the state.

How governments establish stability and law and order across the country and secure their borders in the post-conflict period, will determine the degree to which alternative security systems will remain or emerge. Failure may cause armed groups to remain mobilised, private citizens to keep their weapons, and ex-combatants to become easy recruits for criminal groups and militias. Looting, petty and opportunistic crime and revenge killings may also take place to varying degrees. But where governments have successfully established local security this chokes off alternative informal policing.

The constraint of development programmes

A large number of development organisations, international and national, are increasingly engaged in policing and ordering. With their financial muscle and pool of expertise they are in a strong position to influence the direction of government policy and to take initiatives themselves. Their action, therefore, can significantly shape the policing environment. In the past their focus has been mainly on the state system of policing, but increasingly they have shown interest in maximising the strengths of informal non-state policing, whether customary or based on new reconciliation forums.

Programmes initiated by international organisations and donor governments, may undertake reform of the entire justice and security sectors in a country (Rauch and van der Spuy, 2006). Some Security Sector Reform (SSR) is still state focussed and ignores the customary and even commercial elements of the sector (e.g. UNMIL in Liberia). Others, such as the UK's Department for International Development (DFID), are more innovative. Their Malawi Access to Safety, Security and Justice (DFID-MaSSAJ) addresses all aspects of the safety, security and justice system through a single co-ordinated programme. Its purpose is to improve safety of the person, security of property, and access to justice, particularly for the poor and vulnerable. The goal is improved quality and accessibility of primary justice services, by undertaking to change, *inter alia*, customary values concerning gender discrimination, domestic violence and corporal punishment.

Interventions that select suitable customary systems and informal ways of settling disputes and give training to paralegals and customary authorities, clearly alter the dynamics of local policing. As Nyamu-Musembi (2003) argues, even using as an entry point those 'caretakers' of the customary institutions that already recognise the need for change is problematic, given the resistance that may be found from many others. Training by large-scale programmes of customary leaders and civic groups in human rights and legal standards, not only has important cultural consequences, but is likely to preserve these customary systems in rural Africa. The same outcome is to be expected if those calling for the full harmonisation of customary law and liberal constitutions have their way.

There will also be significant consequences following from the current popularity among donors of viewing security holistically and as an effective entry-point to development projects. This approach conceptualises security problems more broadly than just the concern of state policing. It recognises that a large array of government and non-government agencies are concerned with security and have a role to play in designing and delivering safer communities. If this development approach becomes popular, then it will mark the first serious recognition of the potential contribution of non-state policing by government agencies and of the need for all such agencies to work together using their core strength.

There is evidence that on an *ad hoc* scale others concerned with development are experimenting with partnerships between state and non-state policing. In Mzuzu, Malawi, the local government has attached community-workers (ndunas) to local government elected councillors. Their role is 'to keep their ear to the ground' as an early warning system about the functioning of the local authority. When births and deaths occur they should alert their councillor, and when urban facilities are broken, or when people erect illegal structures on their properties, the ndunas are dispatched to negotiate a solution to the problem. It has parallels with the peacekeepers of South Africa who are paid a small monthly sum to assist the community in mediating domestic conflict, reporting crime to the police, conducting foot patrols, and teaching schoolchildren on domestic/sexual abuse and crime prevention. Such a policy environment at the local or national level, where state and non-state policing act as partners, would have widespread repercussions on policing.

Other NGOs and CBOs (Community Based Organisations) are shifting their focus from advocacy and guidance in negotiating the formal court system, to training paralegals, civic education to raise awareness on primary justice issues, and equipping decision-makers in community-based justice forums. Through the training and employment of 'advice officers', people can be helped to access common law courts and customary dispute resolution mechanisms. The NGOs and CBOs also advocate that customary law should be brought into conformity with international and constitutional human rights standards.

Another area of involvement by NGOs has been in peace committees or new reconciliation forums, found in South Africa and Sierra Leone. In South Africa it is known as the Zwelethemba Model of dispute resolution, named after Zwelethemba, a residential suburb of Worcester, a town north of Cape Town. The model promotes and facilitates the resolution of disputes within very poor communities through the mobilisation of local capacity and knowledge. As a result of the Community Peace Programme it has been introduced into a number of other South African townships.

Inevitably much of the development finance, values and training agenda, together with the personnel who administer these programmes, originate outside of Africa. Yet the impact of foreign assistance on the development of local systems of criminal justice is little understood. Some fear that extensive foreign training programmes might undermine the development of innovative local responses to crime problems, and impose solutions fashioned in, and therefore more applicable to, Western societies. Certainly there is often an explicit attempt to overturn certain contemporary values as regards policing. Most Western-led development activities have sought to broaden participation in non-state policing and ordering systems to include women and youth. Opposing these Western values may be traditions of rapid justice or new ideologies of social order originating from elsewhere in the developing world, such as more fundamentalist interpretations of Islam concerning the definition of crime, the role of women, and appropriate forms of punishment. How these ideological battles play out will be crucial in determining the forms of non-state policing that prevail.

These 'modernising' programmes raise more than just the ownership of the underlying values. Nyamu-Musembi believes that many of the positive innovations have been made possible by crises (such as armed conflict) and that this context makes it easier for people to accept them as crisis responses. However, he asks what will happen after the crisis has subsided. For instance, will the women's role continue to be accepted in intervention in ordinary day-to-day informal justice delivery? With concern he notes that when conflict in Laikipia, Kenya, diminished, the peace elders undertook land and family disputes that were not necessarily related to the armed conflict (Nyamu-Musembi, 2003:25).

This activity on the part of donors and NGOs outside state policing is still small, but it is beginning to open new avenues of policing and to reinterpret older processes in a way that can only continue the process of fragmentation.

The constraint of commercial opportunities

Where there are valuable fixed assets or lucrative businesses (legal or illegal) to be defended, policing will arise, whether provided by the asset owners or offered by formal and informal commercial security groups, protection racket mafias, or state policing operating on a formal or informal basis. An obvious example is the strict policing of large mines and plantations by company police. Thus the De Beers company town of Kleinzee in Namibia is, to all intents and purposes, cut off from the outside world. Workers are under constant and close scrutiny to prevent the smuggling of diamonds (Carstens, 2001). When the mines are owned by the state, they may seek security from commercial firms and make the payment in the form of a share of the assets themselves. During Sierra Leone's civil war this required commercial military force and it has been alleged that Executive Outcomes accepted mining rights in Sierra Leone as part of their remuneration for removing the rebel groups from their control of the mining areas (Zarate, 1998; Brooks, 2000). Since the war, the company has continued in mining through its links with Diamond Works Inc and maintains site security of government diamond mines through another linked company, Lifeguard. Or again a number of Zimbabwean state-run industries and businessmen well connected with ZANU-PF secured lucrative deals in the DRC as 'payment' for their protection of the regime and resources of President Kabila Snr. (Baker, 2000). Payment may also take the form of goods seized, as with both bandits and customs officers on the Chad/Cameroon border (Roitman, 2004).

Other resources apart from minerals include timber, hence the forest guards of Kenya, authorised by the Forest Department. The forest guards protect the 20 gazetted forest reserves of Mau from gangs of armed illegal loggers who often attack them violently. Usually, a forest guard operates alone and is expected to 'effectively' police some 600 hectares of forest.

Despite the danger, most guards policing the Mau forests are neither armed nor equipped with communication equipment.[2]

Another industry that has required extensive security in Africa is the development industry. Many of the commercial security companies profit from providing escort facilities and site protection for NGOs and international government organisations.

Even the tourist industry is now recognised as too economically important to be left to the policing of general duty police. Western visitors are deemed to require higher standards of policing than is available to the local population, to be more at risk because of the wealth they carry and to be potential sources of political dissent if allowed too much access. As a result The Gambia, whose economy is heavily dependent on tourism, formed in 2003 a Tourism Security Unit of the Gambia National Guards.

The state as well as commercial enterprises are concerned to preserve revenue sources. Rarely are the general duty police suitable for this task, hence the proliferation of special units of the state police or specialised commercial security firms. As Garland has noted: once security ceases to be guaranteed to all citizens by a sovereign state, it tends to become a commodity which like any other is distributed by market forces rather than according to need (Garland, 1996:463).

Conclusion

The current condition of the state, the presence or absence of internal conflict, the nature of the development programmes and the type of commercial opportunities, together constitute the social structures that constrain the choices of individual authorisers and providers of policing. They are the predictable elements that the unpredictable elements are filtered through. It is this combination of contrasting individuals working within diverse structures that produces the complex and overlapping array of policing that I call multi-choice policing.

---

2. *The East African*, Nairobi, August 18, 2003.

— CHAPTER 9 —

The Social and Political Implications

The institution of the 'police' is not in itself a public good – rather, the outcome of security is. (Shearing and Kempa, 2000)

The governance of security is both an indicator of the quality of political life and a major determinant of it. (Bayley and Shearing, 2001)

In this concluding chapter I examine the social and political implications of the presence of multi-choice policing in Africa. What does this fragmentation and overlapping pattern of public and private policing mean for society and government? First I look at its social implications. Who gains and loses in terms of public safety as a result of multi-choice policing? Are the human rights of individuals more at risk when policing is provided by some groups rather than others?

The obvious social gain of there being a choice of policing, besides that of the state police, is that it provides a broad social safety net when states lack the capacity (or will) to keep the social contract. This need not be threatening. It can be as much complementary to state services as competitive. In addition, there are gains that can be made at the community level in terms of providing locally sensitive governance. Community governance of policing in some circumstances can deepen democracy. Members of community controlled policing groups have access to communal decision-making processes, the outcomes of which have a direct bearing on both the security they receive and the method of their provision. 'In the abstract, markets for goods can be seen as a good thing because they promote active citizenship and create choices, as long as the goods provided do not have harmful effects on consumers and others' (Shearing and Wood, 2003). However, as against these positive gains, there are a number of serious negative implications, which I consider in the following sections.

Unequal provision

When policing is the monopoly of the state, the theory is that it is based upon the promise of universal protection. The corollary of this is the fundamental presumption that those who do not violate state law have the rightful expectation of enjoying equal liberty without interference. However, once policing is undertaken by non-universalistic providers, inequality becomes an issue. Their 'governance deficits' have been identified as three-fold: deficits of community self-direction (inequities in the determination of, and access to, common goods), deficits of community capital (inequitable access to economic and social capital to support community governance), and deficits of regulation (the absence of community-based mechanisms of regulation) (Shearing and Wood, 2003). Neither the market nor the voluntary sector can guarantee that there is equal provision and access.

Policing providers work to promote their authorisers sometimes narrowly private interests, but more often common interests (such as the interests of a neighbourhood or a business community). Sometimes these common interests overlap with public interests, so that the goods they pursue are compatible with public goods. At other times, certain common interests may not be compatible with other common interests. For example, the interests of business may conflict with those of ethnic minorities, the unemployed, homeless and youth. They may even be in conflict with the pursuit of public goods, as when in-house private security fails to report employees' theft to the police so as to avoid adverse publicity. Access is another area where common interests are not necessarily public interests. It depends on local initiative and how non-discriminatory their practice is. This is true for community self-help groups as well as business. Neither commercial nor community policing can guarantee equality; although it should be remembered that state policing in Africa has never been equal across the rural/urban divide, class boundaries or gender divide (Clapham, 1999).

In cases where non-state policing undertakes adjudication, such as customary courts, religious courts, community courts and dispute resolution forums, there are inevitably concerns about standards of investigation, scrutiny of evidence, discrimination against women and minorities, the sanctions available and a consistency of treatment for citizens (Brogden and Shearing, 1993:162–63). Not that state courts have escaped bribery, prejudice and carelessness. Nevertheless, as choice in policing expands, it is likely that the gap will widen between those who can afford a high quality of protection and those who have not got the same resources; and between those in urban centres and those in rural areas. The so-called 'commodification of security' (Loader, 1999) allows those with buying power to determine individual and common interests and to exercise choice in the manner in which these interests are secured.

Intolerance of 'outsiders'

Once policing is diffused across many agencies, universalism is replaced by particularism: security is only offered to the members/clients of the policing organisation and, by definition, 'outsiders' are ineligible. Indeed, their very 'outsiderness' may be a cause of suspicion and exclusion in the name of protecting the group. Communities have long defended themselves by a cultivated wariness of the stranger. In some security circles risk assessment techniques are used to identify, classify and manage groups categorised according to levels of 'dangerousness'. This approach shifts the focus from the individual offender, to targeting 'suspect' populations, based upon risk assessments of their likelihood of offending in particular circumstances or when exposed to certain categories of opportunity (Feeley and Simon, 1992; Zedner, 2003).

In Africa the risk assessment techniques may be missing, but 'common sense' calculations may mean that 'no-go areas' keep the state police, opposition political groups and 'undesirables' from neighbourhoods and villages. In developed countries, of course, the deterrent costs can be set so high as to inhibit deviant behaviour. In Africa such deterrence is rarely sufficient. The stigmatised in the poorer context have little to lose or at least dare not starve for want of trying to steal bread. Communities, therefore, resort to labelling and the exclusion of the 'unwanted'. Policing organisations frequently denigrate and criminalize whole social groups. Membership of the outsider group alone then becomes sufficient to warrant discrimination and the assumption of guilt, along with the justification of heavy-handed treatment. As a result there is a vicious cycle of deviance amplification and the promotion of social antagonism. People are divided by affiliations of age group, race, ethnicity, religion, language and class, irrespective of actual conduct. And it is around these affiliations that victim groups and law and order groups are polarised (Shearing and Stenning, 1981; Jones and Newburn, 1999).

In the case of East African pastoralist societies, the conflict has been ethnicised. Hence discrimination and violence is used against civilians for no other reason than their ethnic identity. Cattle raiding is perceived in terms of the ethnic antagonism, whether it is Karamojong against the

Pokot or the like. Elsewhere there are more localised versions of the same negative labelling. The 'hoodlums' dens' of Anambra state, Nigeria, are the two particular settlements, Umuleri and Umuoba Anam (Baker, 2002c). Seeing that both communities are deemed 'evil', they forfeit their civil rights and their members are told to leave the towns and go back to their villages. In South Africa 'undesirables' (whether non-residents or drug dealers) are kept away from the township streets that vigilantes control by force. In wealthy city suburbs physical barriers patrolled by guards are used to establish 'gated communities'. These are areas fenced or walled off from their surroundings, either prohibiting or controlling access to these areas by means of gates or booms. They are often residential areas with restricted access so that normal public spaces are privatised or use is restricted. However, they may also control access to office parks, shopping malls and recreational centres. There are an increasing number of gated communities in Nigeria, Kenya and South Africa (Landman, 2003).

Security particularism is thus often associated with the insulation of sections of society. With it goes the loss of dialogue across political, class, and racial divides. Security fragmentation denies the dialogue, inclusiveness and sense of a common identity, which must be the foundation for democracy.

Endorsement of violence

Policing in Africa too often uses violence or the threat of violence and for many non-state organisations that means with only minimum constraints and supervision. Such policing assumes the powers of state police, prosecutor and judge and disregards the presumption of innocence. The common practice is that once a suspect is identified and apprehended, he/she is asked to prove his/her innocence, often after having been subjected to torture. Violence is intended to serve as a warning and as a punishment. It is premised on instant, retributive justice, rather than corrective justice. Violence is commonly regarded as a legitimate way in which to solve problems, so that the victim of crime seeks revenge (Harris, 2001b).

The instruments of violence, especially knives and firearms, are widely owned in Africa for defence and assault. Despite firearms being illegal in many countries, it is very easy to obtain both guns and gun licences. It is within this weapon-carrying culture that policing operates. Not surprisingly, policing authorisers commonly allow their agents to carry instruments of coercion, whether chemical sprays, handcuffs, batons and licensed pistols in the case of commercial security firms; or a variety of weapons in the case of informal non-state policing. Even among the most 'responsible' groups the training is minimal and the guidelines for use are basic. At the other end of the spectrum, there are very few restraints at all.

There is also a tendency to mete out violence indiscriminately to communities irrespective of individual guilt. Thus once a crime is identified as originating from a particular community, policing agencies may feel justified in threatening or carrying out violence on the whole community, as in the case of anti-cattle rustling vigilantes against 'guilty' villages. This communal punishment is often claimed to be consistent with customary practice.

When policing engages in illegal and unjust violence, it provokes violent responses in self-defence and retaliation. Criminal violence threatens and angers people: threatened they try to defend themselves; angered they want to retaliate (Gurr, 1970:232). Each injury or death in East Africa at the hands of cattle vigilantes has provoked further raids. Vigilante violence may deter armed robbery in the short period of its existence, but the evidence suggests that criminals are prepared to return, intent on meeting violence with violence. A society with a wide and widening range of policing means, in part, the carrying of instruments of coercion by a larger number of minimally supervised policing agencies. It is therefore the harder to control their responsible use.

Inadequate accountability

The issue of accountability only multiplies when a wide variety of policing agencies exist. Accountability raises a series of questions: Do the various policing agencies have standards of conduct that they adhere to; are there records that can be examined; to whom are the agencies answerable for such adherence; are those served by these agencies familiar with those standards so that they can call for compliance? Is there community consultation to determine policing goals and objectives? And beyond the local community, are policing agencies accountable for actions (such as the use or threat of force) that impinge directly on public interest objectives such as human rights and rights to privacy?

Formal accountability is more likely with state policing, although it is even more likely to be accountability upward (to the Inspector General or Minister of Interior and Parliament) than accountability downward (to citizens). Likewise, the keeping of detailed records by such bodies, despite legal requirements, varies widely. Few state approved policing systems have structures such as Uganda's LCs, where councillors who exercise policing and judicial roles are elected every 5 years. And even this does not address on-going accountability for their actions. With respect to NGO-sponsored policing the question arises as to whether those in authority are accountable to the NGO (and perhaps its foreign parent organisation) from whom the resources come, or to the communities the bodies serve.

The nature of community policing agencies makes it difficult to put in place accountability mechanisms. At first glance the desire of citizens to engage in policing reflects their desire to acquire greater control over their circumstances. The initial motive may have been to enhance the local accountability of policing through a greater level of local control, but negotiating loyalties to self-interest, family community, state laws and religious/ethnic identities, is fraught with difficulties. In practice, local policing arrangements often come about on an *ad hoc* basis, without the initial approval or leadership of the community. Host neighbourhoods may even be unaware of the nature and extent of community policing activities.

The fact that such policing is often imposed on residents and only gains respect and legitimacy from them later, is partly due to their style of leadership. Local policing groups may well attract those who have a prior interest in security and who are assertive by nature. Such groups may lack transparent decision-making and the leadership may not be elected or removable. Such a situation curtails complaints by the users over practice.

Where policing groups expect all community adults to participate in the patrols, this provides both a broad base and some level of consent if not accountability. In the case of the Nairobi community policing, those who fail to commit to the watch, or who disappoint in their responsibilities toward the watch (for example, paying dues, attending meetings or feeding the dogs) are censured or even ostracised by the watch members. Other community policing groups, to ensure participation, bring those arrested before an assembly of the whole community. Whatever the standards of investigation and apprehension, at least the whole community participates in the judging and sentencing processes.

It is true that some sectors of the public are prepared, for a greater sense of neighbourhood security, to sacrifice due process and the rights of the accused (including the wrongfully accused). Accountability is taken to be at the expense of their effectiveness. Put differently, faced with a choice between safeguarding the trappings of democracy and protection of family, home and property, many favour the latter. This is not ideal in a democratic state, yet with states struggling to make their own police organisation accountable downwards as well as upwards, it seems a tall order to imagine they can ensure the compliance of a multitude of policing organisations. Even when legislation is passed, there is still the problem of enforcement.

Facilitation of illegal activity

Ironically more policing groups may mean more crime. Armed policing groups that are unaccountable can easily switch from law enforcement to law breaking, confident that they are not subject to state law and can intimidate would-be informers. The material rewards associated with anti-crime groups, whether in the form of 'service fees' charged by the police agents, 'payments' to kangaroo courts, or 'compensation' to the 'plaintiff' in the form of confiscated property, 'suggest motives beyond the pursuit of crime-fighting' (Harris, 2001b). This is 'crime prevention' for criminal gain.

An overview made by the South African Police Service of 267 cases brought against members of Mapogo a Mathamaga between 1996 and mid-2000, revealed charges that include murder, assault, robbery, stock theft, kidnapping, housebreaking and theft, and arson. The pursuit of criminals and rebels can, therefore, provide a cover for personal revenge, sexual abuse and economic exploitation.

In East Africa there is little difference between criminal cattle raiders and policing vigilantes – the two roles being almost inter-changeable. In Lesotho some chiefs are suspected of working with the local police in a racket that steals cattle so as to be involved in their recovery at a price. Further, the gap is small between legitimate protection and protection racket, as was demonstrated by the Bakassi Boys in Nigeria. The possession of weapons for crime prevention provides a temptation both to state and non-state policing agents to use them for crime participation. The Human Rights Committee of South Africa claims that crime statistics for 1997 indicate that police officers are 'almost three times more likely to be involved in criminal activities than members of the general public'.[1]

Leaders of police groups may have the power over life and death; over the right to stay in a community or to be expelled; and to determine guilt or innocence. The fact that considerable local power resides in local policing no matter who authorises it, means that the resident who wishes to resist or challenge their actions has to think very carefully about the social

---

1. *Mail & Guardian*, 18 August, 2000.

consequences for the future allocation of resources (e.g. access to land, development projects and food aid) or exposure to violence.

A non-state policing group that takes a dislike to a person can use its powers to their disadvantage. Yet such power may be in the hands of an unelected person; possibly a power-seeking individual; or worse, in the hands of a person prone to violence. A report on vigilante-style violence at the Amplats Platinum Mines in South Africa, revealed that many of the central figures had a history of violent actions within the area. These actions included murder, attempted murder, and intimidation. Many also held key positions within political organisations and the mining structures (Network of Independent Monitors, 1997, quoted in Harris, 2001b). It seems that violent history, powerful positions and individual personality traits go a long way to explaining specific manifestations of vigilantism at local and regional levels. If the fragmentation of policing gives opportunity to such individuals to exert an influence over local communities it must be a backward step.

Having looked at the social implications of multi-choice policing, I now look at the political ones. What does multi-choice policing mean for governments? What are the political implications? What opportunities and what challenges does it present to them? What controls and mechanisms of accountability and public-private relationships are necessary to maximise the benefits and minimise the dangers?

The impossibility of state monopoly

The prolonged existence of multi-choice policing only confirms how fragile and incomplete the sovereignty of the state is. States are not in a position to establish a monopoly on policing for their territorial sovereignty is too incomplete, too contested, too fictional. Yet they continue to make grand exclusive claims. The Nigerian Constitution asserts: 'There shall be a police force for Nigeria, which shall be known as the Nigeria Police Force, and … no other police force shall be established for the Federation or any part thereof'. Sierra Leone's 1991 constitution optimistically assures that, 'the security, peace and welfare of the people of Sierra Leone shall be the primary purpose and responsibility of Government, and to this end it shall be the duty of the Armed Forces, the Police, Public Officers and all security agents to protect and safeguard the people of Sierra Leone'.

The Western model of policing has proved unattainable in Africa. It has run aground for two reasons, one practical and one normative. The practical issue is that, for all the fine words of constitutions asserting the right to freedom and security of person, states are not in a financial position to provide these through the sole use of their own police forces. Even governments of the wealthiest economies now admit that it is beyond them. 'Having taken over social control functions and responsibilities which once belonged to the institutions of the community, the state is now faced with its own inability to deliver the expected levels of control of criminal conduct' (Garland, 1996:449). Given the additional limitations on African state budgets and the widespread conflict and social upheaval on the continent, the provision of exclusive policing is an even more unlikely proposition.

The other reason why the Western system of policing has failed in Africa is normative. Multi-state policing is not only about a response to the inadequacy of the quality and strength of the state police. It also highlights different normative modes of ordering. The rise of legal positivism in the nineteenth century shifted the source of law away from local, moral/social norms to legislation. Colonialism transplanted foreign legal cultures alien to many local customs and indigenous legal systems. Subsequently Western standards have been adopted by African states. Yet despite these trends many communities are still committed to a self-definition of acceptable order. Indeed, 'many South African communities view control over the definition of local ordering as a gain of the [anti-apartheid] struggle which they are reluctant to relinquish' (Nina and Schwikkard, 1996:71).

Many new laws have adopted an individual-rights approach and falsely assumed a community of nuclear families. In Ethiopia, imposing a rights-based value system on people applying different customary rules to govern personal relationships and property meant that the more egalitarian principles of the new Civil Code never took root. Resistance, however, should not be interpreted as a rejection of the rule of law. This is to assume that the rule of the law means the upholding of state norms only. Yet as Woodman observes:

> The rule of law cannot be limited to the rule of state law. If the law of a state is largely disregarded because subjects consider it to be an alien element which enjoins them to flout their own sense of right, but general rules expressed in a customary law are largely observed, the conditions for the rule of law would appear to be present (Woodman, 1996:4, 6).

Ironically, as has been pointed out, non-state policing has always been present in the West and the idea of a state policing monopoly never existed there, but was part of the myth that states were keen to perpetuate to bolster their argument that they were the supreme authority in any society. Since the illusion is now almost universally recognised for what it is, the first practical step for all African states would be to concede their own failure to secure a monopoly.

Partnership opportunities

Given that multi-choice policing is already the established pattern, a further question is to ask what contribution can multiple authorisers and providers of policing make to both the protection of person and property, and to restorative and punitive responses to abuses? Governments have much more to gain from acknowledging the potential of multi-choice policing and incorporating it into an integrated internal security policy, than in suppressing it.

The partnership, however, has to be thought through beforehand. Investing in reform of non-formal systems should not be seen simply as a 'low-cost' substitute for making state policing accessible and effective. Indeed, as Zedner notes, the greater the number of policing agencies, the more suspects are trawled into the criminal justice net (Zedner, 2003). Non-state policing may significantly extend surveillance and prevention, but much of it still relies upon state police back-up to detain, investigate, and prosecute suspects, and to supervise their licensing and inspection. In other words, non-state policing does not reduce state duties in the security sector.

Multi-choice policing means overlapping policing; overlapping in territory and in service. These relationships must be handled with care, for whilst they offer potential for co-operation, they can also become sites of unproductive rivalry or conflict. Rivalry, whether between state agencies, state and non-state agencies, or non-state and non-state agencies, inhibits exchange of information and crucial intelligence never reaches those who could use it. Co-operation, on the other hand, can enhance effectiveness, as the resources and specialist skills of one agency are drawn upon by another. The challenge for a society faced with multi-choice policing is, through the state or some other authority, to maximise the co-ordination of practices, the harmony of standards, the free exchange of information and joint operations. Neither criminal elements nor self-regarding political actors must be allowed the opportunity to exploit inter-agency rivalry or lack of communication.

Partnership certainly offers extended service but it comes at a cost in terms of demands on co-ordination and supervision. If states are not willing to pay that cost they will reap the consequences of rivalry and futile duplication.

Oversight requirements

By its diverse nature, multi-choice policing suggests the need for some kind of single supervisory body and national policy to make the most of it strengths. This is a role that the state is in a strong position to fulfil, contrary to what is claimed by those who deny the state has any role to play in the provision of policing (Rothbard, 1978). Some would go so far as to say that *only* the state can provide sole supervision:

> The state (alone) possesses the knowledge and expertise required both to 'steer' the delivery of services among diverse policing forms, to co-ordinate the relationship of policing agencies to other government authorities, and to ensure that the increasingly complex institutional pattern of policing does not present a closed and self-corroborating bureaucratic system, opaque and unresponsive to its wider public environment. It exhibits, in particular, the capacity to bring reflexive coherence and forms of democratic accountability to the inter-organizational networks and multi-level political configurations with which the police are now situated, and represents as such a prerequisite of equitable and effective policing (Loader and Walker, 2001:27).

These words, written for a Western audience, may sound too optimistic when applied to the African state, but they could be argued as an ideal to aim for.

Governments are confronted with the fact that in the new social conditions of the 21st century, policing is much more complex and dynamic than before. Managing it will take high levels of co-ordination and innovative relationships between the many authorisers and providers and must be based on sector-wide research audits and strategic planning. Coordination means it can no longer be sufficient to undertake Security Sector Reform without looking beyond state agencies, or to have human rights training just for the police; or Security Boards that only cover commercial private providers; or judicial legislation that does not come to terms with alternative justice systems such as customary courts and NGO dispute resolution forums. In societies with multi-choice policing there is much to be said for a broad, integrated conception of state-regulated policing which emphasises an accountable government in the delivery of equitable internal security. This is not to imply that it is only at the national level that oversight must be undertaken. Multi-choice policing is typically about local policing, therefore local government should take a proactive role, supplementing the role of the state in 'coordinating the fight against violence, seeking long-term solutions and at the same time addressing immediate needs' (Kisia, 2004:4).

Beyond supervision, there is the need to consider the future in terms of national internal security policy. African states must face the fact that there is going to be an exponential increase in the demand for policing services in the next 20 years. Increased levels of schooling will leave people much more aware of their legal rights, of government performance and of international standards. Likewise, legal aid NGOs, community policing initiatives and media publicity are deepening not just understanding, but expectations. So too is the general democratic climate. This is the age of human rights, of possessions that are to be protected, and of professional standards that preclude corruption, incompetence and inefficiency. All these trends point in only one direction. People will want a higher quality of personal and property protection and a fuller sense of security than ever before. It may be that the array of policing agencies now emerging is the best hope of realising such expectations. But it should not happen by chance but by choice.

What would a policy based on the acceptance of multi-choice policing mean in practice? Below, four possible avenues, based on state policy options raised by the South African Law Commission's project team on non-state justice, (reported in Schärf, 2003) are explored.

Policy option of partnership

Policies of partnership, as indicated earlier, take multi-choice policing as an opportunity to extend order and security. The challenge is to work with a range of policing groups so that they perform a genuine service to society and do not become too independent and self-serving. The positive approach is captured well by Schärf:

> The celebration of the rich diversity of non-state justice systems should be the policy that is adopted and promoted, as long as they fall within constitutional limits. There might have to be some monitoring and training, which should be conducted in the spirit of positive development as opposed to curtailment and control (Schärf, 2003:38).

For many policy makers cooperation means a suitably vague 'community policing' that will 'bring the police closer to the people' since 'the police cannot win the war against crime alone'. This has been called by Shearing and Wood, 'the iconic responsibilization program'. That is, it is part of the responsibilization agenda, by which governments seek to harness civil and private activities so as to meet public interest objectives. Community policing, is thus, 'a state-led "co-production" initiative that, while involving "consultation" with citizens, retains the position of the police as the bastion of security expertise and know-how and as bearers of public interest concerns' (Shearing and Wood, 2003).

There can be no doubt that community policing has been popular with the public and politicians. In Malawi the number of district or sub-district level Community Policing Forums (CPFs) increased from 17 in 1999 to over 350 in 2000. In addition, thousands of Crime Prevention Committees and Panels at the village and group-village levels sprung up in 2000 to support the CPF (Wood, 2000). But what are their objectives? Four are normally given. First, mobilisation: to enrol the public as the unpaid informers and surveillance personnel of the state police. Second, improved trust: to remove the legacy of suspicion between police and some communities emanating from the past. Third, consultation: to bring together the police and citizens to agree on the security needs and on ways to meet them. Fourth, monitoring: to engage communities in the monitoring of police effectiveness and efficiency and in evaluating its service provision.

In practice, community policing is primarily seen as a policy of enhancing the state police only and remains 'police property' (Reiner, 2000), that is, a police-led and state-centred initiative against crime and disorder. This has led to frustrations on both sides (for the experience of Sierra Leone, see Baker, 2007b). Citizens expect to be included in police initiatives and to have some control over the setting of local security priorities. In the Western Cape of South Africa '60 per cent of the Crime Prevention Panels currently in place in the province were not engaged in problem identification or prioritisation; and 65 per cent were not engaged in problem-solving' (Altbeker, 1998:3). Yet for their part, the police forces have found the forums and negotiations too time-consuming and too threatening to their management and operational independence (for South Africa see Pelser, 1999; Shaw, 2002). Further, state police agencies in Africa are often reluctant to let civilians meddle in 'their' domain, or to closely scrutinise how the police agency operates.

More fundamentally, the very concept of 'community' is problematic. Stephen Friedman noted:

> In reality 'the community' is not a uniform, definable entity: communities are extremely divided with little commonalties in terms of needs and aspirations

... if one measure of the effectiveness of safety and security strategies is to be their acceptability among the 'community', the result could be approaches which are sensitive to the needs of particular interests, but not all or even most citizens (Friedman, quoted in Pelser 1999).

Community implies shared beliefs and values; direct, many-sided relationships between members; and reciprocity. But given Africa's frequently divided and fragmented societies, it is not certain whether such relationships exist. Yet, as Lyons points out, 'the logic of community policing assumes communities to be a form of association capable of informal social control'. It assumes that shared values can be used to regulate individual activities for the common good. In addition, there are issues as to whether all communities have the social capital to effectively undertake informal control.

Regarding policing partnership policies more generally, the first difficulty is determining which groups meet the basic requirements or at least have the potential to achieve such. Those policing groups who work within the law may be brought into some form of alliance with the state. In this vein the Mozambique Minister of the Interior called, in 2002, for private security companies to cooperate with the police, requesting security guards to act as police officers in the fight against crime and to share their vehicles in emergencies. Another approach is to prioritise partnership groups informed by what Nyamu-Musembi calls 'following the "paths" of the people themselves'. This will almost certainly place the priority on local delivery and possibly on local leadership such as village headmen and clans (Nyamu-Musembi, 2003:5). The danger of using the latter, however, is the appearance of supporting customary leaders when in much of Africa the restitution of customary structures of authority is still controversial.

Partnership policies not only have to tackle the issue of 'who' but of 'how'. There are many different ways in which policing groups can work together. There is the possibility of *open cooperation*. For instance, if a community dispute resolution organisation requires a responder to pay back money to the complainant, should or could the state's enforcement machinery be summoned to enforce the 'judgment'? A much tighter partnership is *incorporation*. An example would be the community/lay assessor system of having two community-members as lay assessors, as occurs in Zimbabwean and South African magistrates courts. They can familiarise the magistrates of the circumstances prevailing in, and peculiar to, that community and can overrule them on the facts, although the magistrate remains the authority on the law. Another form of partnership is *co-optation* by the state of 'approved' private initiatives. This has the advantage of bringing them operationally under the umbrella of the state police so that excesses can be more readily controlled and the activities can receive central or local government funding. Initially the Tanzanian state, for instance, was intensely wary of anti-rustling vigilantes ('sungusungu'). Its official line was to praise them for their initiative, whilst insisting that they hand over suspects to the police and leave the determination of guilt and punishment to the courts. In time, however, the Tanzania state saw the benefits of co-optation so as to neutralise their threat, and they were formalised in 1990 (Abrahams, 1987; Bukurura, 1994; Heald, 2006).

It takes more radical thinking to conceive of partnerships in which the state police would not have automatic claim to sovereignty. Policing could be opened up to autonomous non-state providers whose services would be coordinated with – but not subordinated to – those provided by state police. Specialised elements of commercial security might be granted limited legal power to supplement state police resources or the police could divest some of their services, such as traffic control, forensic laboratories and court transport.

Partnership with informal policing groups that do not always work within the law but are prone to use violence is much more problematic. In most cases, informal non-state policing would fall away if the safety threat were tackled successfully. South Africa and Zambia's approach to such groups has been to 'harness' them into a law-abiding path. The strategy requires establishing training, cooperation protocols with the police, and opening communication channels so that accountability to lawful working practices is assured. An alternative approach is to assist informal groups to transform into 'private security' companies, in which case they are required to conform to commercial law and the standards of commercial security professional bodies. This has been used in Cape Town.

The most difficult forms of vigilantes to 'transform' through partnership are those linked to chiefs and ethnic organisations or those that are ideologically driven, both of which can be violent. The best option may be some form of community policing in which co-operation with and accountability to both the police and local authority ensures that their actions remain largely within the law. Zambia has used registration with the police for urban neighbourhood watches as a means of control.

Establishing partnerships with customary leaders and customary law has its own particular problems. Seeing that most Africans have access only to customary courts to seek justice, a policing policy must be constructed within a comprehensive policy on customary leaders and customary law.

Some African countries, such as Zimbabwe, Malawi, Sierra Leone and Liberia, have made some attempt to establish a formal relationship between common law and customary law (Schärf, 1999). In those countries there is an appeal process whereby a case from a customary process can be taken to a state court. More commonly, customary law and liberal constitutions clash and the underlying conflicts need to be resolved by dialogue.

Since ideologically driven groups can become rapidly politicised, the state needs to engage with them as soon as they emerge. The South African government's attempt to co-opt PAGAD into a law-abiding partnership failed in part because, in Schärf's view, they focussed more on the violent symptoms of the problem, rather than at the drug dealing causes. In addition, the police raised expectations beyond their ability to deliver when they promised to investigate all 189 drug-dealers named by PAGAD. When it became apparent they could only mount four covert investigations, PAGAD began murdering drug-dealers. The police turned to prosecuting them, but this only provoked retaliation and an increasing politicisation of PAGAD by Islamists (Schärf, 2003:37–38). It was a salutary lesson in how not to handle problematic policing groups.

The policy option of regulation

Non-state policing is often not constituted in ways that further public interest objectives. Its agents often impinge directly on public interest objectives such as human rights and rights to privacy. These agents are primarily accountable to the auspices that pay them (Bayley and Shearing, 1996), with inadequate regulatory mechanisms in place to ensure that public interests are respected.

Beyond different degrees of alliance between state and non-state policing, governments may extend regulation to bring all policing and law and order systems under legislative control. That much non-state policing is illegal is because provision outside of the state and commercial sector is outlawed. States should explore new regulatory strategies. Accountability, for instance, can be required of all non-state policing using local oversight, legislation, licensing and ombudsmen (Sarre and Prenzler, 1999; Stenning, 2000; Nell and Williamson, 1993), or state codes of conduct. Compulsory registration of security service providers, however, has resource implications and may not be implemented thoroughly.

Currently, few African countries have specific legislation to control policing outside the commercial security sector. An exception is Tanzania where they regulate the arrest powers of self-policing groups. They also require them to work together with the state, so that suspects of crime are handed over to the Ward tribunal, and if it is a very serious crime, to the police for prosecution in the formal courts.

Even the commercial sector has only minimal control beyond being subject to general commercial laws. The tightest legislative control of the commercial security industry on the continent is in South Africa where, not co-incidentally, the commercial security industry is the most established. In South Africa, legislation, regulations and training specifications exercise control over large parts of the private security industry and its employees. Since 1987, the Security Officers' Board has exercised control over security personnel and from 2002 all private security businesses are required to register with the Board. Requirements for registration are strict: a person must be a citizen or permanent resident; be over 18 years of age; have complied with the relevant training requirements; and have no criminal record within the last 10 years. The legislation also makes it an offence to employ an unregistered person and company, meaning that the client can also be prosecuted. South Africa's 1998 Debt Collectors Act provides for the establishment of a Council for Debt Collectors that exercises control over the occupation of the debt collector.

Elsewhere in Africa regulation is basic. In Ghana the ease with which registration can be acquired from the Ministry of the Interior has led to concern. Some companies, exploiting the lack of law enforcement, do not in fact renew their licences annually. There is little supervision of training, with some companies offering their own schemes whilst others call in state police expertise. Similarly, there is little vetting of personnel, whether of owners or guards. Research of private security companies found that some had owners with mercenary backgrounds, though Ghanaian personnel provided the public face of the company.[2] It found, further, that with no reliable data bank on criminal records, adequate searches on prospective employees were impossible and such as were done by the police were inefficient and slow. The same issue of unenforced regulations applies to Nigeria. Security organisations are required to be registered as a company, to have a government licence and to be wholly owned by Nigerians. An owner must not have a criminal record and no employee may wear any uniform similar to those of the police or armed forces. Beyond these regulations there is supposed to be self-regulation by the private security professional associa-

2. www.africansecurity.org/governing-security.

tion. As one private security provider comments: 'good as the intention of government is, the advent of some security firm operators ... has in no small measure blighted the gains of this ancillary force. As private guard companies mushroom, so has the flagrant disregard for ethics' (Akingbade, 2003).

Regulation, like licensing and accreditation, in practice often means additional responsibilities for the police, yet it is by no means clear that an already over-committed police want (or have the resources) to engage in such bureaucratic processes. There is also a conflict of interest. To what extent do police want to license or register non-state security providers with whom they are competing directly for a share of the local security market? Of course, regulation need not be tied to statutory regulation, for accountability can be market based as well as juridical.

The policy of deregulation and delegation

Further statutory regulation is not seen as the best policy by all. Some have argued for delegation to sub-state, private or community auspices. In the opinion of Nigerian political scientist Peter Ekeh, the Nigerian prohibition on any policing organisation other than the Nigeria Police is foolish since the state does not have the resources to deliver. He argues that policing should be devolved to provincial state and local governments where it can be operated in a locally sensitive and effective way (Ekeh, 2002). Whether local authorities would be any more effective than federal authorities in the African state is a moot point, though the cases of Uganda and Rwanda are encouraging. Not all government decentralisation programmes have been successful, owing to the lack of professional staff and auditing failures. This would be as likely in policing as in other areas.

Schonteich goes much further than Ekeh's call for decentralisation. He argues for deregulation and for extending privatisation. He would place most policing functions, apart from where the use of firearms is required, in the hands of commercial companies. He claims such a strategy would release state police to specialise in 'bandit catching' (Schonteich, 1999a). Superficially it is attractive to consider tapping into the expanding resources of the commercial security industry. There are as many commercial security guards as uniformed police in many African countries, but their quality is very poor outside the largest companies. Further, it is unlikely to be attractive to those states committed to the principle that all social services should be offered on the basis of universal provision, rather than being no more than a guaranteed minimum provision. Many, too, would be uneasy with accountability being essentially only to clients, rather than to the wider public, though tough auditing procedures could be introduced.

Brogden and Shearing (1993) opt for control of policing to pass to local 'communities', whether territorial or not. In other words, they argue for giving the major role of ordering communities to communities themselves. The argument has as its premise that policing is everybody's business. This would mean that within the overarching principles of the constitution, the neighbourhood can determine what is acceptable, for instance, in terms of dress code, noise, or licensing hours; the football club or trade union can decide what levels of marshalling they want at match or march; the business company can have its own policy as regards employees caught stealing company property; the Muslim community can ban alcohol sales/use from its locality; and the tribal authority can determine its customary rules on age of marriage, land rights and the like (Zwane, 1994; Stack, 1997).

Nyamu-Musembi seeks to divert criticism of deregulation heightening unaccountability by calling for it to run alongside 'an empowerment approach that equips the people who are served by these systems with knowledge that enables them to demand accountability' (Nyamu-Musembi, 2003:7). Such empowerment would have to ensure that users knew what the scope of the policing group's authority was; what their own rights were in relation to that authority; and where they may lodge complaints when they are aggrieved. There still remain, however, the difficulties of enacting delegation to local communities where there are not homogenous communities.

In a subsequent paper Shearing clarifies his own views of accountability under deregulation (Shearing and Wood, 2003). He advocates a model where states retain control over non-state providers, but in such a way as to constitute, 'security markets that enable disadvantaged communities to participate as "customers", thereby experiencing the benefits of enhanced self-direction and choice in the provision of common goods'. It is a model that attempts to address the criticism that deregulation favours wealthier communities who have the physical and social capital to identify and provide for common goods. Poor collectives, it is argued, find it more difficult than more affluent ones to mobilise the resources that sustain policing programmes. His answer, therefore, is to create small businesses among poor communities that have a policing function. In the light of his experience of setting up Peace Committees in 20 very poor communities in developing countries, he claims these are capable of identifying the sources of the conflict and of gathering together persons in the community who have the capacity and knowledge to contribute towards a solution. He argues that the 'clients' of these Committees, 'are both the persons whom the conflict is affecting as well as local governments who see this conflict as contributing to crime and other problems'. Whether they function as auspices or providers of policing depends on the available resources and capacities. Because common security is consistent with, and enhances, public goods, he calls for local governments to fund them as long as they comply with the terms of a Code of Good Practice e.g. have not used force or the threat of force; have worked within the law; have respected human rights; and have acted impartially. In other words, he envisages a market-based form of accountability operating such that the payment system translates compliance with the public interest into a commodity that these security businesses market to state governments:

> In 'new regulatory' fashion it retains the role of the state in the protection of public interests through a tax-based payment system that supports the community governance budgets of Peace Committees. As well, it retains the role of the state, and the police specifically, as the bearers of legitimate, non-negotiable force. In so doing, it retains the role of the state as the central regulator of coercion (Shearing and Wood, 2003).

The policy option of criminalization

To argue that multi-choice policing offers a potential solution to law and order issues does not mean a blanket acceptance of all providers. Governments have to clearly define the desired relationship between the different policing structures and set the parameters. Those non-state policing systems that operate outside of the law must be persuaded to abandon values contrary to the constitution and international standards of human rights. Those not prepared to work within the law should be proscribed and continued activity prosecuted.

This, however, is easier to legislate for than to enforce. In Nigeria the outlawing of militias and vigilante groups like the Bakassi Boys and OPC did not remove them. A year after the dismantling of the Bakassi Boys in Anambra State, the state government simply established a new vigilante outfit, claiming (as it had done for the Bakassi Boys) that it would be run in collaboration with the Nigeria Police (Baker 2002c).[3] Again, the Nigerian

---

3. *Daily Champion*, 19 September, 2003.

federal government announced a ban on the OPC in 1999. Yet although the police regularly raided and broke up OPC meetings and scores of OPC members were either killed or arrested, the OPC continued to function clandestinely (Human Rights Watch, 2003).

The problem of enforcement of laws against unregulated or illegal policing is not just one of lack of resources. At times it is a lack of will. The existence of a mixed bag of multi-choice policing can promote an instrumental attitude to lawless law enforcement. Buur (2003) claims that the police at times 'farm out' dirty work, which they are not entitled to perform, to less accountable policing groups. And the International Council on Human Rights Policy (2003) tells of influential politicians in Nigeria highjacking vigilante groups and turning them into personal militias.

With states lacking the capacity to bring such policing under full and effective accountability, it can be a temptation for them to rationalise the bending of the rules and withhold prosecution as part of the necessary evil to crush a worse evil. The public may hold similar views in certain circumstances. If lawless policing 'works' and, perhaps more to the point, does not affect the 'innocent', then many are willing to turn a blind eye. In South Africa it was found that 36.4 per cent thought 'it might be better to ignore the law and solve problems immediately, rather than wait for a legal solution' (Gibson and Gouws, 1997:179). Nor is this tolerance simply a matter of an uneducated public. It is also found among the police themselves. Police in South Africa, faced with a youth-led violent vigilante group in 2002, chose not to act.

> They knew about the happenings but not as police officers: 'You see, when I am here [at a meeting of the group], I am a resident of the area. When I put my uniform on, I am a police officer, and I need to uphold the law'. Yet another police officer, charged with investigating the incidents, asserted, 'We don't fold our hands. We attend complaints and open dockets. We arrest people from the community if we have to. To me crime is crime and nobody is above the law. If there is a crime there are procedures to be followed. These people took the law into their own hands and we investigate it. If it ever transpires that one, two, three were involved, we have no choice but to open a case. But we must understand that people are fed up with crime and violence. For me it was the right thing they did. It was a good thing. But law is law' (Jensen, 2003).

There was similar ambiguity when the same force was faced with a tribal vigilante group that was equally violent. The local commander of a small station with 35 police officers covering an extensive area was only too glad to have the cooperation of local residents, especially the tribal authorities. She told Jensen:

> That is also why the sub-forum works well. They are really working hard. They do case handling. They investigate cases, apprehend the suspects and then hand them over to the police. So as a result we only have had one case in the last month.

So how did she justify the violence?

> Sometimes you have to turn the blind eye for the sake of crime. If you for instance have someone coming in accused of raping a three year old and he has been beaten up, then you do turn the blind eye. You know that it is like victim support.

It might have been an issue if the public or even other officers had complained, but none did. In these circumstances, the legitimacy accorded those who break the law to enforce the law will be variable. Put another way, once the focus is on the end, irrespective of the means, then lawlessness by security groups is immune from local censure and investigation by outside bodies is near impossible.

The politics of addressing root causes

Controlling policing is not just about supervising organisations, but tackling some of the underlying social issues that cause conflict and precipitate the need for policing alternatives to the state police. In the first instance, legislation will not suffice until there is a mechanism put in place for investigating and punishing complaints against state police abuse. Yet only a few countries have state police complaints boards or ombudsmen (e.g. Mauritius, Namibia, South Africa, Uganda and Zambia). Even those complaints institutions that do exist only have the power of recommendation and often do not receive co-operation from ministries and institutions in dealing with enquiries.[4] In Malawi, the Presidential Working Group on Police Reform surveyed complaints against police. They found that 66 per cent of the respondents said they never complained against police. Of the 33 per cent who had complained, 88 per cent said they were dissatisfied with the result because they got no help or no action was taken (Wood, 2000). In a situation where action against a police officer is supposed to

---

4. *The Namibian*, 3 March, 2004.

be taken by the officer in charge of the offending officer's police station, this is inevitable. Only an independent Complaints Board/Ombudsman can tackle this sort of problem with individual officers. There is also the additional problem of complaints not against individual officers, but about police operations in general, such as the tear-gassing of crowds. The public must be re-assured that complaints against the police will be investigated and wrongdoing disciplined.

Another fundamental issue to be dealt with is ignorance of the law. For instance, bail laws are often misunderstood and it is assumed that suspects taken to the police are simply allowed to go free. Or again there are serious problems in Africa over the widespread belief that women can be sexually harassed and assaulted. These particular roots of disillusion with the state legal and policing system can be addressed by civic education. Independent or state-partnered large-scale civic education programmes can keep citizens, particularly ones with limited access to the media, abreast of developments and encourage positive citizenship. Malawi's National Initiative on Civic Education is one such example. It has offices throughout the country and is an important source of citizen education about government policies and civic issues, especially political rights and social issues. Civic education is a role that can be taken up by NGOs, many of whom have a human rights arm and an education arm. Human rights education offers individuals:

> Alternative, non-violent options for vigilante incidents that are explained as emotion-driven i.e. motivated by revenge, anger, jealousy, prejudice and fear. Similarly, the social promotion of non-violent role models and activities is also important to delegitimising violence as the primary solution to emotional frustrations. Beyond the individual level, community-based reconciliation strategies, coupled with human rights education, may work to address vigilantism that is either fuelled by revenge, underpinned by politics, and/or a product of transmigration from certain rivalries in specific areas (Harris, 2001b).

Further, people will be reluctant to abandon non-state procedures until better physical, financial and procedural access to justice in the state courts is provided. Unfortunately the current common-law system requires a high level of resources to make it fair. For instance, its adversarial form of criminal procedure assumes that the scales of justice will be balanced insofar as every accused person will be represented by a defence counsel. Yet a survey of eight Southern African countries revealed that only two had a form of legal aid and then only for serious cases (Schärf, 1999). The simplest way to improve accessibility is to enhance the availability of legal services through legal aid schemes that provide legal services free of charge, assuming that there are enough qualified lawyers available, which is unlikely.

South African experience shows these legal services can be effectively provided through a mixture of private, government, university and NGO initiatives working together. A more radical approach operates in Malawi, where paralegals without formal legal qualifications have been employed to promote awareness and understanding of basic legal rights. Since paralegals help to reduce backlogs in the system, their contribution is valued by the police and judges.

Non-state policing and justice systems will always thrive whilst they have features that are popular and that are absent in the state provision. There are several avenues of reform worth exploring by governments. The operation of the formal court system, for instance, could become more user friendly to the poor. Procedures could be simplified; evidence could be presented in narrative form; and the presiding officer could adopt an inquisitorial approach to the presentation of evidence and assist with eliciting the required evidence from the parties. Courts could also be given the option of conducting proceedings in the vernacular. In addition, members of the accused person's community could be allowed to serve as assessors, or be part of the decision as to the best sentence for the accused. In so doing, the best effects of re-integrative shaming can take place and the destructive effect of imprisonment can be avoided. Another attraction of local systems, such as customary law, is that they look at a problem as a whole rather than focussing on the single event that triggered the immediate dispute. One way forward would be to reform the state system in such a way as to adopt some of these non-state justice features.

Though reform of state policing will not take away all recourse to non-state provision, it will mean that it will not be motivated by suspicion and hatred of the state system.

Holistic politics

The politics of security and policing is intimately connected with poverty eradication. It has been argued in recent years that poverty is not just a lack of income; it is the experience of multiple forms of vulnerability, including exposure to crime, disorder and violence (Deepa, 2000). It is very often the poorest that are least protected from discrimination, official corruption, theft, sexual abuse, violence and denial of land/inheritance rights. It is the poorest who are most exposed to extortion and unjust treatment by policing agents. Hence it is not just at the macro-level that investment is deterred by disorder and crime. At the micro-level, too, the poor have their confidence undermined and may hold back from developing their resources. Such vulnerable households can scarce afford to use their limited disposable income for risk-avoidance strategies (e.g. bribes and weapons) or on paying for policing. For these reasons peace and security is no longer seen by development experts as the sole preserve of the state police and the justice system. It is now set in the context of human dignity and human rights. If human development is the provision of choices and opportunities, 'human security means that people can exercise those choices safely and freely'. Human security is therefore people-centred and communities are seen as having the leading role in promoting safety and security (Kisia, 2004:5).

If policing is an important element of development, then it is important that it is integrated with development programmes. Recognising this and the fact that policing is in reality usually multi-choice policing, has led to programmes designed to harness the resources of all those engaged in policing in its widest sense. Indeed, it is now becoming popular to regard law and order issues as an entry-point to development projects. In other words, it is argued that law and order should be addressed holistically as a development issue and not only as a policing issue. The premise is that a general improvement in the standard of living should reduce crime.

Justice may not only be offered by a state, but also by an NGO. There are development NGOs that aim to enhance the prospects for better safety and security of person and property, as well as significantly increasing access to justice. Examples of such NGOs would be an organisation offering legal aid for women or victim support; or a church mediation forum. Zambia is a good example of such NGOs. The Legal Resources Foundation mediates more than 1,000 cases a year; Women for Change empowers village women to understand their rights and to find the appropriate forum for their problem; Legal Resources Foundation and National Women's Legal Aid Clinic assist women to navigate the complex court structures; and Zambia Civic Education Association provides legal advice, civic education, legal representation and advocacy work.

Support for community-policing initiatives by independent NGOs can be of enormous benefit. They have promoted public discourse on security threats; organised civic education programmes; raised knowledge of the issues by distributing materials on security issues; commissioned research on the legislative control and policing practices; obtained financial contributions from the business sector for crime prevention work with youth; lobbied parliamentarians to support specific measures and resources to promote crime prevention; and developed pilot schemes to take these activities forward.

Forums can bring together every local community organisation, international NGO and government agency concerned with improving the quality of life in the community. Together they can develop a community safety plan, share human and physical resources, and create channels for referral to services provided by one another. Once a need is identified, options can be sought that are both state and non-state, or joint projects. Brogden and Shearing speak of it as 'dual policing' (Brogden, 1995; Brogden and Shearing, 1993). The dual model envisages the state police bearing primary responsibility for enforcement, while problem-orientated (community) policing would be provided by state police in conjunction with commercial, municipal and voluntary elements. Overall responsibility for coordination and integration of policing networks would lie with local government, though authoritative force would remain with the state police and national criteria would be established to determine the legitimate limits of local civil autonomy. An example of this approach is South Africa's Community Safety Forums. Since 2002 all justice system structures, all relevant local government structures, education representatives and community-based organisations meet monthly and identify problems and generate solutions (Schärf, 2003).

Another initiative is the Safer Cities Programme. This was launched in 1996 in response to calls from mayors of large African cities who wanted to address urban violence and were looking for a prevention strategy at the city level. It has been implemented in Abidjan, Antananarivo, Dakar, Dar-es-Salaam, Durban, Johannesburg, Nairobi and Yaoundé. It seeks to create awareness, sensitise communities and build local capacity in urban safety in partnership with other stakeholders. NGOs and CBOs at community level have drawn up proposals with neighbourhood leaders for job creation as a means of tackling the root causes of crime, as well as organising communities to promote urban safety. As Kisia observes, the safer cities approach 'requires radical institutional reform, partnership, a major shift in attitude among civic leadership and genuine and broad-based participation in decision-making, which enhances citizenship and inclusion' (2004:13). Yet when he examined Johannesburg and Nairobi it was this that he found to be missing:

An effective approach to promoting peace and security requires an empowered local government especially the civic leadership, and an empowered and fully recognized citizen intervention through civil society. The Civil Society's initiatives always seem to have more impact but are most often hampered by lack of effective support from the local government (Kisia, 2004:14).

Though holistic programmes offer enormous potential, the logistics of joined-up-governance are difficult to initiate and sustain against a background of individual fiefdoms, rivalry, suspicion and overstretched resources.

Conclusion

The policy options outlined above are not mutually exclusive. Combinations of them can be used. The over-riding principle, however, is the need for a national strategy of law and order that integrates, regulates, mobilises, and empowers all those willing to preserve law and order in an acceptable manner. There are few today who see non-state policing as appropriating state sovereignty and as a challenge to state mechanisms of state control that must be rolled back. Many more see multi-choice policing as an opportunity to extend the range of state social control. For them the immediate task is, therefore, to bring the 'responsible' elements under thorough statutory legislation, so that they are accountable to the public and can form an alliance with state policing agencies. Alternatively, others argue for a middle way in which non-state policing is allowed a degree of autonomy from the state, but at the same time acknowledges the legitimacy of the state (Merry 1988; Fitzpatrick 1992; Nina and Schwikkard, 1996).

One thing is certain, whether governments take account of multi-choice policing and seize the initiative to maximise its advantages and minimise its hazards, or whether they ignore it, it will continue to play a significant part in the social, economic and political development of their countries. Whether there is government action or inaction it will also have wide-scale repercussions on the lives of ordinary citizens. Security of person may be a basic human right, but for millions it is something they must attempt to secure against the odds and with or without the assistance of their governments. Their degree of success in negotiating a measure of security for person and property from the array of security providers on offer, will determine in large measure the quality of their human experience.

Bibliography

For a complete bibliography on Africa policing see: www.africanpolicing.org

Abrahams, R., 1987, 'Sungsungu: Village Vigilante Groups in Tanzania', *African Affairs*, 86, 179–90.

—, 1998, *Vigilant Citizens: Vigilantism and the State*. Oxford: Polity Press.

—, and M. Williams, 2005, *The Globalisation of Private Security. Country Report: Sierra Leone*. Aberystwyth: The University of Wales.

Ade Ajayi and Crowder, M. (1974), *History of West Africa*, Vol.2, London: Longman.

Adu-Mireku, S., 2002, 'Fear of Crime among Residents of Three Communities in Accra, Ghana', *International Journal of Contemporary Sociology*, 43, 2, 153–68.

Agnew, R., 1990, 'Adolescent Resources and Delinquency', *Criminology*, 28, 535–66.

Ahire, P., 1990, 'Re-Writing the Distorted History of Policing in Colonial Nigeria', *International Journal of the Sociology of Law*, 18, 45–60.

—, 1991, *Imperial Policing in Colonial Nigeria, 1860–1960*. Milton Keynes: Open University.

Akingbade, T., 2003, *Industrial Security in Nigeria : Challenges & Prospects for the 21st Century*. Milton Keynes: Authorhouse.

Albrecht, P. and M. Malan, 2006, *Post-Conflict Peacebuilding and National "Ownership": Meeting the Challenges of Sierra Leone*. Accra: Kofi Annan International Peacekeeping Training Centre.

Alemika, E., 1993, 'Colonialism, State and Policing in Nigeria', *Crime, Law and Social Change*, 20, 187–219.

—, 1998, 'Policing and Perception of Police in Nigeria', *Police Studies*, 11, 4, 161–76.

Allen, C., 1999, 'Warfare, Endemic Violence and State Collapse', *Review of African Political Economy*, 81, 367–84.

Altbeker, A., 2001, 'Who Are We Burying? The Death of a Soweto Gangster', in J. Steinberg (ed.), *Crime Wave: The South African Underworld and Its Foes*. Johannesburg: Witwatersrand University Press.

—, 1998, *Solving Crime: The State of the SAPS Detective Service*. Pretoria: Institute for Strategic Studies (ISS), monograph 31.

Alvazzi del Frate, A., 1998, *Victims of Crime in the Developing World*. UNICRI publication 57. Rome: United Nations Interregional Crime and Justice Research Institute.

Amnesty International, 1998, *Senegal: Climate of Terror in Casamance*. New York: Amnesty International.

—, 2002, *Southern Africa: Policing to Protect Human Rights: A Survey of Police Practices in Countries of the Southern African Development Community, 1997–2002*, available at web.amnesty.org/library/index/ENGAFR030042002

Anderson, D., 2002, 'Vigilantes, Violence and the Politics of Public Order in Kenya', *African Affairs*, 101, 531–55.

Anderson, M., 2002, 'Getting Rights Right. Is Access to Justice as Important as Access to Health or Education?', *ID21 Society and Economy*, available at http://www. id21.org/society/Insights43Editorial.html

Anderson, T. and R. Bennett, 1996, 'Development, Gender and Crime. The Scope of Routine Activities Approach', *Justice Quarterly*, 32, 343–63.

Appiahene-Gyamfi, J., 2003, 'Urban Crime Trends and Patterns in Ghana: The Case of Accra', *Journal of Criminal Justice*, 31, 1, 13–23.

Astrow, A., 1983, *Zimbabwe: A Revolution That Lost Its Way?* London: Zed Press.

Baker, B., 2000, 'Going to War Democratically: The Case of the Second Congo War (1998–2000)', *Contemporary Politics*, 6, 3, 263–82.

—, 2002a, 'Living with Non-State Policing in South Africa: The Issues and Dilemmas', *Journal of Modern African Studies*, 40, 1, 29–53.

—, 2002b, *Taking the Law into Their Own Hands.* Aldershot: Ashgate.

—, 2002c, 'When the Bakassi Boys Came: Eastern Nigeria Confronts Vigilantism', *Journal of Contemporary African Studies*, 20, 2, 1–22.

—, 2003, 'Policing and the Rule of Law in Mozambique', *Policing and Society*, 13, 2, 139–58.

—, 2004a, 'Protection from Crime: What Is on Offer for Africans?', *Journal of Contemporary African Studies*, 22, 2, 165–88.

—, 2004b, 'Post-Conflict Policing: Lessons from Uganda 18 years on', *Journal of Humanitarian Assistance*, available at www.jha.ac posted July.

—, 2004c, 'Multi-Choice Policing in Africa: Is the Continent Following the South African Pattern?', *Society in Transition*, 35, 2, 204–23.

—, 2004d, 'Popular Justice and Policing from Bush War to Democracy: Uganda 1981–2004', *International Journal of the Sociology of Law*, 32, 333–48.

—, 2005, 'Multi-Choice Policing in Uganda', *Policing and Society*, 15, 1, 19–41.

—, 2006, 'The African Post-Conflict Policing Agenda in Sierra Leone', *Conflict, Security & Development*, 6, 1 (2006), 25–50.

—, 2007a (not yet published), 'Reconstructing a Policing System out of the Ashes: Rwanda's Solution', *Policing and Society*.

—, 2007b (not yet published), 'Community Policing in Freetown, Sierra Leone: Foreign import or local solution?', *Journal of Intervention and Statebuilding*.

—, and R. May, 2004, 'Reconstructing Sierra Leone', *Commonwealth and Comparative Politics*, 42, 1 (2004), 35–60.

—, and E. Scheye, 2007 (forthcoming), 'Multi-layered justice and security delivery in post-conflict and fragile states', *Conflict, Security and Development*.

Barya, J. and J. Oloka Onyango, 1994, *Popular Justice and Resistance Committee Courts in Uganda.* Kampala: New Visions Publishing.

Bassett, T., 2003, 'Dangerous Pursuits: Hunter Associations (*donzo ton*) and National Politics in Côte d'Ivoire', *Africa,* 73, 1, 1–30.

Bayart, J., S. Ellis and B. Hibou, 1999, *The Criminalization of the State in Africa.* Oxford: James Currey.

Bayley, D. and C. Shearing, 1996, 'The Future of Policing', *Law and Society Review*, 30, 585–606.

—, 2001, *The New Structure of Policing: Description, Conceptualization and Research Agenda*. Washington: US Department of Justice, Office of Justice Programs, National Institute of Justice.

Beattie, J., 1986, *Crime and the Courts in England, 1660–1800*. Oxford: Clarendon Press.

Bekker, J., 1989, Customary Law in Southern Africa. Cape Town: Juta.

Biddle, K., L. Clegg and J. Whetton, 1998, Evaluation of ODA/DFID Support to the Police in Developing Countries – Synthesis Study. Swansea: Centre for Development Studies.

Biddle, K., L. Clegg and J. Whetton, 1999, *Evaluation of ODA/DFID Support to the Police in Developing Countries – Synthesis Study*. Swanea: Centre for Development Studies.

Bierschenk, T. and O. de Sardan, 2003, 'Powers in the Village: Rural Benin between Democratisation and Decentralisation', *Africa*, 73, 2, 145–73.

Birkeland, N. and A. Gomes, 2001, 'Angola: Displaced in the Province of Huambo', in M. Vincent and B. Sorensen (eds), *Caught Between Borders: Response Strategies of the Internally Displaced*. London: Pluto Press, 33–41.

Bouman, M., 1987, 'A Note on Chiefly and National Policing in Botswana', *Journal of Legal Pluralism*, 25&26, 275–300.

Brantingham, P. and P. Brantingham, 1984, *Patterns in Crime*. New York: Macmillan.

—, 1993, 'Environment, Routine and Situation: Toward a Pattern Theory of Crime', in R. Clarke and M. Felson (eds), *Advances in Criminological Theory*, Vol.5. New Brunswick: Transaction Publishing, 259–93.

Brogden, M., 1995, 'An Agenda for Post-Troubles Policing in Northern Ireland – the South African Precedent', *The Liverpool Law Review*, 17, 1, 3–27.

—, 2004, 'Commentary: Community Policing: A Panacea from the West', *African Affairs*, 103, 413, 635–49.

—, and C. Shearing, 1993, *Policing for a New South Africa*. London: Routledge.

Brooks, D., 2000, 'Write a Cheque, End a War: Using Private Military Companies to End African Conflicts', *Conflict Trends*, available at http://www.foxnews.com/world/062300/un_broder.sml

Bruce, D. and J. Komane, 1999, 'Taxis, Cops and Vigilantes: Police Attitudes towards Street Justice', *Crime and Conflict*, 17, 39–44.

Bukurura, S., 1994, 'The Maintenance of Order in Rural Tanzania: The Case of Sungsungu', *Journal of Legal Pluralism*, 34, 1–29.

Burman, S. and W. Schärf, 1990, 'Creating People's Justice: Street Committees and People's Courts in a South African City', *Law and Society Review*, 24, 3, 693–744.

Buur, L., 2003, 'Vigilantism and the Policing of Everyday Life in South Africa', paper presented for ROAPE conference: Africa: Partnership as Imperialism, September 5–7 2003, Birmingham University.

—, and S. Jensen, 2004, 'Vigilantism and the Policing of Everyday Life in South Africa', *African Studies* 63, 2, 139–52.

Call, C., 2002, 'Competing Donor Approaches to Post-Conflict Police Reform', *Conflict, Security & Development*, 2, 1, 110–10.

Carlston, K., 1968, *Social Theory and African Tribal Organization*. Urbana: University of Chicago Press.

Carstens, P., 2001, *In the Company of Diamonds: De Beers, Kleinzee, and the Control of a Town*. Athens: Ohio University Press.

Center for Strategic and International Studies (CSIS) and the Association of the United States Army (AUSA), 2002, *Post-Conflict Reconstruction*, available at www.twq.com/02autumn/hamre.pdf

Chazan, N., 1988, 'Ghana: Problems of Governance and the Emergence of Civil Society', in L. Diamond, J. Lintz, and S. Lipset (eds), *Democracy in Developing Countries: Africa*. Boulder: Lynne Rienner.

Chesney, K., 1972, *The Victorian Underworld*. London: Pelican.

Childs, R., 2001, 'Private Security: Is the Service up to the Challenge?', *Policing Today* 7, 2, 26–27.

Chukwuma, I., 2001, 'Police Transformation in Nigeria: Problems and Prospects', paper presented at 'Crime and Policing in Transitional Societies', Conference held 30 August – 1 September 2000, South Africa, available at www.kas.de/proj/home.

Center for Strategic and International Studies/the Association of the US Army, 2002, *Meeting the Challenges of Governance and Participation in Post-conflict Settings*. Washingon DC: CSIS/AUSA.

Clapham, C., 1999, 'African Security Systems: Privatisation and the Scope for Mercenary Activity', in G. Mills and J. Stremlau (eds), *The Privatisation of Security in Africa*. Johannesburg: South African Institute of International Affairs, 23–45.

Clayton, A., 1989, 'Law Enforcement and Colonial Police Forces', in A. Clayton and D. Killingray, *Khaki and Blue: Military and Police in British Colonial Africa*. Athens: Ohio University Center for International Studies, 67–78.

—, and D. Killingray, 1989, *Khaki and Blue: Military and Police in British Colonial Africa*. Athens: Ohio University Center for International Studies.

Cliffe, L. and R. Luckham, 1999, 'Complex Political Emergencies and the State: Failure and the Fate of the State', *Third World Quarterly*, 20, 1, 27–50.

Coalition on Violence against Women , 2002, *In Pursuit of Justice: A Research Report on Service Providers' Response to Cases of Violence against Women in Nairobi Province*, COVAW- Kenya.

Cohen, P., 1979, 'Policing the Working Class City', in B. Fine et al. (eds), *Capitalism and the Rule of Law*. London: Hutchinson.

Cohen, S., 1985, *Visions of Social Control*. Cambridge: Polity Press.

—, 1986, 'Bandits, Rebels, or Criminals: African History and Western Criminology', *Africa*, 54, 468–83.

Cooney, M., 1994, 'The Informal Social Control of Homicide', *Journal of Legal Pluralism*, 34, 31–59.

Crowder, M., 1978, *Colonial West Africa: Collected Essays*. London: Frank Cass.

Currie, E., 1992, 'Market Society and Social Disorder', in B.D. MacLean and D. Milanovic (eds), *New Directions in Critical Criminology*. Vancouver: Collective Press.

—, 1997, 'Market, Crime and Community: Towards a Mid-Range Theory of Post-Industrial Violence', *Theoretical Criminology*, 1, 2, 147–72.

Danish International Development Assistance (Danida), 1998, *Baseline Survey on the Local Council Courts Systems in Uganda*. Final Report. Copenhagen: Danida.

Das, D. and A. Verma, 1998, 'The Armed Police in the British Colonial Tradition: The Indian Perspective', *Policing: An International Journal of Police Strategies and Management*, 21, 2, 354–67.

Davey, B., 1983, *Lawless and Immoral: Policing a Country Town 1838–57*. Leicester: Leicester University Press.

Davis, J., 1989, 'From Rookeries to Communities: Race Poverty and Policing in London 1850–1985', *History Workshop Journal*, 27, 66–85.

Davis, R., N. Henderson C. and Merrick, 2003, 'Community Policing: Variations on the Western Model in the Developing World', *Police Practice and Research*, 4, 3, 285–300.

Deepa, N. with R. Patel, K. Schafft, A. Rademacher and S. Koch-Schulte, 2000, *Voices of the Poor: Can Anyone Hear Us?* New York: Published for the World Bank, Oxford University Press.

Department for International Development (DFID), 2002, *Safety, Security and Accessible Justice: Putting Policy into Practice*. London: DFID.

Draper, H., 1978, *Private Police*. Sussex: Harvester Press.

Dugard, J., 2001, *From Low Intensity War to Mafia War: Taxi Violence in South Africa (1987–2000)*. Violence and Transition Series, vol. 4. Johannesburg: Centre for the Study of Violence and Reconciliation (CSVR).

Ekeh, P., 2002, A Review of HRW's and Cleen's Report 'The Bakassi Boys: The Legitimization of Murder and Torture' on State Sponsored Vigilante Groups in Nigeria, available at www.waado.org/NigerDelta/Documents/ConstitutionalMatters/ PoliceVigilante/ReviewBakassiBoys-Ekeh

Emsley, C., 1987, 'Policing the Streets of Early Nineteenth-Century Paris', *French History*, 1, 257–82.

—, 1997, 'The Nation-State, the Law and the Peasant in Nineteenth Century Europe', in X. Rosseaux and R. Lévy (eds), Le Penal dans tous ses états. Justice, états at sociétés en Europe (XIIe-XXe siècles). Brussels: Facultés universitaires Saint-Louis, 153–78.

—, 1999, *Gendarmes and the State in Nineteenth Century Europe*. Oxford: Oxford University Press.

Ero, C., 2000, 'Vigilantes, Civil Defence Forces and Militia Groups: The Other Side of the Privatisation of Security in Africa', *Conflict Trends*, 1, 25–29.

Etannibi, E.A., 2005, *Police Oversight Organizations in West Africa.* Report commissioned by the African Policing Civilian Oversight Forum (APCOF).

Farah, A. and I. Lewis, 1993, *Roots of Reconciliation – Local Level Peace Process in Somaliland.* London: ACTIONAID.

Fayemi, K., 2004, 'Governing Insecurity in Post-Conflict States: The Case of Sierra Leone and Liberia', in A. Bryden and H. Hanggi (eds), *Reform and Reconstruction of the Security Sector.* Geneva: Geneva Centre for the Democratic Control of the Armed Forces (DCAF).

Feeley, M. and J. Simon, 1992, 'The New Penology: Notes on the Emerging Strategy of Corrections and Its Implications', *Criminology,* **30**, 4, 449–74.

Fitzpatrick, P., 1992, 'The Impossibility of Popular Justice', *Social & Legal Studies,* 1, 2, 257–82.

Forrest, J., 1998, 'State Inversion and Nonstate Politics', in L. Villalon and P. Huxtable (eds), *The African State at a Critical Juncture: Between Disintegration and Reconfiguration.* Boulder: Lynne Rienner.

Garland, D., 1996, 'The Limits of the Sovereign State: Strategies of Crime Control in Contemporary Society', *British Journal of Criminology,* 36, 4, 445–71.

—, 1999, '"Governability" and the Problem of Crime', in R. Smandych (ed.), *Governable Places: Readings on Governability and Crime Control.* Aldershot: Ashgate.

Gastrow, P., 1998, Organized Crime in South Africa. Pretoria: Institute for Strategic Studies (ISS), monograph 28.

—, 1999, 'Main Trends in the Development of South Africa's Organised Crime', *African Security Review,* 8, 6, available at http://www.iss.co.za/Pubs/ASR/8No6/ Contents.html

Gbla, O., 2006, 'Security Sector Reform under International Tutelage in Sierra Leone', *International Peacekeeping,* 13, 1, 79–83.

Gibson, J. and A. Gouws, 1997, 'Support for the Rule of the Law in the Emerging South African Democracy', *International Social Science Journal,* 152, 173–91.

Giddens, A., 1990, *The Consequences of Modernity.* Cambridge: Polity Press.

Ginifer, J., 2006, 'The Challenge of the Security Sector Reform Process in Democratic Transitions: The Case of Sierra Leone', *Democratization,* 13, 5, 791–810.

Global Witness, 2001, *Review of the Sierra Leone Diamond Certification System and Proposals and Recommendations for the Kimberley Process for a Fully Integrated Certification System (FICS)* April 25, 2001, available at www.globalpolicy.org/ security/issues/sierra/report/2001/0425gw.htm

Gluckman, M., 1973, *The Judicial Process among the Barotse of Northern Rhodesia.* Manchester: Manchester University Press.

Goldsmith, A., 2003, 'Policing Weak States: Citizen Safety and State Responsibility', *Policing and Society,* 13, 1, 3–21.

Government of National Unity, 1998, *In Service of Safety, 1998–2003.* White Paper on Safety and Security. Pretoria: Government of National Unity, South Africa.

Gurr, T., 1970, *Why Men Rebel.* Princeton: Princeton University Press.

—, P. Grabosky and R. Hula, 1977, *The Politics of Crime and Conflict.* Beverly Hills: Sage.

Halevy, E., 1974, *A History of the English People in the Nineteenth Century,* Volume 1. London: Ernest Benn.

Harris, B., 2001a, 'A Foreign Experience: Violence, Crime and Xenophobia during South Africa's Transition', *Violence and Transition* Series, 5, available at www. csvr.org.za/papers/papvtp5.htm.

—, 2001b, 'As for Violent Crime That's our Daily Bread': Vigilante Violence during South Africa's Period of Transition, Violence and Transition Series, 1. Johannesburg: Centre for the Study of Violence and Reconciliation.

Harvey, R., 2000, *Juvenile Justice in Sierra Leone,* available at www.essex.ac.uk/ armedcon/story_id/000039.doc

Heald, S., 1998, *Controlling Anger: The Anthropology of Gisu Violence.* Oxford: James Currey.

—, 2003, 'Domesticating Leviathan: Sungusungu Groups in Tanzania', Research paper, Crisis States Programme, available at www.dfid.gov.uk.

—, 2006, 'State, Law and Vigilantism in Northern Tanzania', *African Affairs,* 105, 419, 265–83.

Hellweg, J., 2004, 'Encompassing the State: Sacrifice and Security in the Hunters' Movement of Côte d'Ivoire', *Africa Today* 50, 4, 3–28.

Hendrickson, D., R. Mearns and J. Armon, 1996, 'Livestock Raiding among the Pastoral Turkana of Kenya', *IDS Bulletin,* 27, 17–30.

Hills, A., 1997, 'Policing, Enforcement and Low Intensity Conflict', *Policing and Society,* 7, 291–308.

—, 2000, *Policing in Africa: Internal Security and the Limits of Liberalization.* Boulder: Lynne Rienner.

—, 2001, 'Police Reform in Post-Colonial States', paper prepared for the Workshop on 'Democratic Control of Policing and Security Sector Reform', Geneva, Switzerland, available at http://www.dcaf.ch , Geneva Centre for The Democratic Control of Police Reform in Post-Colonial States.

Hochschild, A., 1998, *King Leopold's Ghost: A Story of Greed, Terror, and Heroism in Colonial Africa.* Boston: Houghton Mifflin.

Home Office, 1999, *Information on the Criminal Justice System in England and Wales: Digest.* Vol. 4. London: HMSO.

Honwana Welch, G., 1985, 'Beyond Pluralism: The Mozambican Experience', in A. Sachs and G. Honwana Welch, *Liberating the Law: Creating Popular Justice in Mozambique.* London: Zed Books.

Howe, H., 2000, 'African Private Security', *Conflict Trends,* 6, 22–24.

Human Rights Committee, 2001, 'Popular Justice', *HRC Quarterly Review,* January.

Human Rights Watch/CLEEN, 2002, *The Bakassi Boys: The Legitimization of Murder and Torture.* Vol. 14, No. 5(A).

Human Rights Watch, 2003, *Nigeria: The O'odua People's Congress: Fighting Violence with Violence,* Vol. 15, No. 4(A).

Humphries, R., 2000, 'Crime and Confidence: Voters' Perceptions of Crime', *Needbank ISS Crime Index*, 4, 2, 1–6.

Igbinovia, P., 1981, 'Patterns of Policing in Africa: The French and British Connection', *Police Journal*, 54, 2, 123–56.

—, 2000, 'The Future of the Nigeria Police', *Policing*, 23, 4, 538–54.

International Council on Human Rights Policy, 2003, *Crime, Public Order and Human Rights*. Geneva: International Council on Human Rights Policy.

International Crisis Group (ICG), 2004, *Côte d'Ivoire: No Peace in Sight*. Africa Report No. 82. Dakar/Brussels: ICG.

International Labour Office (ILO), 2003, *Global Employment Trends*. Geneva: ILO.

Irish, J., 1999, *Policing for Profit: The Future of South Africa's Private Security Industry*. Pretoria: Institute for Strategic Studies (ISS), monograph 39.

Isaacman, B. and A. Isaacman, 1982, 'A Socialist Legal System in the Making: Mozambique before and after Independence' in R. Abel (ed.), *The Politics of Informal Justice*, Vol 2. New York: Academic Press.

Jefferson, T., 1990, *The Case against Paramilitary Policing*. Milton Keynes: Open University Press.

Jeffries, C., 1952, *The Colonial Police*. London: Allen and Unwin.

Jemibewon, D., 2001, 'The Nigerian Experience', Crime and Policing in Transitional Societies, Seminar Report, Johannesburg: Konrad Adenauer Stiftung.

Jensen, S., 2003, 'Through the Lens of Crime: Land Claims and Contestations of Citizenship on the Frontier of the South African State', available at wwwserver. law.wits.ac.za/ workshop/workshop03/WWLSJensen.doc

Johnston, L., 1992, *The Rebirth of Private Policing*. London: Routledge.

—, 1996, 'What Is Vigilantism', *British Journal of Criminology*, 36, 2, 220–36.

—, 1999, 'Private Policing in Context', *European Journal on Criminal Policy and Research*, 7, 2, 175–96.

—, 2001, 'Crime, Fear and Civil Policing', *Urban Studies*, 38, 5–6, 959–76.

—, and C. Shearing, 2003, *Governing Security: Explorations in Policing and Justice*. London: Routledge.

Jones, G., 1984, *Outcast London*. London: Penguin.

Jones, T. and T. Newburn, 1998, *Private Security and Public Policing*. Oxford: Clarendon Press.

—, 1999, 'Urban Change and Policing, Mass Private Property Reconsidered', *European Journal on Criminal Policy and Research, 7*, 225–44.

—, 2002, 'The Transformation of Policing? Understanding Current Trends in Policing Systems', *British Journal of Criminology*, 42, 129–46.

Justice Initiative, 2003, *Sierra Leone: Access to Justice*, available at www.justiceinitiative. org/activities/ncjr/atj/sierraleone_atj.

Kabwegyere, T., 1995, *The Politics of State Formation and Destruction in Uganda*. Kampala: Fountain Publishers.

Kande, J., 1999, 'Ransoming the State: Elite Origins of Subaltern Terror in Sierra Leone', *Review of African Political Economy*, 81, 349–66.

Kane, M. et al., 2002, *Sierra Leone: Report on Preliminary Review of Justice Sector: joint DFID/World Bank visit*. Washington DC: World Bank.

Kanyeihamba, G., 2002, *Constitutional and Political History of Uganda: From 1894 to the Present*. Kampala: Centenary Publishing House.

Kasozi, A., 1994, *The Social Origins of Violence in Uganda*. Kampala: Fountain Publishers.

Kempa, M., R. Carrier, J. Wood and C. Shearing, 1999, 'Reflections on the Evolving Concept of "Private Policing"', *European Journal on Criminal Policy and Research*, 7, 197–223.

Kennedy, L. and D. Forde, 1990, 'Routine Activities and Crime: An Analysis of Victimization in Canada', *Criminology*, 28, 137–69.

Killingray, D., 1986, 'The Maintenance of Law and Order in British Colonial Africa', *African Affairs*, 85, 411–37.

—, 1997, 'Securing the British Empire: Policing and Colonial Order, 1920–1960', in M. Mazower (ed.), *The Policing of Politics in the Twentieth Century*. Providence and Oxford: Berghahn Books, 167–90.

—, 2003, lecture to IFRA Nairobi, available at www.ifra-nairobi.org/english/new/cdrom/pp/papers/killingray.pdf

Kinnes, I., 2000, *From Urban Street Gangs to Criminal Empires: The Changing Face of Gangs in the Western Cape*. Pretoria: Institute for Strategic Studies (ISS), monograph 48.

Kirk-Greene, A., 1980, 'Hereditas Damnosa: Ethnic Ranking and the Martial Races Imperative in Africa', *Ethnic and Racial Studies*, 3, 4, 393–413.

Kisia, P., 2004, 'Promoting Peace, Safety and Security: The Role of Communities and Local Governments', paper prepared for Africa Local Government Action Forum, available at www.worldbank.org/wbi/publicfinance/documents/ALGAF/KISIA.pdf

Klipin, J. and K. Harrison, 2003, *The Future for Policing and Crime Prevention in SADC*, Canadian International Crime Prevention Centre, available at http://www.crime-prevention-intl.org/publications.php?type=OTHER

Knighton, B., 2003, 'The State as Raider among the Karamojong: "Where There Are No Guns They Use the Threat of Guns"', *Africa*, 73, 3, 427–55.

Kraska, P. and V. Kappelar, 1997, 'Militarising American Police: The Rise and Normalisation of Paramilitary Units', *Social Problems*, 44, 1, 1–18.

Kwame, A., 1985, *Traditional Rule in Ghana: Past and Present*. Accra: Sedco.
Kynoch, G. and T. Ulicki, 2000, 'It Is Like the Time of Lifaquane: The Impact of Stock Theft and Violence in Southern Lesotho', *Journal of Contemporary African Studies*, 18, 179–206.

Landman, K., 2003, 'Alley-Gating and Neighbourhood Gating: Are They Two Sidesof the Same Face?', paper presented at Conference on 'Gated Communities: Building Social Division or Safer Communities?', available at www.gatedcomsa.co.za/docs/Glasgow_paper_v5.pdf

Lawi, Y., 2000, 'Justice Administration Outside the Ordinary Courts in Mainland Tanzania: The Case of Ward Tribunals in Babati District', *African Studies Quarterly*, 1, 2.

Leach, P., 2003, 'Citizen Policing as Civic Activism: An International Inquiry', *International Journal of the Sociology of Law* 31, 3, 267–94. Linebaugh, P., 1991, *The London Hanged*. London: Penguin.

Llewellyn, J. and R. Howse, 2002, *Restorative Justice – A conceptual framework*, prepared for the Law Commission of Canada, available at http://www.lcc.gc.ca/en/themes/sr/rj/howse/

Loader, I., 1999, 'Consumer Culture and the Commodification of Policing and Security', *Sociology*, 33, 2, 373–92.

—, 2000, 'Plural Policing and Democratic Governance', *Social & Legal Studies*, 9, 3, 323–45.

—, and N. Walker, 2001, 'Policing as a Public Good', *Theoretical Criminology*, 5, 1, 9–35.

Louw, A. and M. Shaw, 1997, *Stolen Opportunities: The Impact of Crime on South Africa's Poor*. Pretoria: Institute for Strategic Studies (ISS), monograph 14.

—, M. Shaw, L. Camerer and R. Robertshaw, 1998, *Crime in Johannesburg: Results of a City Victim Study*. Pretoria: Institute for Strategic Studies (ISS), monograph 18.

Lumina, C., 2006, 'Police accountability and policing oversight mechanisms in the Southern African Development Community', *African Security Review* 15, 1, 92–108.

Lund, C., 2001, 'Precarious Democratization and Local Dynamics in Niger', *Development and Change*, 32, 5, 845–69.

MacNair, J., 1956, *Livingstone's Travels*. London: Dent.

Maloba, W., 1993, *Mau Mau and Kenya*. Indiana University Press: Bloomington.

Malan, M., P. Rakate and A. McIntyre (eds), 2002, *Peacekeeping in Sierra Leone: UNAMSIL Hits the Home Straight*. Pretoria: Institute for Strategic Studies (ISS), monograph 68.

Mamdani, M., 1996, *Citizen and Subject, Contemporary Africa and the Legacy of Late Colonialism*. Kampala: Fountain Publishers.

Marks, M., 1998, 'Policing for Democracy: A Case for Paramilitary Policing in Africa?', *Crime and Conflict*, 11, available at www.und.ac.za/und/indic/ archives/crime/issue11/moniqu2.html

Marx, K., 1978, 'The Eighteenth Brumaire of Louis Bonaparte', in R. Tucker (ed.), *The Marx-Engels Reader 2*. New York: Norton.

Massaquoi, J., 1999, 'Building Mechanisms for Conflict Resolution in South-East Sierra Leone: Sulima Fishing Community Development Project', paper presented at the First Conference on All African Principles of Conflict Resolution and Reconciliation, Addis Ababa, available at www.reliefweb.int

Mbembe, A., 1992, 'Afrique des comptoirs, ou Afrique du development?', *Le Monde diplomatique*.

McCracken, J., 1986, 'Coercion and Control in Nyasaland: Aspects of the History of a Colonial Police Force', *Journal of African History*, 27, 127–48.

McMullan, J., 1987, 'Policing the Criminal Underworld: State Power and Decentralized Social Control in London 1550–1700', in J. Lowman et al. (eds), *Transcarceration: Essays in the Sociology of Social Control*. Aldershot: Gower, 119–38.

—, 1998, 'Social Surveillance and the Rise of the "Police Machine"', *Theoretical Criminology*, 2, 1, 93–117.

Meek, S., 2003, *Policing Sierra Leone*, in M. Malan, S. Meek, T. Thusi, J. Ginifer, and P. Coker (eds), *Sierra Leone: Building the Road to Recovery*. Pretoria: Institute for Strategic Studies (ISS), monograph 80.

Merry, S., 1988, 'Legal Pluralism', *Law and Society Review*, 22, 869–96.

Menkhaus, K. and J. Prendergast, 1995, 'The Stateless State', *Africa Report*, May–June, 22–25.

Meyer, A., 1998, *Crime Prevention at Modal Interchanges*. Pretoria: CSIR Transportek.

Migdal, J., 1988, *Strong Societies and Weak States: State-Society Relations and State Capabilities in the Third World*. Princeton: Princeton University Press.

Mirzeler, M. C. and Young, 2000, 'Pastoral Politics in the Northeast Periphery in Uganda: AK-47 as Change Agent', *Journal of Modern African Studies*, 38, 407–29.

Mondelane, L., 2000, 'The Growth, Extent and Causes of Crime: Mozambique', paper given at the conference Crime and Policing in Transitional Societies, South Africa, available at www.kas.org.za/Publications.

Mqeke, R., 1995, 'Customary Law and Human Rights', *The South African Law Journal*, 113, 2, 364–69.

Museveni, Y., 1997, *Sowing the Mustard Seed: The Struggle for Freedom and Democracy in Uganda*. London: Macmillan.

Neild, R., 2000, 'Democratic Police Reforms in War-Torn Societies', *Conflict Security and Development*, 1, 21–43.

Nell, V. and G. Williamson, 1993, 'Community Safety and Community Policing: Achieving Local and National Accountability', paper presented at the Centre for the Study of Violence and Reconciliation, Seminar No. 6.

Newburn, T., 2001, 'The Commodification of Policing: Security Networks in the Late Modern City', *Urban Studies*, 38, 5–5, 829–48.

NIM (Network of Independent Monitors), 1997, unpublished report on violence in the Amplats Mines.

Nina, D., 2001, '*Dirty Harry* Is Back: Vigilantism in South Africa – The (Re)Emergence of "Good" and "Bad" Community', available at www.iss.co.za.

—, and P. Schwikkard, 1996, 'The "Soft Vengeance" of the People: Popular Justice, Community Justice and Legal Pluralism in South Africa', *Journal of Legal Pluralism*, 69–87.

—, and W. Schärf, 2001, 'Introduction: The Other Law?', in W. Schärf and D. Nina, *The Other Law: Non-State Ordering in South Africa*. Lansdowne: Juta.

Nyamu-Musembi, C., 2003, *Review of Experience in Engaging with 'Non-State' Justice Systems in East Africa*. Commissioned by Governance Division, DfID (UK),

Institute of Development Studies, Sussex University, available at http://www. ids.ac.uk/ids/law/pdfs/eanyamu.pdf

O'Donnell, G., 1999, 'Polyarchies and the (Un)Rule of Law', in Latin America: A Partial Conclusion', in J. Mendez, G. O'Donnell and P. Pinheiro (eds), *The(Un)Rule of Law and the Underprivileged in Latin America*. Notre Dame: University of Notre Dame Press.

Oloka-Onyango, J., 1989, Law, 'Grassroots Democracy and the National Resistance Movement in Uganda', *International Journal of the Sociology of Law*, 17, 465–80.

Oomen, B., 1999, 'Vigilante Violence in Perspective: The Case of Mapogo a Mathamaga', *Acta Criminologica*, 12, 3, 45–53.

O'Malley, P., 1997, 'Policing, Politics and Post-Modernity', *Social and Legal Studies*, 6, 3, 363–81.

Pavlich, G., 1992, 'People's Courts, Postmodern Difference and Socialist Justice in South Africa', *Social Justice*, 19, 3, 29–45.

Peake, G., 2006, 'Security Sector Reform in Sierra Leone' in G. Peake, E. Scheye and A. Hills (eds), *Managing Insecurity: Field Experiences of Security Sector Reform*. London: Taylor and Francis.

Pelser, E., 1999, *The Challenges of Community Policing in South Africa*, Pretoria: Institute for Strategic Studies (ISS), monograph 42 available at www.iss.co.za/Pubs/Papers/42/Paper42.html

—, A. Louw and S. Ntuli, 2000, *Poor Safety: Crime and Policing in South Africa's Rural Areas*. Pretoria: Institute for Strategic Studies (ISS), monograph 47.

Peters, R., 2001, *The Reintroduction of Islamic Criminal Law in Northern Nigeria: A Study Conducted on Behalf of the European Commission*, available at http://europa.eu.int/comm/europeaid/projects/eidhr/pdf/islamic-criminal-law-nigeria_en.pdf

Philip, K., 1989, 'The Private Sector and the Security Establishment', in J. Cock and L. Nathan (eds), *War and Society: The Militarisation of South Africa*. Cape Town: David Philip.

Philips, D., 1989, 'Good Men to Associate and Bad Men to Conspire: Associations for the Prosecution of Felons in England 1760–1860', in D. Hay and F. Snyder (eds), *Policing and Prosecution in Britain 1750–1850*. Oxford: Clarendon Press, 113–70.

Phiri, K., 2000, 'A Case of Revolutionary Change in Contemporary Malawi: The Malawi Army and the Disarming of the Malawi Young Pioneers', *Journal of Peace, Conflict and Military Studies*, 1, 1, 41–50.

Plunkett, M., 2005, 'Reestablishing the Rule of Law', in G. Junne W. and Verkoren (eds), *Postconflict Development: Meeting New Challenges*. Boulder: Lynne Rienner, 73–115.

Pospisil, L.,1971, *The Anthropology of Law: A Comparative Theory of Law*. New York: Harper and Row.

Poulantzas, N., 1978, *State, Power, Socialism*. London: Verso.

Ranger, T., 1983, 'The Invention of Tradition in Colonial Africa', in T. Ranger and E. Hobsbawm (eds), *The Invention of Tradition*. Cambridge: Cambridge University Press.

Rauch, J. and E. van der Spuy, 2006, *Recent experiments in police reform in post-conflict Africa: A review*. Pretoria: Institute for Democracy in South Africa (IDASA).

Read, D., 1979, *England 1868–1914*. London: Longman.

Reiner, R., 1992, 'Policing a Post-Modern Society', *Modern Law Review*, 55, 6, 761–81.

—, 1997, 'Policing and the Police', in M. Maguire, R. Morgan and R. Reiner (eds), *The Oxford Handbook of Criminology*. Oxford: Clarendon Press, 997–1049.

—, 2000, *The Politics of the Police*. Oxford: Oxford University Press.

Reno, W., 2004, *Countries at the Crossroads: Country Profile of Sierra Leone*, available at unpan1.un.org/intradoc/groups/public/documents/nispacee/unpan016206.pdf

Report of the Panel of Experts Appointed Pursuant to UN Security Council Resolution 1306 in Relation to Sierra Leone, 2000.

Report of the Panel of Experts on the Illegal Exploitation of Natural Resources and Other Forms of Wealth of the Democratic Republic of Congo, 2002.

Roberts, R., 1973, *The Classic Slum*. Handsworth: Penguin.

Roche, D., 2002, 'Restorative Justice and the Regulatory State in South African Townships', *British Journal of Criminology*, 42, 514–33.

Roitman, J., 2004, 'Power is Not Sovereign: The Pluralisation of Economic Regulatory Authority in the Chad Basin', in B. Hibou (ed.), *Privatising the State*. London: Hurst.

Rothbard. M., 1978, *For a New Liberty: The Libertarian Manifesto*. New York: Collier Macmillan.

Ruteere, M. and M. Pommerolle, 2003, 'Democratizing Security or Decentralizing Repression? The Ambiguities of Community Policing in Kenya', *African Affairs*, 102, 587–604.

Sachs, A., 1984, 'Changing the Terms of the Debate: A Visit to a Popular Tribunal in Mozambique', in *Journal of African Law*, 28, 1 & 2, 99–108.

—, and W. Honawa, 1990, *Liberating the Law: Creating Popular Justice in Mozambique*. London: Zed Books.

Salamone, F., 1998, 'The Waziri and the Thief. Hausa Islamic Law in a Yoruba City: A Case Study from Ibadan, Nigeria', *Journal of Legal Pluralism*, 42, 139–56.

Salgado, G., 1977, *The Elizabethan Underworld*. London: Book Club Associates.

Samara, T., 2005, 'Youth, Crime and Urban Renewal in the Western Cape', *Journal of Southern African Studies*, 31, 1, 209–27.

Samatar, A., 1994, 'Civic Disembowelment and the Collapse of the State in Somalia', in A. Samatar (ed.), *The Somali Challenge: From Catastrophe to Renewal*. Boulder: Lynne Rienner.

Santos, B de Souza, 1984, 'From Customary Law to Popular Justice', *Journal of African Law*, 28, 1&2, 90–98.

Sarre, R. and T. Prenzler, 1999, 'The Regulation of Private Policing: Reviewing Mechanisms of Accountability', *Crime Prevention and Community Safety: An International Journal*, 1, 3, 17–28.

Schapera, I., 1957, 'The Sources of Law in Tswana Tribal Courts: Legislation and Precedent', *Journal of African Law*, 1, 3, 150–62.

Schärf, W., 1999, Report on the Consultative Group Meeting on Access to Justice and Penal Reform in Africa Kampala, Uganda 18th to 20th March 1999, Penal Reform International, London.

—, 2000, 'Community Justice and Community Policing in Post-Apartheid South Africa. How Appropriate Are the Justice Systems of Africa?', paper delivered at the International Workshop on the Rule of Law and Development: Citizen Security, Rights and Life Choices in Low and Middle Income Countries, Institute for Development Studies, University of Sussex 1–3 June 2000, available at www.ids.ac.uk/ids/govern/accjust/ pdfs/scharf%20paper.pdf

—, 2001, *Police Reform and Crime Prevention in Post-Conflict Transitions. Learning from the South African and Mozambican Experience*, www.um.dk/upload/english/ DP3cScharf.

—, 2003, *Non-State Justice Systems in Southern Africa: How Should Governments Respond?*, available at www.ids.ac.uk/ids/law/pdfs/scharf.pdf

—, and D. Nina, D., 2001, *The Other Law: Non-State Ordering in South Africa*. Lansdowne : Juta.

Schmidt, E., 1992, *Peasants, Traders and Wives: Shona Women in the History of Zimbabwe. 1870–1939*. Portsmouth: Heinemann; London: James Currey; Harare: Baobab.

Schonteich, M., 1999a, *Unshackling the Crime Fighters: Increasing Private Sector Involvement in South Africa's Justice System*. Johannesburg: South Africa Institute of Race Relations.

—, 1999b, 'Age and Aids: South Africa's Crime Time Bomb', *African Security Review*, 8, 4, 33–44.

—, 2000, *Justice versus Retribution: Attitudes to Punishment in the Eastern Cape*, ISS, monograph 45.

Seekings, J., 1992, 'The Revival of People's Courts', in G. Moss and I. Obery (eds), *South African Review 6: From 'Red Friday' to Codesa*. Johannesburg: Ravan Press, 186–200.

—, 2001, 'Social Ordering and Control in the African Townships of South Africa: An Historical Overview of Extra-State Initiatives from the 1940s to the 1990s' in W. Schärf and D. Nina (eds), *The Other Law: Non-State Ordering in South Africa*. Lansdowne : Juta.

Seymour, S., 1970, *Bantu Law in South Africa*. Cape Town: Juta.

Shapland, J. and J. Vagg, 1987, *Policing by the Public*. London: Routledge.

Shaw, M., 1995, 'Partners in Crime'? Crime, Political Transition and Changing Forms of Policing Contro*. Johannesburg: Centre for Policy Studies.

—, 2000, 'Conference Summary and Overview', in Crime and Policing in Transitional Societies, proceedings of a conference, *Crime and Policing in Transitional*

Societies conducted in conjunction with the South African Institute for International Affairs, available at www.kas.de/proj/home

—, 2002, *Crime and Policing in Post-Apartheid South Africa: Transforming under Fir.,* London: Hurst.

—, and A. Louw, 1997, *Stolen Opportunities: The Impact of Crime on South Africa's Poor.* Pretoria: Institute for Strategic Studies (ISS), monograph 14.

Shearing, C., 1992, 'The Relation between Public and Private Policing', in M. Tonry and N. Morris (eds), *Modern Policing: Crime and Justice: A Review of Research,* Vol. 15. Chicago: University of Chicago Press, 399–434.

—, and M. Farnell, 1977, *Private Security: An Examination of Canadian Statistics 1961–1971.* Toronto: Centre of Criminology, University of Toronto.

—, F. Jeffries, S. Arthurs and P. Stenning (eds), 1974, *Private Policing and Security in Canada.* Toronto: Centre of Criminology, University of Toronto.

—, and P. Stenning, 1981, 'Modern Private Security: Its Growth and Implications', in M. Tonry and N. Morris (eds), *Crime and Justice: An Annual Review of Research,* Vol. 3. Chicago: University of Chicago Press, 193–245.

—, and P. Stenning, 1983, 'Private Security: Implications for Social Control', *Social Problems,* 30, 5, 480–502.

—, and M. Kempa, 2000, 'The Role of "Private Security" in Transitional Democracies', paper given at 'Crime and Policing in Transitional Societies', Conference held August 30 – September 1 2000, South Africa, available at www.kas.de/proj/home

—, and J. Wood, 2003, 'Governing Security for Common Goods', *International Journal of the Sociology of Law ,* 31, 3, 205–25.

Sheptycki, J., 1999, 'Policing, Postmodernism and Transnationalization', in R. Smandych (ed.), *Governable Places: Readings on Governability and Crime Control.* Aldershot: Ashgate.

Shubert, A., 1981, 'Private Initiative in Law Enforcement: Associations for the Prosecution of Felons', in V. Bailey (ed.), *Policing and Punishment in Nineteenth Century Britain,* London: Croom-Helm, 25–41.

Sierra Leone Police, 2004, *An Investigative Perception Survey on the Performance of the SLP for the First Half of the Year 2004: A Case Study of the Western Area and the Provincial Towns of Makeni, Bo and Kenema.* Freetown: Sierra Leone Police.

—, 2005, *The Annual Crime Report for the Year 2004.* Freetown: Sierra Leone Police.

Sierra Leone Truth and Reconciliation Commission, 2004, *Sierra Leone Truth and Reconciliation Commission Report.* Freetown: SLTRC.

Simons, A., 1998, 'Somalia: The Structure of Dissolution', in L.Villalon and P. Huxtable, *The African State at a Critical Juncture.* Boulder: Lynne Rienner.

Small Arms Survey, 2003, *The Small Arms Survey 2003: Development Denied,* available at www.smallarmssurvey.org

South, N., 1988, *Policing for Profit.* London: Sage.

Spearin, C., 2001, 'Private Security Companies and Humanitarians: A Corporate Solution to Securing Humanitarian Spaces?', *International Peacekeeping,* 8, 1, 20–43.

Spitzer, S. and A. Scull, 1977, 'Privatization and Capitalist Development: The Case of Private Police', *Social Problems*, 25, 1, 18–29.

Stack, L., 1997, *Courting Disaster? Justice and South Africa's New Democracy*. Johannesburg: Centre for Policy Studies.

Steedman, C., 1984, *Policing the Victorian Community: The Formation of English Provincial Police Forces, 1856–80*. London: Routledge.

Stenning, P., 2000, 'Powers and Accountability of Private Police', *European Journal on Criminal Policy and Research*, 8, 325–52.

Stevens, J., 2001, *Access to Justice in Sub-Saharan Africa – The Role of Traditional and Informal Justice Systems*. London: Penal Reform International.

Storch, R., 1975, 'The Policeman as Domestic Missionary', *Journal of Social History*, 9. 481–509.

—, 1981, 'The Plague of the Blue Locusts: Police Reform and Police Resistance in Northern England, 1840–59', in M. Fitzgerald, G. McLennan and J. Pawson (eds), *Crime and Society*. London: Routledge and Keegan Paul.

Tamuno, T., 1970, *The Police in Modern Nigeria: 1861–1965*. Ibadan: Ibadan University Press.

Tanner, M., 2000, 'Review Article. Will the State Bring You Back in? Policing and Democratization', *Comparative Politics*, 101–24.

Tanzanian Ministry of Labour in collaboration with the National Bureau of Statistics, *Integrated Labour Force Survey 2000/01*, conducted by the www.tanzania.go.tz/newf.html.

Integrated Labour Force Survey 2000/01, conducted by the Tanzanian Ministry of Labour in collaboration with the National Bureau of Statistics, available at www.tanzania.go.tz/newf.html.

Taylor, I. , 1999, *Crime in Context: A Critical Criminology of Market Societies*. Cambridge: Polity.

Throup, D., 1992, 'Crime, Politics and the Police in Colonial Kenya, 1939–63', in D. Anderson and D. Killingray (eds), *Policing and Decolonisation: Politics, Nationalism and the Police, 1917–1965*. Manchester: Manchester University Press, 127–57.

Tignor, R., 1971, 'Colonial Chiefs in Chiefless Societies', *Journal of Modern African Studies*, 9, 3, 339–59.

Touré, A., 1998, 'Conflict Prevention and Management in Africa', in H. Grandvoinnet, H. and H. Schneider (eds), *Conflict Management in Africa. A Permanent Challenge*. Paris: OECD, 49–56.

Tsebo, M., 1999, 'Lesotho Death Squads in the Mountain Kingdom', *New People African Feature Service,* available at http://ospiti.peacelink.it/npeople/may99/pag2may.html

Tshehla, B., 2001, Non-State Ordering in the Post-Apartheid South Africa – A Study of Some Structures of Non-State Ordering in the Western Cape Province, Master's thesis, Law Faculty, University of Cape Town, available at http://web.uct.ac.za/depts/sjrp/publicat/nonstate.htm

Turner, R., 1955, 'Law Enforcement by Communal Action in Sukumaland, Tanganyika Territory', *Journal of African Administration*, 7, 4.

United Nations Development Programme (UNDP), 1996, *Human Development Report 1996*. New York: UNDP.

UN-HABITAT, 2001, *Crime in Nairobi – Results of a Victim Survey.*

—, 2003, *Global Report on Human Settlements 2003: The Challenge of Slums.*

US Department of State, annually, Bureau of Democracy, Human Rights, and Labour, *Country Reports on Human Rights Practices.*

UNDP, 1999, *Management Development and Governance Division, Bureau for Development Policy, Governance Foundations for Post-Conflict Situations.* New York: UNDP.

Van Binsbergen, W., 1997, *Virtuality as a Key Concept in the Study of African Globalisation: Aspects of the Symbolic Transformation of Contemporary Africa* available at http://www.shikanda.net/general/gen3/virtuality_map/virt_6.htm

Van Dijk, J., 1996, 'Responses to Crime across the World, Results of the International Crime Victim Survey', University of Leyden, Netherlands Ministry of Justice.

Van Ness, D. and K. Heetderks Strong, 1997, *Restoring Justice.* Cincinnati: Anderson Publishing.

Van Onselen, C., 1973, 'Collaborators in the Rhodesian Mining Industry', *African Affairs*, 72, 289, 401–18.

—, 1976, *Chibaro, African Mine Labour in Southern Rhodesia, 1900–30.* London: Pluto Press.

Vaux, T., 2003, *European Aid Agencies and Their Use of Private Security Companies*, available at www.international-alert.org

Vera Institute of Justice, 2003, *Measuring Progress toward Safety and Justice: A Global Guide to the Design of Performance Indicators across the Justice Sector*, available at www.vera.org/indicators.

Villa-Vicencio, C., 1996, 'Identity, Culture, and Belonging: Religious and Cultural Rights' in J. Witte and J. van der Vyver (eds), *Religious Human Rights in Global Perspectives: Religious Perspectives.* The Hague: Martinus Nijhoff Publishers.

Vogler, R., 1991, *Reading the Riot Act.* Milton Keynes: Open University Press.

von Schnitzler, A., G. Ditlhage, L. Kgalema, T. Maepa, T. Mofokeng and P. Pigou, 2001, *Guardian or Gangster? Mapogo a Mathamaga: A Case Study.* Violence and Transition Series, 3, available at http://www.csvr.org.za/papers/papvtp3.htm.

Waddington, P., 1991, *The Strong Arm of the Law: Armed and Public Order Policing.* Oxford: Clarendon Press.

Waller, R., 1999, 'Pastoral Poverty in Its Historical Perspective', in D. Anderson and V. Broch-Due (eds), *The Poor Are Not Us.* Oxford: James Currey.

Washington Office on Latin America, 2002, *From Peace to Governance: Police Reform and the International Community* (2002), available at http://www.wola.org/publications/police_reform_report.pdf

Washington Office on Latin America (WOOLA), 2002, *From Peace to Governance.* Washington DC: WOLA.

Wood, B., 2000, *Malawi Security Sector Reform Pilot Project Report: Sept 1999 – Aug 2000*, available at www.nisat.org/security%20sector/August_Project_report. htm.

Woodman, G., 1996, 'Legal Pluralism and the Search for Justice', *Journal of African Law*. 40, 2, 152–67.

Woodrow Wilson School of Public and International Affairs, 2003, *The Missing Priority: Post-Conflict Security and the Rule of Law*, prepared for the US National Security Council, by Princeton University, available at www.wws. princeton.edu.

Woods, J., 1998, 'Mozambique: The CIVPOL Operation', in Oakley, R., M. Dziedzic and E. Goldberg (eds), *Policing the New World Disorder: Peace Operations and Public Security*. Washington: National Defense University, available at http:// www.ndu.edu/inss/books/Books%20%201998/Policing%20the%20New%20 World%20Disorder%20-%20May%2098/chapter5.html.

World Bank, 1998, *Participatory Poverty Assessment for Ethiopia*. Washington DC: World Bank.

—, 2003, *African Development Indicators (ADI) 2003*. Washington DC: World Bank.

—, 2004, *World Development Report 2004. Making Services Work for Poor People*. New York: Oxford University Press.

Wunsch, J. and D. Ottemoeller, 2004, 'Uganda: Multiple Levels of Local Governance' in D. Olowu J. and Wunsch, *Local Governance in Africa: the Challenges of Democratic Decentralization.*, Boulder: Lynne Rienner.

Young, C., 1988, 'The African Colonial State and Its Political Legacy', in D. Rothchild and N. Chazan (eds), *The Precarious Balance: State and Society in Africa*. Boulder: Westview Press.

Zarate, J., 1998, 'The Emergence of a New Dog of War: Private International Security Companies, International Law and the New World Disorder', *Stanford Journal of International Law*, 34, 75–162.

Zartman, W. (ed.), 1995, *Collapsed States: The Disintegration and Restoration of Legitimate Authority*. Boulder: Lynne Rienner.

Zedner, L., 2003, 'Too Much Security?', *International Journal of the Sociology of Law* 31, 3, 155–84.

Zolberg, A., 1992, 'The Specter of Anarchy: African States Verging on Dissolution', *Dissent* 39, Summer.

Zvekic, U. et al. (eds), 1995, *Criminal Victimisation in the Developing World*. UNICRI Publication 55. Rome: United Nations Interregional Crime and Justice Research Institute.

Zwane, P., 1994, 'The Need for Community Policing', *African Defence Review*, 18, 38–43.

Acronyms

ADF	Alliance of Democratic Forces
AFRC	The Armed Force Revolutionary Council
BBC	British Broadcasting Corporation
BPRM	Bo Peace and Reconciliation Movement
BSAP	British South Africa Police
CAR	Central African Republic
CBO	Community Based Organisation
CCSSP	Commonwealth Community Safety and Security Project
CDF	Civil Defence Forces
CDIID	Complaints Discipline and Internal Investigation Department
CFA	Communauté française d'Afrique (French community of Africa) franc
CGG	Campaign for Good Governance
CLO	Community Liaison Officer
CMI	The Chieftaincy of Military Intelligence
CPP	Community Peace Programme
CSAS/AUSA	Center for Strategic and International Studies/Association of US Army
DFID	Department for International Development
DPC	District Police Commissioner
DRC	Democratic Republic of Congo
ECOMOG	Economic Community of West African States Cease-Fire Monitoring Group
FRELIMO	Liberation Front of Mozambique; Frente de Libertação de Moçambique
IBEACO	Imperial British East African Company
IDP	Internally Displaced Person
IMF	International Monetary Fund
ISO	Internal Security Organisation
LAP	Local Administrative Police
LDU	Local Defence Unit
LRA	Lord's Resistance Army
LUC	Local Unit Commanders
MMO	Mines Monitoring Officer
MOCKY	Movement of Concerned Kono Youth
MYP	Malawi Young Pioneers
NGO	Non-Governmental Organisation

NRA	National Resistance Army
NRM	National Resistance Movement
OPC	O'odua People's Congress
OSD	Operational Support Division
PAGAD	People against Gangsterism and Drugs
Renamo/ RENAMO	Resistência Nacional Moçambicana
RUF	Revolutionary United Front
SADF	South African Defence Force
SAP	South African Police
SLP	Sierra Leone Police
SPC	Special Constable
UK	United Kingdom
UN	CivPol United Nations Civilian Police
UNAMSIL	United Nations Mission in Sierra Leone
UPDF	Ugandan Peoples' Defence Force
UTODA	Uganda Taxi Operators and Drivers Association
VCCU	Violent Crime Crack Unit
WOLA	Washington Office in Latin America

Index